PRAISE FOR T

M000158797

"*The Silent Rebellion* is an outstanding book, exploring why our current leaders, whether in politics or business, have failed us, and what we need in our future leaders."
Professor Sir Cary Cooper CBE, Alliance Manchester Business School and Chair of the National Forum for Health and Wellbeing at Work

"Leadership in the time of dramatic change requires deep insight into the human experience. The authors highlight the inner knowledge that is required by leaders to help their people navigate uncertainty and unstable times."
Donna Hicks, Ph.D., author of *Dignity: Its Role in Resolving Conflict* and *Leading with Dignity: How to Create a Culture That Brings Out the Best in People*

"*The Silent Rebellion* offers a fascinating new perspective on leadership. This refreshing collaboration is a must-read that invites us to reimagine the definition of a modern leader."
Judge LaDoris Cordell (Retired), author of *Her Honor: My Life on the Bench... What Works, What's Broken, How to Change It*

"Excellent leadership has never been more important across all sectors of society. We have all experienced where bad leadership can take us. Leaders must read this brilliant book to appreciate what qualities and attributes are required, and to recognize the leadership skills of others. Sometimes these skills are not always recognized when building a team."
Professor Russell Foster CBE, FRSB, FMedSci, FRS

"*The Silent Rebellion* explores how effective leaders foster a culture of innovation, resilience, and agility, turning challenges into opportunities. The result is a must-read for leaders who aspire not only to survive but to thrive in the face of uncertainty."
Sharon E. Horton, Ph.D., Neurosciences, Stanford University School of Medicine

"No other field, more than medicine, has changed as much in the wake of COVID. *The Silent Rebellion* provides a new perspective of leadership in a unique format. It's a multi-media experience that takes the reader beyond the pages of the book. The partnership between Chris Lewis and Inez Odom has resulted in a co-created voice to shape modern leadership."
Daniel Jacobson, MD, Assistant Professor, Department of OB-GYN, Division Chief, Community OB-GYN Medicine, University of Colorado School of Medicine

"*The Silent Rebellion* is brilliantly relevant in a post-pandemic era. With insightful analysis, compelling narratives and actionable strategies, it illuminates the path for leaders. *The Silent Rebellion* fosters resilience, encourages innovation, and celebrates inclusive cultures that resonate with the aspirations of today's workforce."
Tiffany Truong, Director of Marketing and Communications, Noble and Greenough School

"*The Silent Rebellion* offers us a much-needed perspective on leadership. The book takes an honest look at what is actually happening in the world of the post-pandemic era and provides a guide for how an innovative and inclusive kind of leadership can be used to address our toughest problems."
Lorri Sulpizio, PhD, Director, The Conscious Leadership Academy at the University of San Diego

"I do not know any leader in any sphere who would not be better for reading this wise book."
Sir Anthony Seldon

The Silent Rebellion

Becoming a Modern Leader

Chris Lewis and Inez Robinson-Odom

KoganPage

Publisher's note

Every possible effort has been made to ensure that the information contained in this book is accurate at the time of going to press, and the publishers and authors cannot accept responsibility for any errors or omissions, however caused. No responsibility for loss or damage occasioned to any person acting, or refraining from action, as a result of the material in this publication can be accepted by the editor, the publisher or the authors.

First published in Great Britain and the United States in 2024 by Kogan Page Limited

2nd Floor, 45 Gee Street
London
EC1V 3RS
United Kingdom

8 W 38th Street, Suite 902
New York, NY 10018
USA

www.koganpage.com

Kogan Page books are printed on paper from sustainable forests.

ISBNs

Hardback	978 1 3986 1774 2
Paperback	978 1 3986 1773 5
Ebook	978 1 3986 1775 9

British Library Cataloguing-in-Publication Data
A CIP record for this book is available from the British Library.

Library of Congress Cataloging-in-Publication Data
Names: Lewis, Chris, 1961- author.
Title: The silent rebellion : becoming a modern leader / Chris Lewis and Inez Robinson-Odom.
Description: London ; New York, NY : Kogan Page, [2024] | Includes bibliographical references and index.
Identifiers: LCCN 2024026007 | ISBN 9781398617735 (paperback) | ISBN 9781398617742 (hardback) | ISBN 9781398617759 (ebook)
Subjects: LCSH: Leadership. | Management.
Classification: LCC HD57.7 .L47585 2024 | DDC 658.4/092–dc23/eng/20240701
LC record available at https://lccn.loc.gov/2024026007

Typeset by Integra Software Services, Pondicherry
Print production managed by Jellyfish
Printed and bound by CPI Group (UK) Ltd, Croydon CR0 4YY

Tradition is not the worship of ashes, but the preservation of fire.
Gustav Mahler

CONTENTS

03 What Actually is Leadership? 62

04 How Does Leadership Need to Change? 80

05 Understanding the Leader's Thinking 101

08 The Future and Hope 192

FOREWORD
HOW DO WE HEAL THE DIVIDE?

by *Professor Sir Cary Cooper, University of Manchester*

The Silent Rebellion: Becoming a Modern Leader is a book for our time. It explores the many recent events that have divided us, from the pandemic to Brexit in the UK to political orthodoxy vs populism to the rise of disinhibition in social media to extreme ideologies. At the root of all of these, and many other divisive events, is the role (or lack thereof) of leadership. For example, post-pandemic, the hybrid world of work emerged, with many managers and leaders unable to cope with staff split, some working from home and others in the office. This highlighted the need for more emotionally intelligent leaders who could be more empathic, resilient, and adaptable. In politics globally, leaders with simple solutions and extreme ideologies have emerged in many countries, as "the people" yearned for magic-bullet solutions to complex problems. Most of the issues that divide us are complex, with change difficult to achieve.

As Machiavelli wrote in *The Prince*: "It should be borne in mind that there is nothing more difficult to arrange, more doubtful of success and more dangerous to carry through, than initiating change… The innovator makes enemies of all those who prospered under the old order, and only lukewarm support is forthcoming from those who would prosper under the new."

The questions that this book poses are the questions of this time and into the near future: How did we end up so divided? What actually is leadership? How does leadership need to change? What does leadership look and sound like? And what do we need in future leaders? We have had difficult and divided times in the past. One of the great political figures of the 20th century, Eleanor Roosevelt, said: "Surely, in the light of history, it is more intelligent to hope rather than to fear, to try rather than not to try. For one thing we know beyond all doubt: nothing has ever been achieved by the person who says, 'It can't be done.'" She understood the dangers of a divided nation, and how policies during the Depression and in the Second World War brought people together. The final chapter echoes this call.

This book highlights the background to what divides us but also provides a clear pathway to bring us together through leaders who provide hope and positivity, and not self-serving behavior. The Taoist Lao Tzu wrote: "A leader is best when the people barely know he exists. When the work is done, his aim fulfilled, the people will say 'We did it ourselves.'"

This is a must-read for all interested in the "Great Divide" and how leadership can, and needs to, bridge this divide.

2020 VISION

The further we get from 2020, the clearer it becomes. For some, the pandemic opened their eyes. For too many, it closed them permanently. Multiplied by the loss of fellowship, the fear remains unforgettable even among the fortunate. The legacy of the pandemic shows in more instances of anger. It shows in despair. It can appear as polarization, alienation, and social division. Or it can show as disengagement—an apathy toward everything and everyone. It's present in many different industries and ways of life.

If there were gaps before between the rich and poor, old and young, male and female, healthy and infirm, urban and rural, COVID-19 widened them all. If there were differences between nations, it magnified those, too. The pandemic changed us all. We're only just beginning to understand how. Even before COVID-19, we were under strain.

The pandemic force-fed us technology with unpredictable side effects. It created a new transparency. Companies could see us more clearly. Yet we could see them more clearly, too. It showed us social media companies profiting from misinformation and harmful content.[1] It revealed our politicians' behavior. It showed us an elite that appeared to prioritize global goals over local ones.

The pandemic disrupted supply chains which wars disrupted further. The massive public spending to offset this caused yet more collateral damage with inflation. This triggered the highest interest rates in 20 years and yet more damage. Of course, we'd never seen this before. But we had. We just didn't remember.

In 1918, the Spanish Flu epidemic killed more Americans than any war before or since. Globally, it killed 10 times the number of people who were killed by COVID-19. Epidemics are wide and shallow. Wars are deep and narrow. We make films about the latter. The Spanish Flu filled graveyards with solitary tragedies, but few collective memorials.

It's an ill wind that blows nobody any good. By February 2024, the great business leaders, ranked by wealth, had done well. According to the Bloomberg Billionaires Index, 131 billionaires doubled their net worth during COVID-19. At the same time, charities saw demand increase by more than 50 percent[2] while losing more than half their income.[3] Notwithstanding, third-sector leadership has responded with dedication and resourcefulness. Thousands of community groups all over the world sprung up to defend their communities. Their motivation is not profit, return on investment or status. They are seldom seen. It is their example that is profiled in this book—a new type of modern leadership focused primarily on a wider benefit to the community.

This type of leadership brings people together. It embraces ethics, divinity, and spirituality. It redresses the balance and incentives between the short and long term. It is diverse, imaginative, and inspiring to anyone who sees it.

The pandemic is behind us. The opportunities, though, remain in front of us. Leadership and capital need to change. Questions are being asked, not least by the young. Less convinced by the alphabet soup of CSR, DEI or ESG, they ask *cui bono?* What is the role of leadership, not just in the solution of problems, but in their provenance as well? If words are weapons, then let them be our sword.

INTERESTING POINTS

- COVID-19 was one of the largest transfers of wealth from the public to private sectors.
- The wealth transfer from Baby Boomers to Millennials is the largest ever.
- The pandemic allowed more than 131 billionaires to double their net worth.
- 30 percent of small charities lost more than half of their income during COVID-19.
- Millennials and Gen Z give more to social causes than any other generation.
- Gen Z is the first generation to prioritize purpose over salary.
- 58 percent of the global workforce will be Gen Z or Millennials by 2030.
- Mental health issues are more prominent in Millennials and Gen Z.
- Mental health problems affect twice as many women as men.
- 98 percent of all CEOs are university or college educated.
- 72 percent of people want their lives to change significantly after COVID-19.
- It takes leaders five positive leadership acts to offset just one negative one.
- Social media is a recognized cause of the mental illness epidemic.
- The US Army War College: "Hope is not just a strategy: it is the only strategy."

HOW TO MAXIMIZE YOUR USE OF THIS BOOK

We live in a digital age. We want the experience of reading this book to reflect that. We've used summaries and many graphics. We've also tried something new. We've used QR codes to link videos and examples of related content to bring the material to life.

Here's an example. Point the camera on your phone at the image below. It should take you to a video from Sir Ken Robinson.

 **RSA ANIMATE: Changing Education Paradigms—Sir Ken Robinson**

SOURCE RSA, https://www.youtube.com/watch?v=zDZFcDGpL4U

This QR code takes you to the video podcasts by the authors for each chapter:

 Video Podcasts

SOURCE TEAM LEWIS

This one takes you to the audio-only podcasts:

Audio-Only Podcasts

SOURCE TEAM LEWIS

You're encouraged to watch or listen to learn more about the chapters.

We invite you to create your own "digital toolbox" as you engage with the book. Why not create a digital folder for a piece of video or audio content that resonates? Perhaps we introduce you to a historical figure or person you've never heard of before? Maybe share a concept that you want to examine further?

Finally, there's an added page of QR codes at the end of the book that will take you to a music playlist compiled by the authors. Music can be an inspiring and important outlet, however eclectic!

ABOUT THE *TEAM LEWIS* FOUNDATION

TEAM LEWIS Foundation Impact
Report 2023

This book supports an idea, so you'd better know what it is.

Every leadership profile in this book has been selected and sponsored by one of our colleagues at TEAM LEWIS. They identify causes that matter to each of them personally. The only requirement is that it is a registered charity. Every year, each of them has a lump sum of cash to donate to a cause of their choice. They are then given the same amount again as a bonus. In some cases, colleagues elect to give that sum to the charity as well.

Finally, we ask the charities, "How else can we help?" The help given is pro bono and is entirely employee-led. Whether it's a video, website makeover, ad campaign, connections, or other need, we do our best to meet it. Countless hours have been donated to bring passion, positivity, and expertise to these causes. The Foundation has supported thousands of communities to date. The work is inspiration for hundreds of commercial campaigns for like-minded clients.

These communities are full of dedicated, hard-working people who believe in their cause. Their leaders are not well known, but that's our point. Some of the best leaders aren't. They have no Rolex watch, no Lamborghini nor mansion. And yet, they are some of the best leaders in the world. They aren't noisy, super-rich, or globally famous. They're quiet, ordinary people who achieve extraordinary things.

These are the heroes you just helped.

Samuel Dean

CEO

TEAM LEWIS Foundation

WHY WE WROTE THIS BOOK

If you've come to this book seeking change, then you're not alone. According to a recent survey, 72 percent of people want their lives to change significantly after COVID-19.[1] The pandemic changed everything and that's the starting point for this book. It has exposed multiple problems. It exacerbated many more. We want to explain how the world changed and what needs to happen as a result. We also want to show how some leaders are already responding.

Even before COVID-19, leadership had its problems. In the years since 2000, the internet has brought us an enhanced transparency. We can now see our leadership much more clearly. This is a passage from *The Leadership Lab: Understanding leadership in the 21st century*:

> *Since the turn of the century, we've learned that our leaders illegally avoided taxes,[2] rigged interest rates,[3] evaded taxes,[4] laundered drug money,[5] presided over an offshore banking system bigger than anyone thought possible,[6] forced good companies into closure,[7] and destroyed pension funds as they themselves grew wealthier.[8]*
>
> *Collectively, they oversaw an unprecedented destruction of wealth and the collapse of the financial system.[9] They watched as life savings placed into investment funds set up by leaders of previously unimpeachable integrity turned out to be Ponzi schemes.[10] They sold off reserves of gold to compensate for these exercises in corporate greed, while never once convicting any banker.[11] Our spiritual leaders covered up sex abuse in the Church.[12] Our charity leaders sexually abused the vulnerable.[13] Our child welfare leaders have permitted child abuse.[14]*
>
> *Our politicians cheated on their expenses,[15] admitted sexually inappropriate behavior,[16] started ruinously expensive unpopular wars[17] on the basis of false information,[18] and were taken completely by surprise by the Brexit vote[19] then tried to avoid implementing*

it. Our education leaders presided over exam cheating[20] and sexual harassment.[21] Our defence industry leaders settled claims relating to the bribery of government officials.[22]

More CEOs are now being forced out of office for ethical lapse than for any other reason.[23] Leaders of the automotive industry[24] lied about emissions,[25] were imprisoned, broke out of jail and remain fugitives.[26] The leaders of our water utilities polluted rivers then tried to cover it up.[27] Global entertainment leaders have faced multiple allegations of sexual harassment and abuse.[28] Britain's leading broadcaster falsely accused political figures of being child abusers,[29] while allowing actual abusers to commit crimes on their premises.[30] Meanwhile, sporting leaders have been caught cheating and doping.[31] Our medical leaders have chronically mistreated patients.[32]

Human rights lawyers have been struck off for misconduct and dishonesty.[33] In the US, many of the former President's political advisors have been jailed[34] and he has been subject to impeachment proceedings. From the Mossack Fonseca and Paradise Papers revelations it's estimated[35] that $8.7 trillion, or 11 per cent, of global wealth resides in tax havens.[36] Large corporations are routinely shielding money which deprived world governments of approximately $170 billion in tax revenue in 2016 alone (with the US Treasury taking a $32 billion hit). This off-shore tax operation was surprising even to people who were aware of the problem. They felt the problem was a fraction of the individual on-shore economies. It turned out to be a multiple of it. [37]

These events sound fantastic, incredible, unbelievable, even impossible, and yet they all happened. But how? It's almost unimaginable. The pandemic layered on many new instances of waste, greed, and incompetence. The belief and confidence that leadership once enjoyed is ebbing away to be replaced by cynicism.

There is no consensus. There is no unity of purpose. Division has become more common than unity and the lack of trust only grows. Our institutions can only be as good as the people leading them. Leaders just don't seem to be thinking in a joined-up way anymore. The lack of situational fluency affects how leadership has come to be seen. It's become tone deaf. It's striking the frivolity with which some actors invest enormous amounts of capital. India managed to land an unmanned spacecraft on the south pole of the moon, for a project cost of $75 million. This was $15 million less than the price Saudi football club Al-Hilal spent on Neymar.[38]

Once leadership has gained situational fluency, it's in a better position to start repairing the relationship with teams. This is the opportunity for leadership. So, how can we repair the damage that has been done?

When we, as authors, first discussed this, we were struck by how different the experience of the leadership deficit was. Some saw it through the lens of inefficiency and waste. Some through the lens of social injustice. Others through an emotional lens at the futility and sadness of it all. The book you are reading is about how the pandemic changed us, how we ended up with a particular type of leadership, and how COVID-19 made it worse. In doing this, we analyze what leadership is for and how it differs from what we have now. We also reflect on what is needed and how to achieve it.

The picture is not all bad. Far from it. All over the world there are communities quietly reorganizing themselves for renewal and rebirth. The leaders featured here are different though. They're of the people. They're determined, hard-working and modest. Their stories are scattered through the book as "leadership profiles." They were referred to us through our colleagues who were from those communities. We chose to help them with money and skills. These leaders are quietly working to change the world for the better. They deserve our support.

Why do they do it? There's no profit in it. They do it because no one else is going to do it for them. Because they want to do the right thing. Because they *take responsibility* and they do so with communities front and center as the prime beneficiaries. They are brilliant, inspirational, and entrepreneurial leaders worthy of the same attention as an Elon Musk or Mark Zuckerberg, but they don't seek that. They set new examples. They are a new type of modern leader.

Purists will say business has nothing to do with the community. The job of business is making money. Business, however, is there to add value, not just make money. That's different. Money is a by-product of adding value. And if you have to ask what business has to do with your community, then you may not be seeing the bigger picture. Business IS your community.

The orthodoxy is that companies know that it matters. Yet how it's done really matters. The buzzwords of Equity, Sustainability, and Governance (ESG) or Corporate Social Responsibility (CSR) depersonalize the involvement.

There are also some who completely object to this and think it's all a bit "woke"—a sort of virtue signalling. Perhaps they would prefer "vice" signalling? Besides, you don't need to be a victim of injustice to want to fight it. This is not about politics. We don't take a side. We don't have time for that. We don't need a red cat or blue cat. We need a cat that catches mice. We support what works and this really does work. Competence and consideration matter more than politics and policy.

The pandemic propelled massive change. People, and especially young people, need change. Change brings opportunity. However, you have a choice. You can resist change. The only thing is that change happens whether you like it not. Change is the only inevitability.

Using change creatively is also what this book is about. Opportunity is exciting but it always arrives in disguise—usually as trouble. Of all generations, the youngest is the most purpose-driven yet,[39] for good reason. These causes work as a palliative for those whose mental health has suffered from the twin isolations of technology and the pandemic.

This younger generation is also the most digitally skilled and thus also the most accelerated. COVID-19 caused the exodus of older generations and an induction of this younger cohort.[40] Like any generation, however, the whole person comes to work every day. True leaders see them with the same compassion and care as they see themselves. A gesture of kindness can redirect a colleague's day. Seeing and being seen matters. If you get the chance to be decent, take it. Leaders are being watched all the time.

The world has changed and it's important to understand how it has changed us. Even a cursory analysis shows that it is business leaders that are now the true agents of change and progress. Want to put a person on the moon? This used to be a job for the government; now it's the private sector. Need a new electric vehicle? Leave it to the visionary entrepreneur. Need to tackle the climate crisis? Business will create the technology for it and incentivize it. Want leadership in the community?

This is the great opportunity for business leaders, if they can see their wider role in the communities they serve. After all, it's in their interest, provided they can understand that communities work on longer-term thinking. Patient capital is needed. Government is too cumbersome for this. Not only is it too slow but in many instances, politics has become too toxic to be effective. Government could also harness these change-makers for real community renewal, if they don't care who gets the credit.

Living in a world with a broad gender spectrum, gender data is still often available only in a binary sense, referencing male and female. With that awareness, at times we have referenced men and women, but we acknowledge the breadth of the gender spectrum.

It is no accident that our book is laden with quotes. We both find great inspiration in powerful ideas. Language evolves and meanings change. In the end, all we have, all that endures, are our words. Being a modern leader requires a lifelong commitment to learning and a willingness to examine new concepts. Integrating the best of these ideas into our leadership style is both a privilege and a growth edge.

Of all the rare commodities around the world—money, minerals, materials—nothing is in shorter supply than attention. We intend to use yours carefully. That's why this book reaches into the online world with videos, podcasts, and references to further resources. On a point of detail, we've kept sentences short. An eight-word sentence is easy to understand. It's a good rule for writing and speaking.

One last thing: the "F" word. We wanted this book to be fun because competence follows preference. Put more simply, people get good at what they like doing. If you have half the fun reading it as we had writing it, then you're in for a good time.

01

How Did the Pandemic Change Us?

What was learned from living through a global pandemic?

Why didn't we see it coming?

What were the economic changes and their implications?

How did healthcare and overall human health change?

How will understanding these social changes equip the modern leader?

How do we discern what is "true" in an overloaded media landscape?

How has workplace culture shifted forever?

Why Does Leadership Matter More Now?

Change has been accelerating since the turn of the century. The Second Gulf War, the Arab Spring, the financial crisis, Brexit, Donald Trump, the Capitol insurrection, the Ukraine War, the pandemic, the death of Queen Elizabeth II, the Israeli War, and other major global pivotal moments: there has been a lot of change. Much of it has been interconnected internationally as well.

There have been shocks before, but nothing like this. There was the financial crisis of 2008, even the attack on the Twin Towers in 2001. Yet nothing changed our lives more fundamentally for such a long period of time as the pandemic. It changed everything... for everyone. It shook the foundations of everything in our world. It separated us from families and colleagues, in some cases forever.

There's a saying that if change isn't allowed to be a process, it becomes an event. Change had been piling up faster than the ability to assimilate it and the strains were already visible even before COVID-19.

All the same, there was something horribly Darwinian about the pandemic. The strong, educated, knowledge workers adapted relatively easily. Many of the weak, especially the elderly in care homes, for instance, were left to fend for themselves. Even in full view of their loved ones pressed up against the glass. COVID-19 infected everyone but with very different outcomes.[1] Inequality and access to healthcare were made much worse.

Leadership, which is often seen as a source of justice, was noticeably absent. There was a feeling that it was everyone for themselves. There were many cases of injustice. The belief in the system was shaken. COVID-19 took away control from the individual and gave it to those in authority. This heightened the sense of outrage when those in authority used their powers of control frivolously. Laws were either over- or under-applied or, in many instances, completely ignored. When you remove power, you also remove responsibility. Many carers, especially for the elderly, were physically separated from loved ones and in many cases, this included death. The loss of franchise was total.

What Was Learned from Living Through a Global Pandemic?

The true impact of the pandemic is only just now becoming understood. What happened behind closed doors in the corridors of power is also now being pieced together. The revelations are shocking. The stories are of internal fighting, ignorance, arrogance, and bad behavior. It is confirming what a lot of people already suspected—that leaders were ill-prepared, inexperienced, and hence, slow and ineffective. They lacked situational fluency, which is the ability to reconcile and make sense of multiple and often conflicting inputs.

All the ways the pandemic changed us came as a complete surprise to our leaders. Government had held some half-hearted exercises for a pandemic, but it felt chaotic, chiefly because it was. The air of panic was palpable.

Why Didn't We See the 2020 Global Pandemic Coming?

Pandemics are nothing new in history nor are their widespread effects. The Black Death (Bubonic Plague, 1346–1353) radically changed Europe. This was because a 30 percent reduction in population has a big demographic effect. It killed landowners and peasants. In England, at the time, nearly 40 percent of land changed hands because the owners died. There was a shortage of laborers as well, which meant a rise in wages. This led directly to political change, specifically, an outbreak of extremism. There was the Peasant's Revolt of 1381, a key moment in British social history. An out-of-touch government tried to introduce a poll tax to finance the Hundred Years' War with France. The pandemic had killed off taxpayers and peasants alike. This forced fewer people to pay more and the peasants weren't having it. They'd had enough of serfdom. They railed against the monarch, a young King Richard II.

There were strange effects, too, for instance, in fashion. Rising wages for those who survived altered the social mix. The wealthy began to dress more extravagantly in order to distinguish their social standing. There was a backlash against intellectuals. They attacked Cambridge University. There was a technical revolution. The shortage of labor propelled innovation in farming technology, methods, and produce. High wages always attract high technology.

Is any of this sounding familiar?

The last comparable global pandemic was the Spanish Flu in 1918. It was called "Spanish" because it was first reported in Spain. This pandemic infected more than 500 million people and killed 50 million.[2] It killed more people globally than all the wars that went before it and since. In the United States, 675,000 people lost their lives. Again, this was more casualties than World War I, World War

II, the Korean War, and the Vietnam War combined.[3] In one year, the average life expectancy in the United States dropped by 12 years.

The differential impact on the United States for both pandemics was notable. According to Yale University:

> *The COVID-19 pandemic has taken the lives of more than 6.5 million people around the world. Despite containing only 4.25 percent of the global population, the US has accounted for 16 percent of those deaths—more than one million. There was significantly higher mortality among younger Americans than in comparable nations.*[4]

Bizarrely, in the absence of other cures, some doctors said the Spanish Flu could be treated with whiskey. It was a popular prescription during prohibition in the 1920s.[5]

During the period immediately following the Spanish Flu, the lack of law enforcement and the growing divisions between rich and poor were also reflected in a crime wave and civil unrest. In the UK, this labor unrest caused the General Strike of 1926. This eventually resulted in the first Labour Government ever under Ramsay MacDonald.

In the United States, the Roaring Twenties reflected the euphoria of those who survived. There were glamourous new gangsters like Al Capone. There were new inventions in aeronautics, communications technology, and especially in health care, with the adoption of the British discovery of penicillin, which was invented in 1928. Again, the political effect of the period resulted in political change in the United States that led to President Roosevelt's New Deal.

Pandemics really do change things for a decade or more after they happen. They are, though, less studied and less well remembered by history. This is partly because they are incremental rolling events with no clear start or finish. There's also a human desire to celebrate victory and forget defeat. Perhaps also timing is a factor. The Spanish Flu didn't fit the mood. As one soldier put it: "Yes, we fought for democracy, but all we got was Spanish influenza and Prohibition."[6]

Pandemics in the Modern World

For the 2020 pandemic, there were some other factors. There had been scares with the SARS, Bird Flu, and Ebola viruses and perhaps these had "cried wolf" to an over-stimulated audience. In actual fact, COVID-19, when it did arrive, killed a lot less. The World Health Organization[7] estimates suggest the total number of global deaths attributable to the pandemic is around six million. This is a fraction of the deaths from Spanish Flu, despite our modern transport infrastructures. The virus moved more slowly in 1918, but it killed more people. It bears reinforcing that the Spanish Flu killed more people than any war before or since combined.

The difference in our time was that the fear and impact were enormously magnified by our 24-hour news cycle and social media. The world was shocked in March 2020 when Academy Award-winning actor Tom Hanks and his wife Rita Wilson tested positive for coronavirus in Australia. The actor, who was starring in Baz Luhrmann's *Elvis* film, had to isolate. Even movie stars could get the virus. It was a moment felt in the collective psyche.

The pandemic was a health event, but was felt as economic, social, cultural, political, and geopolitical too. It was this generation's World War II, with as many far-reaching consequences. The end of COVID-19, according to the US Centers for Disease Control (CDC), wasn't until May 11 2023.[8]

Let's look in detail at how it changed us.

Economic Change

The pandemic resulted in a massive transfer of wealth from the public to the private sector. From this flowed many enmities and inequities. It was the greatest intervention in public life since World War II. Enormous economic stimulus packages were deployed. On top of this, governments worked with the pharmaceutical companies to accelerate and subsidize the development and cost of vaccines. These payments went largely to the private sector.

The response from the private sector was extraordinary. It reorganized. It accelerated programs. It found new ways of working. Remote working technologies accelerated and developed, especially that of video conferencing.

The main economic effect, though, was that it exacerbated the differences between rich and poor, men and women, urban and rural, those in authority and others, knowledge and manual workers, elderly and young, healthy and infirm. It also imposed physical barriers and stopped travel and trade, forcing nations back onto their own resources.

It made the rich very much richer.[9] It was one of the largest transfers of wealth from the public to the private sector ever. It boosted the share of global wealth held by the super-rich,[10] while dramatically weakening the finances of nations.

The United States alone in 2021 dedicated 26 percent of GDP to soften the effects of the pandemic. This translates to stimulus packages worth $5.54 trillion.[11] In the United Kingdom, there was the COVID-19 Furlough Scheme, "Eat Out to Help Out," and many other schemes which paid companies to keep employees on payroll or stimulated spending. This was estimated by the UK Parliament at £372 billion[12] (the UK government's entire budget for the year was around £1,200 billion, so the stimulus was 30 percent) The pandemic spending from the government drove Pfizer's 2022 revenue to a record $100 billion and other pharmaceutical companies had similar gains. This alone would've been enough to create an inflationary boom. Yet there were two other major effects.

Interest rates had remained low since the 2008 financial crash, encouraging banks and other institutions to lend. The resulting inflationary wave was then hit by another event.

During one of the high points of the pandemic, Russia went to war with Ukraine. This was possibly because Russia felt the European Union was divided and distracted by COVID-19. Each European state had made its own policy, putting up borders against the next. The vaccine response was slow and badly coordinated. Russia had previously annexed Crimea in 2014 and other parts of Eastern Ukraine with little response.

It saw a chance to take Ukraine and it struck at the capital Kyiv. Ukraine is one of the world's largest suppliers of wheat and corn oil, which is widely used for everything from cooking to cosmetics. The world boycotted Russia as a result and thus isolated one of the world's energy economies. The exclusion of Russian energy from global markets triggered a global energy price shock. This drove the prices of all these commodities higher.

The result? A cost-of-living crisis as people were caught between rising costs, disrupted supply chains and static incomes. This was especially the case for those governed by public sector pay agreements. Unsurprisingly, this led to an increased amount of labor disputes and strikes, especially in transport and healthcare in the United States.[13] All governments had to raise taxes and cut spending to balance the books, thus prolonging the strikes.[14]

The inflationary bubble caused by government spending on COVID-19 had to be countered by central banks. They responded with the only lever they have—interest rates. They put up rates faster than ever before.[15] This caught out many banks early in 2023, especially the newer ones. They had huge amounts of cash on deposit, so they did what banks do with spare cash—they put it to work. At the time government bonds were offering long-term returns of less than 1 percent. Suddenly, when faced with depositors asking for 3–4 percent return, the banks had margin calls they could not meet. In the United States, this caused an astonishing three out of the five largest bank failures in US history.[16] They were all forced to go to the Federal Reserve for funding to underpin their short-term positions. Yet more public money flowed into the private sector. This confirmed the fact that government treasuries and central banks were not working together at all. The actions of one forcing the other to emergency responses from the other was a truly bizarre situation.

The division didn't just apply between rich and poor within the United Kingdom. Migration to richer countries fell as borders were closed but then surged as soon as COVID-19 restrictions were lifted. COVID-19 increased the division between rich and poor countries and accelerated migration between them. This surge was

Number of Non-EU, EU and British Nationals Immigrating Into the UK, Between YE June 2012 and YE June 2023

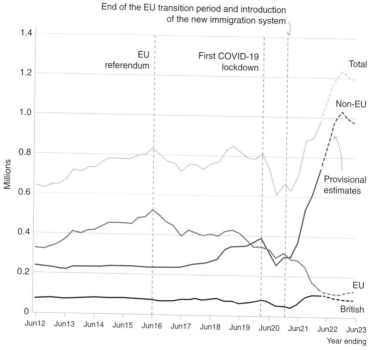

SOURCE Office for National Statistics (ONS), released November 23 2023, ONS website, statistical bulletin, Long-term international migration, provisional: year ending June 2023 https://www.ons.gov.uk/peoplepopulationandcommunity/populationandmigration/internationalmigration/bulletins/longterminternationalmigrationprovisional/yearendingjune2023

Content is available under the Open Government Licence v3.0

also due to the hospitality and construction industries recovering.[17] The same is true in the United States, as the surge in illegal migration has overwhelmed some parts of the US border.[18]

This surge in immigration from poor countries to wealthier ones has been felt all across the world. This is especially the case in the United States and Europe. Of course, COVID-19 has not been the sole driver of this. Wars, domestic instability, and rising commodity prices have all contributed.

LEADERSHIP PROFILE
Iolanda Chirico: Refugee Café (now Plateful Café)

Plateful Café Website

SOURCE platefulcafe.co.uk

Iolanda Chirico, founder of the Refugee Café (now Plateful Café), says:

> Whatever we have gone through, we all have something beautiful to offer. It doesn't matter where we come from, what we're going through and what trauma we might be experiencing. We still have a valuable contribution to make to the place we live and to the people around us.

Encouragement and perseverance are her watchwords as Chirico works with refugees from all over the world at her café in Lewisham, London.

The Plateful Café provides an opportunity for refugees to prepare food and develop marketable skills as well as receive a living wage. The healthy, vibrant menu introduces and celebrates the communities and cultures of the cooks. Community events, workshops, and feasts are central to relationship building. It's based on the idea that when you know your neighbor, you don't fear them. When you break bread with them, you're more likely to see their humanity.

Providing employment opportunities from creating delicious food is the mission of the organization. Bringing people together through food, the café has given refugees a way to support themselves, break stereotypes, and find inclusion in their new communities. At first, they started with community dinners, which sold out right away. When refugees had a chance to cook traditional food from their countries, attitudes changed, both for those who ate and for those who prepared the food. Barriers were broken. Relationships were forged. Chirico remembers:

> For the first time, I saw the refugees relaxed and I saw they were sitting down at the dinner table with the guests. They were laughing and talking with each other. They were not afraid, not embarrassed anymore for not speaking the language because they could talk about the ingredients of the particular dish.

Creating a permanent café where local refugees could showcase their cuisine and culture to become a more integral part of the local community is the goal. Rather than being seen as refugees with no skills, no experience, and no knowledge, they were able to use the language of food to share their heritage.

Chirico says that some refugees never overcome the trauma of losing everything. Losing their families, homes, jobs, and sense of place from their country of origin. The café currently works with many people fleeing the civil war in Syria. The trauma resides in their hearts, bodies, and minds. The loss shows up in the way they talk. In the way they interact with people, as they remember their previous lives. Chirico shares:

> They keep telling me, even after ten years, I wish I could go back because life in Syria was so much more enjoyable. I had my family around me. But here I'm alone. Still after ten years, they feel so isolated.

Beyond the actual running of the café, Chirico provides care to the people she works with. Many have complex stories. The norm is that they have experienced hardship and loss. Most of the families were smuggled across various borders and countries. Some may have traveled more than a year to arrive. Their journeys were perilous.

To be employable, they have to overcome prejudice and beliefs about who they are. They require constant encouragement and support.

Chirico asks, *"Why make such a journey and then give up?"* In the words of her parents:

> Never give up, even if there are difficulties, even if you're tired or you feel let down. They kept saying to me, if you work hard, you will see the benefits.

It's a powerful reminder to persevere. To consider the journey traveled rather than just the destination.

Chirico grew up in a farming community in Southern Italy. She worked hard. The values instilled by her parents resonate in her work ethic and approach today. Chirico found her calling in human rights work whilst in college. She joined Amnesty International and met two minors from Somalia who changed the trajectory of her life. By mentoring and assisting these young people, she recognized the holistic needs faced by refugees. Beyond employment or housing, the emotional trauma that many refugees have is the real issue.

Getting basic needs met, such as grocery shopping, can be daunting for a refugee. Embarrassment about speaking English can create problems when seeking a job. Even leaving the house and navigating the streets can be overwhelming. Chirico recalls refugees who simply couldn't physically get to the café. They did not know how to navigate the bus system in England. She says:

> I'm working with businesspeople to explore different options in the area. I want us to generate income from other sources so we can open up a pop-up in another place. It's a constant juggling act to try to find different ways in which to generate money.

It's ironic that she works with people who have such complex needs, that can be solved through the simple common denominator that we all share—eating together.

Healthcare Systems Came Close to Collapse

In Britain, existing public health systems were overwhelmed by the pandemic and remain so, with huge backlogs of mental and physical health cases (among health workers, too). COVID-19 revealed the fragility in public health and government.

Places of compassion and understanding became centers of rules, regulations, and authority. In the United States, the healthcare systems coped but shot up in costs. As a result, people took matters into their own hands, looking for their own cures. The disinformation circulating exacerbated this and led to greater distrust of official channels. We can see this in the use of hydroxy-chloroquine as a treatment.[19] The medical emergency elevated and accelerated technology but it also accelerated misinformation. Telecare and telehealth services took off as a result. More people turned to private healthcare than ever before as trust in the usual channels broke down.

At the bottom of the pile were those who worked face-to-face, such as nurses. According to Yale University again:

> [health workers'] complaints echoed many of the experiences nurses faced in 1918. Many were forced to expose themselves without proper protective gear like n95 masks. Hospitals expected nurses to be in the rooms with COVID-19 patients, while physicians waited outside. One nurse told her that "it felt like we were a little bit of a sacrificial lamb."
>
> "Their perception was not far from reality," said Hoffman. Over 3,600 health care workers lost their lives in the first year of the pandemic alone, with nurses and support staff being at significantly greater risk. Health care workers in nursing homes, who are often paid less and are more likely to be immigrants or people of color, were twice as likely to die as someone who worked in a hospital. Once again, the expectation of nurses and low-income health care workers to place themselves heroically at the frontline led to disproportionate amounts of illness and death among these groups.[20]

As one nurse put it:

> "You can't walk through water without getting wet."[21]

It wasn't just nurses, though. The same report highlighted the increased likelihood of infection among farm and food processing workers who were also people of color:

> One of the most hazardous occupations was food production. Farm workers, for instance, were four times more likely to come down with COVID-19. Like nurses, they lacked adequate protective gear and the ability to social distance. And the response to a COVID-19 outbreak in a meatpacking plant in Smithfield, South Dakota highlights the prioritization of industry over the well-being of its workers.

In early April of 2020, just weeks into the pandemic, county health officials planned to close the Smithfield Park processing plant in Sioux Falls as many of its employees fell ill, but then U.S. Secretary of Agriculture, Sonny Perdue, pressured authorities to reopen the plants. Two weeks later, the administration declared meatpacking plants "critical infrastructure." The plant reopened May 7. Following its opening, more than 1,200 workers got sick and at least four died. The meatpacking industry employs about a half million workers nationwide, and most of these employees are people of color.

Knowledge workers and the highly educated were much less affected than these blue-collar groups.

A report from the Pan American Health Organization published in March 2022 summed it up:

The physical and emotional costs of working long shifts in hospitals and the worry about COVID-19 exposure followed many female healthcare workers home, where they were often also responsible for 80 percent of chores. The study points to several research studies that have shown that women working in healthcare are more likely to suffer from anxiety and depression, insomnia, or burnout than their male counterparts.

During lockdowns to curb the spread of the virus, women also spent more time at home, a place which was unsafe for many. Calls to domestic violence hotlines shot up by 40 percent in some countries during these periods. In others, they dropped dramatically, indicating that women could have faced new barriers to seeking help.

Meanwhile, the re-direction of healthcare services to cope with the COVID-19 emergency left too many women and girls without the support they needed to stay healthy. In Latin America and the Caribbean, 1 in 4 adolescents did not have access to family planning services, leaving them exposed to unwanted pregnancies, health risks, and school dropouts, among others.[22]

In monetary terms, the loss suffered by women from COVID-19 equaled $800bn in lost income in one year or the total wealth of 98 nations, according to an Oxfam report which said at the time:

Economic fallout from the COVID-19 pandemic is having a harsher impact on women, who are disproportionately represented in *sectors offering low wages, few benefits and the least secure jobs. Instead of righting that wrong, governments treated women's jobs as dispensable—and that has come at a cost of at least $800 billion in lost wages for those in formal employment.*[23]

The Health Effects

We're still trying to understand the long-term health effects of COVID-19. However, what we do know is alarming. While COVID-19 was mainly a respiratory illness, "Long COVID-19" is increasingly being revealed as a neuropsychiatric disorder. In other words, Long COVID-19 is all about the brain. The Brookings Institute says that our brains have actually changed.[24]

According to Russell Foster, Professor of Circadian Neuroscience at Oxford University: "There are times that we might be so cognitively impaired that we have no idea how cognitively impaired we are."

Ha! It might explain quite a few things about our strange times.

An estimated 22–32 percent of patients who recover from the illness experience brain fog and cognitive challenges. Other research suggests that one-third will have a new onset or recurrent psychiatric problem, often depression or anxiety, in the following year. Additionally, it is not just people with severe COVID-19 that are affected. Studies have found that people, including those who were and were not hospitalized, have experienced challenges with attention, memory, and executive functions:

From a clinical perspective, it is known that several factors can lead to post-COVID-19 cognitive problems and mental disorders, including pre-existing illnesses, damage from the virus itself, neuroinflammation and vascular damage. However, further research is needed to understand the full mechanisms and implications of COVID-19 on the brain.[25]

The Brookings Institute says the decline in brain health has led to and will continue to lead to negative economic and societal implications:

> With colleagues at the Organization for Economic Co-Operation and Development's (OECD) New Approaches to Economic Challenges Unit (NAEC), we have shown—via our Neuroscience-inspired Policy Initiative—that Brain Capital drives economic empowerment, brain performance, social resilience, and emotional connection. Brain Capital is the underpinnings of economic growth and prosperity. It postulates that our brains are our greatest assets, and if we strategically invest in Brain Capital, the payoff is our country's future, economy, innovation, well-being, and even democratic strength.[26]

We're not talking about COVID-19 anymore and we should be. It's almost as if we heard so much about it during the nightmare that we don't want to discuss it. Perhaps we're still too close to it in time that we're not ready to look at its effects objectively? Maybe we'll leave it to the historians? We hope not.

In any case, those interested in and desiring change will draw the conclusions themselves.

Psychological and Social Change

The pandemic deepened divisions in our communities. It differentially attacked racial minorities and people of color.[27] It's no surprise that the response to the murder of George Floyd in May 2020 and the rise of the Black Lives Matter movement coincided with COVID-19.[28] Unsurprisingly, many searched for explanations. It made them more suspicious of our leaders and the elites—with good reason.

Those who dismissed these protests were invariably those who were relatively unaffected by COVID-19. It was once said the definition of a liberal was someone who was "not yet affected." No one understands an emotion until they feel it.

Some of the change was imperative. Many retreated into the online world because they had to. The more people stay inside, the more it becomes difficult to reengage outside. These are long-lived behaviors and there's no sign of this changing.[29] The effects of this are profound. Take local communities for instance. This is a zero-sum game. As online communities grow, local communities, such as retail spaces and high streets, decline. When the majority pulls away from the local community, it also leaves it open to those at the margins of criminality. The same is true of organizations, where they become complacent.

Isolation and Human Behavior

Local communities became much more important during the pandemic. Local, hyper-local, and voluntary organizations have been crucial. That's another reason to feature so many of them in this book. There were, however, inequalities between communities based on the strength of community infrastructures. One of the key lessons here, according to a report from The British Academy, was: "National capacity to respond to changing circumstances and challenges requires effort to sustain a strong web of communities and community engagement at local levels."[30]

The impact of the pandemic was multiplied further as people spent more time on social media during the lockdowns. This created a kind of social media accelerator. Social media and 24-hour mainstream channels dominated information acquisition. The problem with this acceleration is that a universal law of news journalism comes into play—that speed and truth have an inverse relationship. The faster the news, the less truth is likely to be associated with it. That was one effect. The other was that social media companies treated truth as a commodity to be bought and sold on the open market. Social media companies actively reward those with the largest followings. The largest followings do not coalesce around the facts. "Simple solutions" become more popular. And more dangerous.

Humans are social beings. The pandemic disrupted our social nature. Subject to age and disposition, the pandemic had a negative impact on our ability to socialize comfortably. Yet what is the science here? We know, for instance, that physical touch is crucial in babies and children.[31]

Prior to the pandemic, we shook hands. People changed behavior to avoid touch and casual contact. From masking to social distancing, we became further apart in our human interactions than ever.

A survey showed that concerns about the psychological harms of COVID-19 are ranked above those of physical wellbeing. Therefore, it is crucial to fully understand the psychological consequences of a pandemic and associated lockdowns, as well as the role of (social) media in this situation.[32]

Social media has become a primary mode of information seeking, social support, and entertainment for billions of users worldwide. In the absence of human communication, social media filled the vacuum. There is evidence that malevolent state and non-state actors on social media account for a substantial amount of the "news" that is circulating.[33]

The average time an American adult spent looking at a screen each day increased from 60 to 80 percent during the pandemic. That's everything from phones and video calls to the television shows and movies we binge. One view is that we have the world at our fingertips, so why go anywhere or do anything?

Despite its numerous benefits for sharing health information, social media has raised several concerns in terms of posing panic during the COVID-19 pandemic. There are many enemies of democracies that have been actively involved in seeding doubt and division.

Truth... Whose Truth?

Many of these impacts became intermingled with others. It's difficult to know where one ends and the other begins. The psychological impacts were felt in other ways. COVID-19 turned the truth upside down and inside out. The anti-vaccination movement encouraged people not to trust healthcare professionals. Even healthcare professionals started to doubt healthcare professionals.

Here's an extraordinary extract from the US National Library of Medicine:

> *Healthcare workers such as doctors and nurses are expected to be trustworthy and creditable sources of vaccine-related information. Their opinions toward the COVID-19 vaccines may influence the vaccine uptake among the general population. However, vaccine hesitancy is still an important issue even among the healthcare workers. Therefore, it is critical to understand their opinions to help reduce the level of vaccine hesitancy.*[34]

It fuelled conspiracy theories that fed on bored keyboard politicians. These promulgated ever more complex and bizarre explanations for what was happening. There was a microchip in the vaccine. Vodka could be used as a hand sanitizer. COVID-19 had arrived from space. COVID-19 was caused by 5G telephone networks. The United Nations actually issued a rebuttal about that one.[35] There was a false email chain purporting to have been sent by NHS staff, stating that being able to hold your breath for 10 seconds without any discomfort meant you weren't infected. Drinking cow's urine could prevent it. Or taking cocaine. Or eating garlic. A theory that garlic could ward off COVID-19 led to a Chinese woman being hospitalized after she ate 1.5kg of raw garlic in an attempt to prevent the infection. Four percent of Britons surveyed believed that eating garlic would "definitely or probably help prevent coronavirus."[36]

In the United States, the fear felt toward a disease that had its origins in China was projected onto all Asian Americans. Significant increases in hate crimes for this group occurred. Many reported personal incidences of negative comments and acts of exclusion or violence. Unenlightened terms like "the model minority" negate the very real race-based hatred experienced by so many Asian Americans within their own country. Ongoing fear and resentment are felt by many to this day.

This experience on the part of Asian Americans was exacerbated by disinformation about the source of the virus. Former President Trump referred to it as the "Kung Flu."[37] According to the Pew Research Center, about one-third of Asian adults say they personally knew another Asian in the United States who had been threatened or attacked because of their race or ethnicity.[38]

Further disinformation included ideas that there were shadowy cabals who had deliberately engineered the crisis to get rid of poor people. They sought to poison the populations of the world with chemtrails (the idea that condensation trails from high-flying aircraft were being deliberately seeded with toxins). These were entertaining ideas, even sensational, but produced no objective evidence of their presence.[39] Yet that wasn't the point. The conspiracists were aided and abetted in this activity by internet companies that reward creativity, not credibility. For them, volume of audience is more important than verification of truth.

The Legacy of Fear and Anger

We don't yet understand all the long-term effects of COVID-19. However, we know one thing: behavior has been changed. Social vulnerability is part of our collective consciousness. The US National Institutes of Health addresses vaccine hesitancy and acknowledges the important role physicians play in addressing concerns. Our faith has been shaken. It shows in the continued vaccine hesitancy concerning other viruses.[40] There is now a big increase in measles as a result of vaccine hesitancy, affecting one-third of those aged under 16 in the UK. Hundreds of thousands of children have not had vaccines. In January 2024, the result was a surge in measles cases, a disease many doctors thought they would never see again.[41]

We successfully developed a vaccine for the virus, but not for what it left us with—the fear, the uncertainty, and the doubt. This was profound and remains enduring. It left us questioning everything:

- Why do we work like this?
- Why do we go to offices?
- Why did so many people quit their jobs and never return?
- Why was there one rule for some and another for others?

- Why did our leaders not see this injustice?
- Why did so many women lose their jobs?[42]

Psychologists will also tell you something else about fear—it's closely related to anger. They both trigger the same "fight or flight" response. Most people can see that we're becoming angrier; could it be that this is because we're more frightened?[43]

According to *Psychology Today*:

Fear, like other negative emotions, can trigger our anger. For example, we might feel anger in response to our fear when someone suddenly cuts in front of us while driving down the highway. Similarly, fear of COVID-19 can certainly trigger anger toward the virus. Fear of financial pressure can provoke anger with a partner who is perceived as not being frugal. When excessive, fear can morph into ongoing anxiety that undermines our capacity to be fully present with others and ourselves. Ultimately, it can cripple our capacity to be open to many of life's experiences. While fear leads us to feel vulnerable and not in control, anger can be energizing and empowering. As such, it can become the go-to reaction to experiencing fear. Unlike fear, it moves us toward the source of our anger.[44]

That sounds like anger is something practical people use to do something to dissipate their fear. It would make sense. Something else that would make sense is that people fear change. We've had a lot of change, so we've had a lot of fear. Therefore, we have a lot of anger.

Behind the Curtains of the Classroom and Workplace

It wasn't just work that went home during COVID-19. Education, eldercare, and childcare did as well. For the first time ever, parents had a front-row seat for the education of their children. Looking over their child's shoulder at the lessons being taught on the screen pulled parents into the classroom. For the first time, they could see and hear what their children were learning. For the first time, they could see into the black box of their child's educational experience.

And many didn't like it. They opted to home-school their children themselves, even after COVID-19.[45] Teachers could no longer control the space. They were no longer the sole expert. COVID-19 became a two-way mirror into many previously hidden areas.

Home became work and now there was no escape from it. This brought work into an environment of previous sanctuary. Yes, people had more flexibility to work from home, but there was a psychological impact of never being able to fully escape or switch off. A lot has been said about the beneficial impacts of working from home, but not about the problems it created.

For instance, more relationships broke up as a result of constantly being in each other's company.[46] Higher rates of mental health problems prevailed among those working from home.[47] Many people simply started to work more, using the extra time gained from commuting to get through more.[48] Many people used the period of working exclusively from home to move away entirely. This caused significant problems when employers asked them to return to the office after the pandemic.

Many workers took matters into their own hands:

According to the US Bureau of Labor Statistics, over 47 million Americans voluntarily quit their jobs in 2021, spurred by COVID-19, ushering in the Great Resignation. Among workers who quit their job in 2021, the majority reported low pay, no opportunities for advancement, and feeling disrespected as the main reasons for leaving. These factors were especially felt by the low-income workforce. We must redesign and reimagine workforce participation.[49]

The authors went on to say that there was an urgent need for jobs that require intellectual and socio-emotional skills but that do not necessarily require a college education. There's a growing realization that you don't need a degree to get a great job and career.[50] This flexibility on graduate intake might also provide an important means to involve lower-skilled, lower-income workforces:

We urgently need innovation to address COVID-19's effects on Brain Capital. These innovations must span clinical care, neuroscience research, youth mental health, education, workforce participation, and more. To recover from the economic implications of COVID-19, we must prioritize and invest in the brain with a coordinated approach across sectors of government, civil society, and industry. Indeed, Brain Capital is the road to recovery and is necessary to build a more resilient future.[51]

The pandemic loosened the connection between teams, their leaders, and the moderating effect of the community. The necessary separation alone would have this impact. Many leaders did not increase the amount of online communication; in fact they did less. In a study of workplace communications at Baylor University,[52] researchers found:

that while senior managers valued communication, it became less of a priority... The use of Zoom soared... remote work made it harder for them to build trusting new relationships. They, like others, felt isolated, missing critical conversations and small talk.

At the time, leadership were hard-pressed just to keep things going, let alone understand and empathize with their teams. Inevitably, older people fared better psychologically, but drug and substance abuse among older people still increased.[53]

The need for leadership didn't decline; it was just supplied from other sources. Not all of these were beneficial or positive to the team.

The science and politics struggled to catch up with the spread of the weirdness. Logic can never keep up with emotion. The real surprise was how fast basic civil liberties were taken away. This was largely accepted because "we were all in it together." The massive-scale lockdowns and stay-at-home orders forced many to experience unprecedented levels of social isolation, disconnection, and distress. Many physical activities were banned or shifted online.

The economic justification for office space was significantly undermined by COVID-19. WeWork, the short-term office rental company, was badly hit. At its zenith in early 2019, the company was valued at $47 billion. It had more than 700 locations around the world with more than 40 million square feet available to rent.

Just under half of that was in the United States and Canada. In early 2024, its value was $14 million.[54] A lot of people lost a lot of money, but this does not seem to have discouraged its founder Adam Neumann. He has just raised a further $350 million for his next venture, Flow.[55]

The Loss of Confidence

The long-term trends show that faith has fallen dramatically since the 1970s in the following areas: institutions of higher education, large tech companies, big businesses in general, the police, the US presidency, television news, newspapers, schools, Parliament/Congress, banks, the courts, and the church/organized religion.

Trust in Government (Total Percentage, 2022 or Latest Available)

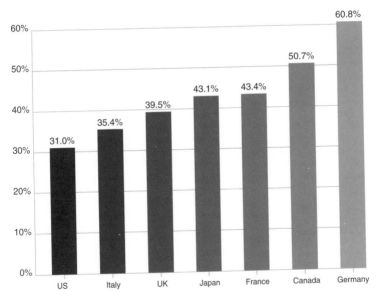

SOURCE Adapted from OECD (2024), Trust in government (indicator). doi: 10.1787/1de9675e-en (Accessed on February 12 2024). DATABASE OECD Social and Welfare Statistics; How's Life? Well-Being https://data.oecd.org/gga/trust-in-government.htm

Do You Approve or Disapprove of the Government's Record To Date?

August 2019 to January 2024

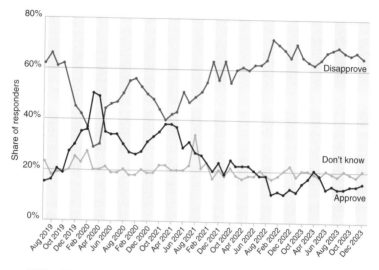

Additional Information:
United Kingdom; August 2019 to January 2024; 1,611-3,326; 18 years and older; GB adults; Online survey

SOURCE YouGov. (January 9 2024). Do you approve or disapprove of the Government's record to date? (August 2019 to January 2024) [Graph]. In Statista. Retrieved February 13 2024, from https://www.statista.com/statistics/1167064/uk-government-approval-rating/

Faith and belief have stayed the same or gone up in the following areas: small business, trade unions, and the military.[56]

In the UK in 2022, trust in government was subject to a specific inquiry.[57] Only 35 percent stated that they trusted national government. Forty-two percent of the population reported that they trusted local government and 55 percent trusted the Civil Service. Trust in public services was higher than trust in the national or local governments, with the NHS the most trusted public service (80 percent), followed by the courts and legal system (68 percent). Seventy-five percent of the population believed that the UK government should place a higher priority on creating conditions for businesses to thrive; 64 percent said they should place higher priority on reducing climate change; 54 percent believed they should place higher priority on reducing the national debt.

Trust in Government in the United States

Share of respondents who say they trust the United States government 'always' or 'most of the time'.

Our World in Data

SOURCE Esteban Ortiz-Ospina and Max Roser (2016) - "Trust". Published online at OurWorldInData.org. Retrieved from: 'https://ourworldindata.org/trust' [Online Resource]

In most institutions, in most countries, faith and trust have declined.

This has led to a new kind of "Special Relationship." According to OECD data, one of the least-trusted [G7] governments internationally is that of the United States.[58]

The trends in both the UK and US are illuminating.

Infrastructure Planning and Transport

Due to social isolation, public transport services were cut because so many weren't using them. Trains, buses, flights, and car journeys were reduced. More cities moved to a pedestrian-based and cycling model in a trend that was accelerating in the form of 15-minute cities, which also spawned its own conspiracy theory.[59]

All Other Priorities Were Ignored

Climate change was relegated to non-urgent. Suddenly, all the airlines had been effectively grounded and global oil consumption collapsed. It's difficult to focus on long-term climate change when your relatives are dying in the here and now.

Although COVID-19 made a slight reduction in carbon dioxide, the challenge remains. According to the National Oceanic and Atmospheric Administration (NOAA) Global Monitoring Laboratory, at Mauna Kea in Hawaii, the amount of carbon dioxide in the atmosphere continues to rise.[60]

Recent Monthly Mean CO_2 at Mauna Lao Observatory

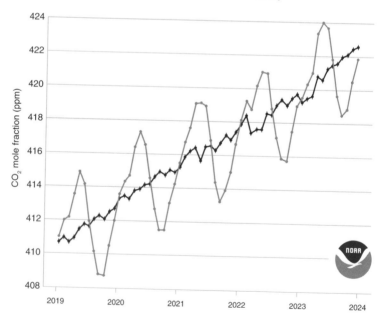

January 05 2024

SOURCE National Oceanic and Atmospheric Administration (NOAA), Trends in Atmospheric Carbon Dioxide, 5 January 2024, https://gml.noaa.gov/ccgg/trends/

What Remains in the Aftermath of a Global Pandemic?

In light of the global pandemic, the usual business of life, including routine healthcare, was deprioritized. Quite understandably, the consequences were kicked down the road and are only being dealt with now. In this respect, COVID-19 gave us the greatest dividing line. There are those who will adapt to a post-COVID-19 world and those who will not. Despite all the mitigations, the COVID-19 pandemic remains a Darwinian event.

What separates society from the savagery of nature and the unregulated power of markets? Civilization, the organization of communities under the rule of law and leadership of the people, by the people, for the people. Is that such an obtuse idea? Would the idealism of the Founding Fathers be tolerated today? Or are we too divided and too cynical? Have we lost our power to understand the complex processes that shape us?

We haven't lost this. We can understand them. We are not animals destined to shout at each other in perpetuity in a social media cage. Our public spaces have got to be better than that. We haven't lost anything. We have just temporarily lost sight of our highest best selves. A kind of madness has gripped us just like it has previous generations. History tells us the madness is usually dissipated by war. The bigger the madness, the bigger the war. We have the division. We have the wars. We have the hatred. However, we also have things that beat all of that. We have love, humor, integrity, decency, and a determination that evil will not win.

SUMMARY: CHAPTER 1

The 2020 pandemic changed everything for everyone. While it was a major health event, it was felt as an economic, social, cultural, and geopolitical event as well. The result of living through a global pandemic was that existing fractures widened. There was an absence of leadership. A marked lack of readiness. Failures of leadership surrounding the pandemic created skepticism in the very institutions tasked to address it. Inequalities in medical access were underscored. Historical experiences with past pandemics were left unexamined.

The pandemic brought about significant economic changes, moving vast amounts of wealth from the public to the private sector in an unprecedented way. Surges in immigration occurred. Permanent shifts in healthcare and overall well-being resulted. The most profound shift occurred in terms of mental health. Other pressing global issues took a back seat during this time.

The landscape of social media was compounded by isolation and created further schisms. The ability to assess what is "true" became increasingly obscured. Profound drops in confidence in government sectors were experienced in the US and the UK.

Workplace culture was forever changed. Work habits were forever altered. From in-person to hybrid to fully remote work, the return to the workplace has been challenging. Also, vast numbers of people opted out of the workplace. The influx of new workers brings its own set of values and needs.

The next chapter examines how we ended up so divided. It explores the remedies as well.

Aspirational Note

- As a result of having read this chapter, what might you do differently in terms of your own leadership style?
- What facts, stories, quotes or points stood out for you?
- What might you explore further?

02

How Did We End Up So Divided?

How did our education system contribute to the divide?

What if our goals weren't so SMART?

How did social media divide us?

How do we navigate all the channels?

What is the role of confirmation bias?

How do we understand the role of identity in order to lead?

How do we talk about "woke"?

What is the value of the emotionally intelligent leader?

The Not-So-Great Divide

As we've seen, the pandemic did a great deal to divide us. In reality, the divisions were there before, and they'd been growing for a while. Everything else had been changing and shaking the foundations of society. There had been social and cultural change layered on top of it. The pandemic accelerated and exaggerated those changes.

Society was already being buffeted by change. This was not just confined to technology. There was also global economic change. For instance, China's economy grew from $1.2 trillion in 2000 to almost $18 trillion by 2022,[1] propelling it from 7 percent of the world's GDP to 18 percent. This meant that many manufacturing jobs left Western economies during this period.[2]

This is now reversing as labor costs in China are higher than in many other countries including Mexico and Vietnam. Amazon grew from a start-up in 1994 to a value of $568 billion over a similar period, with a consequential effect on retail on high streets across the world.

The net result for manufacturing areas and towns has been to hollow them out. This has been written about extensively, most notably in David Goodhart's *The Road to Somewhere: The populist revolt and the future of politics*.[3] This created a clear set of divisions between manual and knowledge workers, town and country, haves and have nots. It explains the growth of populist politics in whole sections of the electorate who feel the systems are no longer working for them. It explains the rise of movements and leaders that sow division and deliberately shun consensus.

How Did Our Educational Systems Contribute to the Divide?

At the same time, other changes were taking place in our education systems which encouraged the level of division. To understand the fundamental problems faced by leadership, we must look at the education system that creates our leaders. It is here where the seeds of division are first sown. The systems we use are designed to atomize us, set us in competition against each other, and value only what can be measured.

Readers of Chris Lewis's previous works will know of the collaboration with educationalist the late Sir Ken Robinson. All of Sir Ken's life, he made the argument for a new approach in education. He argued that the education system was conceived in the intellectual culture of the Enlightenment and to feed the industrial revolution. It was designed for the needs of the 19th century.[4]

The Enlightenment emphasized reason and science. It was, itself, a reaction to an age of faith. At the core of the idea were three principles: reason, individualism, and skepticism. Put simply, it was the idea that Western reductionism could solve all problems. That there was a right answer to any problem because everything was rational. Everything could be broken down into its constituent problems and analyzed further. It became known as the philosophy of Western Reductionism.

Like a swinging pendulum, humanity moved from faith to rationalism in the 18th, 19th, and 20th centuries as the Industrial Revolution progressed. It reached its apogee in the post-war societies of the West. The ultimate triumph of science-based society was the domination of one side's atomic science over the other's inferior and less plentiful technology.

Robinson's point was not to deny the importance of the Enlightenment itself, but to point out that it had run its course and become counterproductive. The education system we still have today resembles the factories that it was created to feed.

A hallmark of such a production line approach would be, for instance, the organization of education by year of birth, by gender, by ability, and by location. Hence schools remain organized by catchment areas. The type of education you receive could simply be an accident of the location or date of your birth. For instance, if you are born toward the end of the academic year, you automatically start out with less experience than others in your cohort.

These education systems are a triumph of bureaucracy, specialization, and factory conditions. It's quite common for public schools in the United States to have well over 2,000 students. Of course, in recent times, the lines have become blurred with co-ed environments, boarding schools, and universities. However, the philosophy of the thinking is still largely in place. It is profound and all-pervasive.

In parallel to this, and because of a need for standardized national and international testing, we have developed universal scores. This allows all schools and all education standards to be broadly comparable. At the cost of these lowest common denominator measures, we have created the ability to assess just one type of intelligence. This is the type of ability that can be measured and it's pretty basic. It is normally speed-based with a set time to answer questions. Thus, the candidate is assessed in two ways: for the quantity of right answers and for the speed at which these right answers are achieved.

It favors the academic approach, one type of intelligence both rational and logical. The most successful in this type of system go on to higher education. This is from where our teachers are selected. The system is self-sustaining and self-replicating, largely because it's made itself so. Attempts to reform it are rebuffed because those who benefit so greatly from it will be the last to want to change it.

Nothing is quite so powerful as rationalism. It yields results that are measurable, provable, repeatable, and comparable. The irony of a system designed to produce such great uniformity is the profound inequality that follows in its wake.

How Can Education Be Reimagined for the Better?

The sorting starts early, usually at around 12 years old, when pupils begin to be selected. And in living memory, it could be brutal. In the UK, there used to be an exam called the "Eleven Plus," sat at the age of 11. Those who passed went to an academic (grammar) school. Those who failed were sent to a secondary modern school. Even today, you still hear politicians saying they made it to the top despite their comprehensive education. In the British educational system, comprehensive education was seen as an equalizer. As Robinson pointed out, if you really cared about the potential of every child, you wouldn't do it this way.

There might've been urgency to sort early when the average life expectancy was 40 years of age, as in the 19th century. Yet modern science has almost doubled this lifespan. We can reasonably expect several phases of education when people are working and living for longer than ever. Why are we still creating a "them" and "us" situation at such an early stage?

This is a system founded on difference. There is a top of the class. There is a bottom. Everyone else knows their place in between. We routinely refer to those who do well in these systems as "gifted," "intelligent" or "smart." The system these days goes to elaborate ends to soften the blow of poor performance. It describes students as "challenged" or having "issues."

The Music Man Project, based in Essex, England, is for musicians with learning disabilities. It is one of the most inspiring, uplifting, life-affirming groups you could ever meet. They may not be virtuoso performers, but they are an example of the tremendous humanity that is lost when such universal sorting methods are applied. Over many years and performances all over the world, this group and its leader, David Stanley BEM, have moved audiences to tears of laughter and joy.

LEADERSHIP PROFILE
David Stanley: The Music Man Project

Music is Magic Documentary:
The Music Man Project

SOURCE TEAM LEWIS Foundation, https://www.youtube.com/watch?v=HgUaM3F6IRM

David Stanley BEM is a disability rights campaigner, musical director, teacher, composer, and concert producer. He studied at the Guildhall School of Music and Drama, King's College University of London, the Royal Academy of Music, and the Institute of Education. Stanley holds a master's degree in musical analysis, a post-graduate certificate in education, and the National Professional Qualification for Secondary School Headship (NPQH). In any walk of life, he would be pre-eminent, but he chooses to spend his time working in the community.

The Music Man Project is a multi-award-winning, world record-breaking international music education charity for people with learning disabilities. It gives grants for accessible arts education and promotes equal access to performance. It carries out research and raises awareness of the achievements of disadvantaged people in the arts. Much more than this, it provides accessible music tuition and inspirational, energetic performances all over the world.

The goal is to focus on what people with learning disabilities can do, not necessarily what they need. The organization shows people, businesses, and society the value of people with learning disabilities and gives them more opportunities. While a lot has been done in terms of equality, education, accessibility, and employment, there still remains a barrier to opportunities.

Yet where did Stanley learn this approach? In many ways, his parents provide the first leadership example. He says they took him to a live performance of the organ, which awakened his desire to make music. The organist turned around, smiled, and vamped with his audience. It was incredibly entertaining. It was visually spectacular as well as musically compelling.

In that moment, Stanley was excited by the flash of this entertainer. He turned to his mother and said, "Mum, one day I want to be able to do that." His parents supported that passion by buying him an electric organ of his own. It was a financial struggle for them to pay for lessons, yet they saw their son's love of music. The organ led to the piano.

Warming hearts became an integral part of Stanley's musical journey. As a teenager, he began performing for senior citizens at nursing homes. He quickly recognized the power and influence of making music with those who are more vulnerable and marginalized.

He went on to receive serious classical musical training at some of the best institutions in the world. He is committed to taking the education he received and making music accessible for people with learning disabilities. It stands up as music in its own right. Nothing watered down. No nursery rhymes. He has high standards and expectations for his students, and they meet the challenge. With composing, it is hugely expressive and allows him to get everything off his chest.

Stanley's initial interaction with people with learning disabilities was with a man named Tony. Stanley played "The Twelve Days of Christmas" multiple times in the middle of July. Tony's reaction overwhelmed Stanley and motivated him to create opportunities for other people with learning disabilities.

Stanley credits his wife and home life as the foundation for his ability to take risks. He is able to come home to love. He advises that leaders must look after themselves physically, spiritually, emotionally, and otherwise:

I think leaders can leave themselves open to burnout. If you're determined and you keep to your dreams and ambitions and you do it with a lot of love and do it in the right way for people that are very vulnerable, then you will get results.

Many of the players have their fair share of problems. Stanley himself is no stranger to tragedy. On October 15 2021, his patron and chief fundraiser Sir David Amess MP was brutally murdered. Suddenly, one of the mainstays of his charity, The Music Man Project, was gone:

I didn't know it then, but there were so many people who wanted our work to carry on. The response was overwhelming. It shows that sometimes, it really is darkest before dawn. I'm motivated by legacy. I'm motivated by impact. I want to leave a mark on the world. What's the point of life unless you can make a difference and change the world?

He makes a difference in many ways. From sweeping and vacuuming the floor to driving the bus to curating the website, Stanley ends up volunteering his time well above any monetary return. Yet, he realizes that it is all in service to the vision and the mission. He teaches and runs a Saturday music school, then he works on the development of the charity. He says, matter-of-factly:

You've got to be willing to go beyond to find success. Giving your time can be transformative for you and for those you help.

The glamor of being on stage in the Royal Albert Hall with HM The King and thousands of people in attendance is gratifying yet humbling as well. Stanley thinks a lot about his students and their lives. He acknowledges that many of them will die young because of their disabilities or physical problems. Many of them struggle with the simplest activities of daily living. Added to this is the discrimination and prejudice that they face based upon their disability. What he has found is that these incredible people can also become impressive musicians and ambassadors. These are people who have had to overcome extraordinary challenges. For Stanley, working with people with learning disabilities is a chance to be surrounded by people who bring joy to the process of making music every day.

In a recent article, Stanley shared six things that define his leadership:

1 Find your inspiration.
2 Be creative and open-minded.
3 Be disruptive.
4 Learn to see failure as a positive.
5 Set goals and aim high.
6 Build your network and credibility.[5]

Stanley wants to see the Music Man Project replicated around the world. Indeed, he receives letters from people who hope for a Music Man Project in their community:

> My music is connecting people with disabilities around the world and connecting them as part of my musical family.

Stanley exudes joy and enthusiasm for the world around him. He speaks of his tenacity as the hallmark of his success. His leadership is disruptive and inspirational in that he believes all things are possible. Stanley believes an attitude of positivity is the superpower of true leaders:

> I'm a yes man. I never shut a door. I really believe in the effect of positive thinking. It's like a law of attraction thing. You kind of attract the positive and good things by thinking that they're happening, or they've already happened.

Is there a secret to this approach? Not really:

> The primary motivation for me is to make a positive difference to the world through my music and that's from a sort of mindset that stands me in good stead. I get a bigger kick out of the events. The impact of the music and the performance, the smiles and the applause are more rewarding than anything that could come in a paycheck. That's my mindset. Working with people with learning disabilities has revealed to me the best of humanity. I'm in constant awe of their bravery and determination and the never-ending struggle faced by their families. So things like that are my motivation. The work of a leader ultimately is to help others see a vision and commit to it.

What Are The Qualities That Matter?

None of this is to say that rationalism should be abandoned. Or that leaders don't need rational ability. They do. However, they also need a wider range of relatable skills. Why? The inputs they are dealing with now are far more complex. This involves being able to read the "math as well as the mood."

The problem is that by the time our formal education is complete, we have become certified by national organizations. They assess marks. Yet consider this for a moment. What are the key qualities of leadership for which no marks are available? You can see this listed in the Education Scorecard here.

Education Scorecard

WE GET SCORES FOR	WE GET NOTHING FOR
RIGHT ANSWERS	EMPATHY
OBEDIENCE	NON-CONFORMITY
INDIVIDUAL ACHIEVEMENT	COLLABORATION
PASSING EXAMS	TEACHING OTHERS
ACTION	ENDURANCE
ATTENTION	IMAGINATION
DEDUCTION	DETERMINATION
MATURITY	HUMOR
INTELLECT	HUMILITY
ORGANIZATION	INTEGRITY
OPPORTUNISM	LOYALTY

SOURCE TEAM LEWIS. First published by Kogan Page Ltd in 2021 in *The Infinite Leader: Balancing the demands of modern business leadership* by Chris Lewis and Pippa Malmgren

Why are these qualities ignored in our assessment system? Is it because they are unimportant? Are they irrelevant? Are they inefficient in a collective enterprise? No. None of this is true. These qualities are neither taught nor assessed because they can't be measured easily, compared, or verified. Nor do they add to school results that will allow them to demonstrate their prowess in academic circles.

If our schools and universities only reward individual performance, why are we surprised that we turn out selfish individualists? We're not saying excellence shouldn't be rewarded. Excellence, though, can't always be measured, especially in interpersonal relationships. It doesn't stop it being important.

At the heart of this is a simple continuum. In previous books by Chris Lewis, we've said that leadership focuses more on the "ship" and less on the "leader." Put another way, in leadership, it's about the crew, not you. Which one are you more focused on—you or the crew?

In the world of rationalism, a sense of humor might be considered frivolous.

For sure, is not easily measured but it indicates some serious qualities. Take for instance emotional intelligence, judgment, and timing. We've all seen what happens when a joke goes wrong. We all prefer to work with teams that are having fun. In fact, you could even say that most people picked their specialist subject at school on the basis of what they enjoyed. How many of those choices were influenced by the teacher of that subject and whether they made it fun? All competence follows preference. Or put another way, we get good at what we like doing. Therefore, a sense of humor is one of the most important leadership qualities and this bleeds into the way we train leaders.

Not-So-Smart Goals

It is received wisdom in management schools that targets or goals should be SMART: Specific, Measurable, Achievable, Relevant, and Time-Bound.

How does a manager or leader achieve the goals of balance or fairness? Or are these not desirable goals? And if they were achieved, would they need to be achieved all over again the next day? This is where we get the to-do list mentality that plagues so many leaders. The leader's goals need to be augmented with things the leader can "be" as well as "do." You can't "do" fair; you can only "be" it. You can't "do" inspiring; you can only "be" inspiring. You can't "do" visionary; you can only "be" visionary. This is the stock-in-trade for the person who does the right things—the leader.

This is the problem with a system based entirely on rationality. It cannot explain faith, trust, belief, sense of humor, charisma, empathy, or determination. And yet this is all the stuff of which great leaders are made.

Our education system is geared around conformity and leaders succeed despite it, not because of it. Not only does the system discriminate against leaders, it cuts against a culture of leadership in general.

The rational approach would say that all people are cynical. They are individual, rational, and motivated only by logical reasons. Yet explain the logic behind a sense of purpose or helping others who are less fortunate. The parable of the Samaritan does not relate to an act of rational behavior. A logical person might see someone in distress and ignore them. Where is the logic of getting involved and giving that person some of your valuable time and resources? Empathy and compassion do not lend themselves to measurement or logic, but they are arguably more powerful than logic. This is the very essence of team building.

Could it be that we're beginning to see a backlash against logic and rationality? We see this in some elections. Convinced that all candidates are the same and have cynical motivations, a voter may decide not to vote or—what we've seen—vote for a candidate that will upset or break up the system—a sort of nihilist option.

The rationalism does lead to the sort of simplistic thinking that is coloring the extremes of political thought. That, for instance, the right answer is always a matter of policy rather than personality. There must be a right policy answer, so therefore there is a logical answer to any political problem. However, it's not necessarily having the right policy that matters, it's being represented by someone that you trust. Someone that you feel is competent and that you believe is honest. This may not just be someone who implements a policy that a voter wants. It's someone whose judgment you trust to do the right thing having considered all available inputs.

The Rise of Social Media – How Social Media Divides Us

The scale and proliferation of social media channels has changed our perception of the world forever. The rise has been rapid and largely uncontrolled, with minimal state intervention. In the age of the individual, rather than the collective, the internet has been a child of its time.

The internet was originally created by the US Defense community and called DARPANET.[6] This stands for the Defense Advanced Research Projects Agency Network. It was the first network to implement the protocols that became the foundation of the modern internet. The World Wide Web was layered over this to create the environment we see today. It was designed to facilitate the sharing of information among learned sources. As such, any governance of these channels—indeed the whole internet—has so far been voluntary and therefore erratic and inconsistent.

Much of the social media division online is caused by "disinhibition." This is the tendency of anonymity to lower the tone of conversation. Where people are identified and verified, the language of discourse tends to be more nuanced. A few brave politicians have tried to clean up social media and picked up this idea. They have embraced the idea of making social media participants identifiable. Many online titles like *The Times* of London have this policy.[7] The conduct has changed greatly now that identities are required. 2024 US Republican Presidential candidate hopeful Nikki Haley had this policy before she decided to drop it.[8] It was widely perceived as wanting to silence the voices of supporters of former President Donald Trump, the very audience she might have been hoping to persuade. Logical, but disheartening.

There's a triple irony here. First, that a tool created for the defense of democracy has arguably become its greatest threat. Second, that the power of the internet was entirely the creation of the US Federal government and is now its largest source of disinformation. And third, that the internet companies now decide the politicians who are allowed to use it. Elon Musk now chooses which politicians are allowed to use Twitter/X as a platform. In the 2010s, personal data belonging to millions of Facebook users was collected without their consent by British consulting firm Cambridge Analytica, predominantly to be used for political advertising.[9]

It turns out that science fact is more relevant than science fiction. We didn't need the fictitious Skynet to become self-aware to threaten humanity, as in *Terminator*. We didn't need the fictitious Orwellian Ministry of Truth to create the hate. The seeds of destruction for democracy are contained within it. Hitler, Stalin, and Pol Pot were all democratically elected.

How Have Algorithms and Social Isolation Led to a More Fractured Global Society?

To understand how and why the internet became so powerful we need to go back in time to 1996, when the US Congress created the Telecommunications Act.[10] The objective was to open markets to competition by removing unnecessary regulatory barriers.

For many years, traditional publishers had been governed by the law of libel. It was feared, though, that the internet could be slowed, if it was subject to these traditional laws. Section 230 in the Act changed everything. It meant that if a news site falsely calls you a liar, you can sue the publisher for libel. If the lie appears on Facebook, you can't sue the company, only the person who posted it (and, of course, they may be anonymous). The company is treated as a telecommunications transmitter, not as a publisher. It was the ultimate in "Get Out of Jail Free" cards in the spirit of the game of Monopoly.® The law stated that "no provider or user of an interactive computer service shall be treated as the publisher or speaker of any information provided by another information content provider."

It shielded companies that can host millions of messages from legal action by anyone who feels wronged by something someone else has posted—whether their complaint is valid or not.

Politicians on all sides have argued that Twitter/X, Facebook, and other social media platforms have abused that protection and should lose their immunity—or at least have to earn it by satisfying requirements set by the government. Only recently in a 2022 ruling, the UK courts investigated whether Meta had a role in the suicide of teenager, Molly Russell, through the content she viewed on her Instagram account. The court ruled that it and other social media platforms had contributed to her death. This was perhaps the first time anywhere that internet companies have been legally blamed for a suicide.[11]

Section 230 also allows social channels to moderate their services by removing obscene posts or ones that violate their own standards, to show they are acting in good faith.

How Do We Navigate All the Channels?

The success of the internet led to a great proliferation of channels, and this led to much greater competition for viewers, readers, and followers. Thus was a vicious circle created. The channels expanded. There was less control over the content and so the channels expanded further. We have now reached the point where social content is largely unregulated, which has led to multiple false stories. We routinely see reports of the deaths of celebrities or of global leaders[12] which are not true,[13] that a country has been falsely accused of an attack,[14] or that it has violated humanitarian codes by attacking a hospital.[15]

This is because sensationalized entertainment has become more important than the truth. Online channels especially have encouraged this. The larger the following, the more the content can be monetized. No rewards for truth. Weirdness, humor, and hatred have become primary ways of getting rapid attention.

No surprise then that these were the two sides of the pandemic coin.[16] The internet went nuts for things that looked like Hitler such as kittens, houses, kettles, Taiwanese cartoon characters, Nintendo zookeepers, power outlets and the like.[17,18]

Social media has grown significantly and has fragmented largely along demographic lines.[19] The growth has been staggering, much faster than any traditional broadcast channel and much more segmented by age.

This graph, although pre-pandemic, shows the scale of the growth.

Number of People Using Social Media Platforms, 2004 to 2018

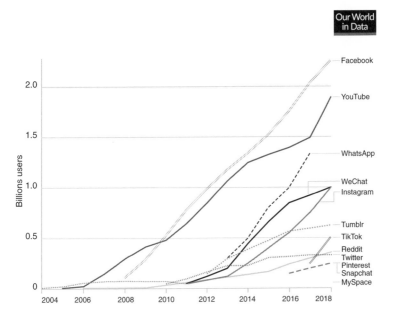

Source:
Statista and TNW (2019)   OurWorldInData.org/internet - CC BY

SOURCE Esteban Ortiz-Ospina (2019) "The rise of social media," https://ourworldindata. org/rise-of-social-media

NOTE Estimates correspond to monthly active users (MAUs). Facebook, for example, measures MAUs as users that have logged in during the past 30 days. See source for more details.

Use of Social Media Platforms by Age Group in the US

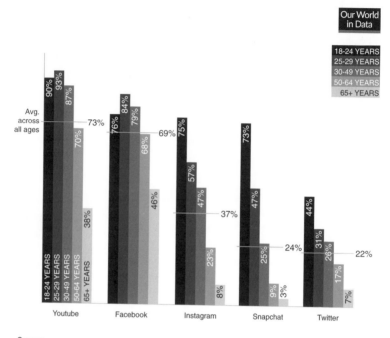

Source:
Pew Research Center (2019)   Licensed under CC BY by the author Esteban Ortiz-Ospina

SOURCE Esteban Ortiz-Ospina (2019) "The rise of social media," https://ourworldindata.
org/rise-of-social-media

NOTE The share of adults in the US who say they ever use the following online platforms or social media apps in 2019. Shown by age group.

Social media and the wider internet have provided a never-ending stream of violent and graphic images. The images coming from the Hamas attack on Israel are a case in point. In this respect, the social media companies have singularly failed in policing the content. There are many effects. Some were there before and were accelerated; others are wholly new effects.

All the Channels, All the Time

For any form of leadership to be heard, it now needs to say the same things on multiple channels but in different ways. For instance, a TikTok video is not going to reach many people over 40 and a Facebook posting won't reach many under that age. Nor is it any use commenting on a fast-moving situation on your YouTube channel, when most would expect that on Twitter/X.

This has made the leader's job of communicating much harder and more time-consuming to do well. For leaders in statutory positions where a requirement to respond is mandatory, such as in public office, it has become a major consideration. This has created an almost permanently open channel, which can cause mischief.

A small, but notable example of this was seen when UK Prime Minister Rishi Sunak visited a jewelry-making workshop. His guide had clearly told the PM to use a hammer sideways to ensure it struck more delicately. The resulting video footage edited out the instruction and just showed the hammer being used sideways. It rapidly became a meme that other social media users jumped on to illustrate how little skill and knowledge the PM had. At last count, the video had received over three million views.[20] It received newspaper reports in its own right.[21] This is monetarized, willful misrepresentation. At first glance, it's funny because it points at an easy stereotypical view that confirms what many might have already thought. It is, though, misleading, unfair, and likely to be repeated many times over, irrespective of the political view. It is the casual, easy misrepresentation of truth which has become so readily accepted. We prefer stories that are less demanding. Like eating donuts rather than health food, it's addictive.

Getting and sustaining awareness are two different things. The awareness, for instance, of the Ukrainian war has dramatically declined since the onset of the Hamas-Israeli war.[22] Media outlets are forced to juggle stories, and this can lead to opinion being laser-focused and then dramatically switched off.

What Is the Role of Social Media Disinhibition?

Generally, younger people are more trusting than older generations.[23] There are enormous variations though. For instance, trust in advanced economies is lower among young people and those with less education.[24] Education and income are generally linked to greater trust in other people. Some countries also have more trust in leaders than others.[25] Denmark expresses the highest trust in its leaders. It is also the highest-taxed country on earth as a percentage of GDP, the former being a necessary condition of the latter.

This lack of trust is directly correlated with voting intentions. For instance, Europeans with favorable views of right-wing parties are less likely to say most people can be trusted. In France, just three in ten supporters of the National Rally party say people can be trusted. In the Netherlands, supporters of two populist parties, Party for Freedom (PVV) and the Forum for Democracy (FvD), are also less likely to say most people can be trusted.

The growth in social media doesn't create a situation that is worse than before its advent; it just creates a situation where everyone's views can now be heard. It has also other important implications. For instance, once committed to a track that is recorded and audited on social media, it becomes much harder to evolve an opinion in the light of fresh evidence. This leads to the doubling-down effect we see on social media, time and time again, where people's positions don't soften or modify over time or experience. They become hardened and entrenched. This leads to the development of Godwin's Law, which states that as the frequency of online interaction increases, so does the tendency of one of the protagonists to liken the other to a Nazi.[26]

Once someone has a publicly reported position, it becomes a matter of vanity or pride that they must stick with it. "Give a dog a bad name" underscores that if a person's reputation has been maligned, they will suffer hardship and difficulty. This process then leads to social media protagonists becoming really nothing like their offline personas. Thus, a Wizard of Oz effect is created. All people then become online a more dramatic version of their offline selves. Sort of like drinking alcohol or taking drugs, they say things they would normally never contemplate in another person's presence or offline. This is the essence of social media disinhibition. It creates an environment where division is not just fostered, it's expected and encouraged.

As an aside, there's an analogy here to the constitution that governs countries. When the United States was established, it was in the spirit of the Enlightenment as well. Rationalism dictated that when attorneys got together to codify the difference between Britain and the US, it was done so in writing. It turned out to be part-declaration, part-contract, with several clauses (amendments) that could subsequently be added. The Second Amendment, the right to bear arms, is a case in point. Did codifying the right to bear arms obscure the intent of the legislation? Britain has no written constitution, which creates problems of its own. However, it does at least allow flexibility for judges to interpret the law for a contemporary age. Law is never applied by statute alone. It is judicial precedence, not written statute, that allows the law to be flexible, as technology and culture change.

More Division Through Confirmation Bias

A minority extremist view might once have been marginalized, but social media also lends itself to a coalition of minorities. You can always find enemies on social media, but you can also find allies. Worse, there are malignant actors, some of which are funded by hostile groups, which will actively try to foment dissent. These actors don't have to be agents of a foreign power; it can be the social media company themselves. They will monetarily reward those who have the highest followings, not those who are telling the truth.

Therefore, controversial and extremist content will be accelerated and rewarded while others are passed over. The more extreme, the greater the conflict, the louder the argument. It's a dangerous development of views, which leads to the misperception that the loudest segment is also the largest, when it's simply not true.

The content itself, though, needs to become ever more extreme to maintain its audience. This was a process we saw with British red top tabloid newspapers in the 1990s. They were driven to greater skullduggery to feed an ever more sensationalist audience. This led directly to the phone-hacking scandal that engulfed News International[27] and several other publishing houses. The effects of this are still being played out in the courts today, with Prince Harry's legal actions against the Mirror Group.[28] That sensation-seeking audience hasn't gone away; it's just become global and changed platform. In the United Kingdom, the *Daily Mail*'s social media platform *MailOnline* is now the most popular news site[29] in the world.

Identity Is the Ideology

All generations have issues that divide them. In the 20th century, generations were often divided by their experience of wars. Nothing is the same after a war. Technology is accelerated. The economy and society change. The Greatest Generation was perhaps the best example. Living through World War II was a defining experience. It involved everyone globally and for the first time, civilians were by far the largest of the casualties. Most of our global institutions date from this time, such as the United Nations, the World Bank, and the World Health Organization.

For the post-war generation living through the Cold War, ideology was the defining factor. Communism faced off with capitalism all over the world. The world split into a simple bipolar existence, with occasional hot wars being fought over control at the margins. This was the world that much of the current leadership grew up with. It was bipolar, post-militaristic, post-imperial, and post-industrial. And now it has changed again. The world has become multipolar with the rise of trading blocs and economies and militaries that rival that of the United States.

With the fall of the Soviet Union came "the end of history," as Francis Fukuyama put it. This was the theory that capitalism and democracy had won. When the Berlin Wall fell, it ushered in a period of disinflation. Large parts of a low-wage Eastern Europe were suddenly available to the West and Europe benefitted enormously. The European Union underwent a long period of expansion incorporating many of the former Soviet satellite states.

The end of history idea was true at least for the Western world. Living standards rose and although haves and have nots still exist, it is no longer the only defining factor. The developing world now wants things the West takes for granted—a viable country, safety, freedom, or even just a roof. The wars and migrations reflect these ambitions. It's difficult to achieve these goals when you only have your labor to sell, and especially so when economic imperatives bump into the politics of immigration.

This is why identity became increasingly important and started to develop its own politics. This is true both at the micro and macro levels. This is reflected in a tendency for those of a particular religion, ethnic group, or social background to form specific alliances away from traditional party politics. We're living with this fragmentation today. If leadership is the ability to focus a disparate group on a unified and collective objective, then identity politics could be seen as a barrier. It need not be.

Dana Washington, Leadership Solutions Partner from the Center for Creative Leadership in San Diego California explained a concept upon which identity can be understood. She described four axes of a matrix as: seen, unseen, given, and selected.

"Seen" identities are those visible identifiers that classify people in terms of race, gender expression, ability/disability, and age. This description is based upon the way people are visibly categorized. This can be more challenging, given gender fluency. Many individuals also have multiple racial identities. Categorization in the space is left to an individual to claim and define.

"Unseen" identities are how people organize themselves by experience or influences. Unseen identities could include the experience of having lost a child, being a recovering alcoholic or drug addict, having survived cancer, having a learning difference, or being a survivor of sexual assault. The identification with this unseen identity may be strong; however, it is only known if shared with others.

"Given" identities are based on factors outside of one's control that may influence a perceived identity. These identities could include being the oldest or youngest in a sibling group, being raised in a particular town, state, or country, having a particular genetic disorder, being left- or right-handed. Many people strongly identify with the place in which they grew up. Others may reject it or feel neutral about it. Yet, that experience can influence them deeply. Does an accent enhance or inhibit potential for instance? Does color blindness impact career selection? Does left-handedness impede sports possibilities?

"Selected" identities are those chosen by an individual. This expresses itself in a variety of ways. People may feel passionately about their political party. Consider the positions of pro-life or pro-choice. Are you a Democrat, Republican, Independent? Wars have been fought over faith. Are you Christian, Muslim, Buddhist, Jewish, or atheist? Sororities or fraternities are expressions of selected identities. Even sports teams can create an identity for fans that, in some extreme instances, results in bloodshed with rivals. Selected identities may be among the most powerful because they are adopted based upon personal choice.

An illustration of a selected identity would include those who choose to celebrate "Kwanzaa." Identities are important in creating norms and standards for community cohesion. Maulana Karenga, an American, Black nationalist who later became a college professor, created Kwanzaa in the 1960s. This was primarily as a way of uniting and empowering the African American community in the aftermath of the deadly Watts Rebellion.[30] Having modeled his holiday on traditional African harvest festivals, he took the name "Kwanzaa" from the Swahili phrase, "matunda ya kwanza," which means "first fruits." The extra "a" was added, Karenga has said, simply to accommodate seven children at the first-ever Kwanzaa celebration in 1966, each of whom wanted to represent a letter.

"Kwanzaa is not a religious holiday, but a cultural one with an inherent spiritual quality," Karenga writes. "Thus, Africans of all faiths can and do celebrate Kwanzaa, i.e. Muslims, Christians, Black Hebrews, Jews, Buddhists, Baha'i and Hindus, as well as those who follow the ancient traditions of Maat, Yoruba, Ashanti and Dogon." According to Karenga, non-Black people can also enjoy Kwanzaa, just as non-Mexicans commemorate Cinco de

Mayo,[31] or Hanukkah for example. Kwanzaa runs from December 26 to January 1 each year.

The seven principles of Kwanzaa, as determined by Karenga, are umoja (unity), kujichagulia (self-determination), ujima (collective work and responsibility), ujamaa (cooperative economics), nia (purpose), kuumba (creativity) and imani (faith).

Kwanzaa also has seven symbols: mazao (crops), mkeka (a straw mat), kinara (a candleholder), muhindi (corn), kikombe cha umoja (a unity cup), zawadi (gifts) and mishumaa saba (seven candles) that are traditionally arranged on a table. Three of the seven candles are red, representing the struggle; three of the candles are green, representing the land and hope for the future; and one of the candles is Black, representing people of African descent. Some families who celebrate Kwanzaa dress up or decorate their homes in those colors.[32]

Understanding "Woke"

A strange battleground has emerged upon which humanity has chosen to fight. It's called "woke." Let's first look to the dictionary definition to define what it is: Merriam-Webster says it is being "aware of and actively attentive to important facts and issues especially issues of racial and social justice." That sounds simple. Why would anyone who is trying to unify a disparate group object to that? Surely an understanding of how people are different and what might be a sensitive issue for them might be useful?

During the 2024 American Presidential campaign, Republican candidate Ron DeSantis defined woke as "the belief there are systemic injustices in American society and the need to address them." In his election night speech DeSantis said: "We reject woke ideology. We will never ever surrender to the woke agenda. People have come here because of our policies." The implicit suggestion seems to be that even the mere attempt to understand someone else's difficulties and motivations is immediately equal to an unfair bias in favor of them. It doesn't take any affirmative action to trigger this rejection, just the mere presence of an intention. Or put another way, trying to redress inequality is itself unfair.

What does the word "woke" really mean, and where does it come from?

SOURCE Domenico Montanaro, NPR News, Washington

It's possible that addressing inequity parallels the economic notion of unfettered free markets. This at least would be an understandable and predictable right-wing reaction. Markets work best when they are open and free. They should therefore not be manipulated. The intention to redress the balance toward those who are economically, racially, or socially disadvantaged could be seen in the context of left-wing politics. This, too, would be understandable.

Yet the split on woke is not based upon economic redress, it is based upon identity. It is a natural phenomenon and hardly a new one either. The notion of similar identities gathering together for protection and support is common in history. Some cities have historically had ghettos. Some still do.[33]

Of course, woke is not confined to race but can be extended to gender, sexual orientation, preference, disability, and other differentiators. This then leads us into the multiple ambiguities over a modern cross-section of people. If we take this as a starting point, then of course an understanding of diversity can be helpful.

The right wing seeks to conflate "woke" with "weak" when it is actually the opposite. It takes a great deal of strength to tolerate ambiguity and remain focused on the outcome. In this respect, the business leader becomes more like the politician.

The other characteristic of those railing against woke is that they are not trying to lead in a modern environment. To lead a diverse, modern group of people with no consideration toward them is irresponsible.

It may be easier to reject diversity when you are not having to work across many different boundaries of race, gender, and age. Talent is so rare that leadership cannot afford to discriminate against its provenance. It must give potential the best chance to be liberated.

Of course, there is an argument that says that talent will always find a way. That may be true but why rely upon the accident of determination and resilience? Leadership should always make it easier for talent to come forward, not harder.

Let's take the example of the scholar, writer, intellectual, poet, lawyer, priest, civil and human rights advocate, Pauli Murray. Her extraordinary story is here:

My Name is Pauli Murray

SOURCE https://www.amazon.com/My-Name-Pauli-Murray/dp/B09DMPMWCP?nodl=1&dp lnkId=3a663af8-02df-456f-b323-e0cc0f5f9e29

Pauli Murray was born a poor, female, non-binary lesbian of mixed racial heritage. She experienced both racial and sexual discrimination. Her mother died when she was three years old. Her father was committed to a mental hospital. She lived in the American South at a time when the lynching of Black people was common and prevalent. She was a Black American although her complexion "passed as

White." She was female but at times "passed as male." She attained wealth but always felt poor. She came from obscurity but found friends at the highest level. It is ironic that someone who lived through segregation should have had so much experience on both sides of so many of the fences society erects.

She went to the University of California Berkeley, got an MA, and set up her own law firm. She became the first African American woman ordained as an Episcopal priest. She was also the first to receive a Judicial Science Doctorate from Yale Law School. Later, she wrote "Jane Crow and the Law: Sex Discrimination and Title VII" and "Roots of the Racial Crisis: Prologue to Policy," both of which proved influential in challenging the legal foundations of racial discrimination. She went on to be one of the co-founders of the National Organization of Women.

Like many of the leaders featured in the leadership profiles in this book, she's largely unknown. But it doesn't make her any less inspiring. When you are a minority in so many ways, you are driven toward embodying the best in common human virtues.

Sadly, there are still many voices that will condemn someone like Pauli Murray. However, if you're a leader, your job is to remove the barriers to talent. You must protect and encourage talent wherever you find it.

The Climate for Cultivating Leadership

Leadership is trying to create the conditions that maximize the chances of achieving the collective objective. This is ensuring not just the correct economic circumstances for success but the creation of a culture that facilitates it.

The "woke" agenda is seen as being a modern fad that adds additional burden to leadership. In fact, it may do the opposite if correctly deployed. There are areas, though, where it definitely can be unhelpful and counterproductive. This is especially the case in the rapidly evolving language of woke. There's a suggestion here that those not fully fluent with the vernacular are excluded on the basis of a language "code." This can also lead to feelings of alienation and anger.

Leadership is nothing but change. This usually involves the navigation from point A to objective B whilst coping at the same time with daily change. Part of this involves adapting to changes in language and this is where the exercise of judgment comes in. There are those who might believe that the woke agenda is a type of evangelical activity that properly divides congregations into saints and sinners. This is wrong. The purpose of leadership is to unify, not divide. Why would any leader seek to exclude any potential asset from a team?

It all comes down to the "J" word—judgment. Leaders are neither Democrats nor Republicans nor Liberals nor Conservatives. This is not only irrelevant to their task, but also unhelpful. Labeling people always is. If you're trying to bring unity to a cause, then an inclusive approach is a matter of practical common sense. You can get more done with consensus than you can with conflict. Said another way, it makes for good business when you bring together diverse voices and perspectives. The more points of view that are considered when planning, the more likely it is that the plan will survive contact with the enemy.

There's a saying that you can pay people to do a job, but they will die for a cause. If you want people to give of themselves, then you need the whole person to show up. Sure, you can pay them, so they provide their time, but this is just the rational approach. You need more than that. You want to get their hearts thrown in for free. You want your team to feel inspired, encouraged, and represented as a result of the words that you use. Words fuel ideas. Inspiring ideas can and should transform situations.

LEADERSHIP PROFILE
Logan Heights Community Development Center

Monte Jones, Logan Heights CDC Website

SOURCE loganheightscdc.org

Lead with sincerity and you'll be a magnet for success.

MONTE JONES

Monte Jones is the President and CEO of the Logan Heights Community Development Corporation (CDC) in San Diego, California. The CDC was originally created by Bethel Church, the oldest African American church in San Diego. The mission of the organization is to provide practical opportunities for disadvantaged community members in terms of economic development.

Jones explains that, as an organization, Logan Heights CDC learned that the community would show up for programming that it found relevant. Initial programs focused on small business development. The blend of services best received was career development, financial literacy, and income support.

Jones reflects:

I like knowing that everyone in our organization has an opportunity to leave a legacy in someone's life. You don't have to be at the helm of an organization to leave a legacy. When people come in at their most vulnerable state and you put them on a path or give them some words of comfort, you have an impact on them. We see that every day.

The only thing different between myself and my colleagues who don't look like me is an opportunity,

He has a military background that is evident in his straightforward delivery and no-nonsense bearing. Leaders invest in the well-being of the people that they serve. Appreciating the softer side of humanity is ultimately the key to being a real leader.

Leadership can look different depending upon who is sitting in the seat. Jones shares:

> One of the keys to success is truly listening and acting upon what the community wants. Creating a climate where people feel well taken care of is key.

Jones speaks passionately about the importance of the work. He shares the struggles he experiences as a Black man at the helm of the organization. While the racial demographics of the community have changed, the poverty has persisted. He acknowledges that, in the non-profit space, it is less common to see Black, male leaders. This can present challenges when fundraising. Assurances must be made to the community being served. Similarly, funding organizations must believe in the organization's capability.

Seeing and being seen is a form of safety in the Black community. This extends into the workplace. Similar to apartheid in South Africa, legal blocks to access existed for Black Americans until the early 1960s. Many American Black leaders have grandparents, parents and relatives who occupied the lowest professional positions and working-class roles out of necessity. This was due to limited access to educational and general opportunities for upward mobility based upon race. Yet in Black churches, sororities, fraternities, and social justice organizations, such as the Urban League and NAACP, these same people held roles that garnered much respect. Many modern-day Black leaders have been socialized to consider everyone in the organization in a holistic sense.

Jones makes this point emphatically:

> Leadership is different for us, so we have to lead differently. We have to lead with a big heart. We have to be open minded. We have to hear what everybody's saying throughout the organization, whether it's the receptionist all the way to the CFO. We've got to hear one another because it's not my organization. It belongs to the people.

Jones speaks about how his team recently received a four-course homemade catered lunch from an Afghan refugee. This individual was so grateful for the work the CDC did to help him keep his home. Gratitude from those whose lives have been transformed was often the only reward at the start of Jones's CDC work:

> For years I didn't take a salary. I worked for free because of my determination to serve this community that had not had representation in any capacity. The leadership really came down to me showing that I could do the work of advocating for people, whether I had the money or not. Because I always truly believe, if you put the work in, the money eventually comes. Now, it took a little bit longer than we expected but it happened. The core of our belief system is that you work hard for people and your work speaks for itself.

Jones also believes strongly in the purpose of his team:

> You want to wake up in the morning and say, "I love going to my job." I like hearing people say how much we've impacted their lives. I think about my parents and the work they've done in their communities. Leave the community better now than how you found it.

The Definition and Importance of a Minority Perspective

This brings us to the subject of minorities. It's not just a matter of social justice. There's an intellectual rationale here. If you're really interested in change, the future always arrives in the form of a minority. Change does not move a majority all at once. This is the principle espoused by John Stuart Mill in his essay *On Liberty*[34] when he talked about the Tyranny of the Majority. In a democracy, minorities have just as much right to pursue their goals. Besides, democracy also relies on "Losers' Consent"—this is an essential for a functioning system. In Mill's view, tyranny of the majority was worse than that of government because it was unchecked politically.

This idea was also embodied in academic Margaret Mead's famous quote:

Never doubt that a small group of thoughtful, committed, citizens can change the world. Indeed, it is the only thing that ever has.

Gillian Johnson is the founder of Recovery Meet-ups, an American non-profit organization designed to help young people manage disordered eating. In 2022, she was recognized by *Vogue* magazine as one of the "21 under 21" to watch. She said:

For anyone wanting to effect change in their communities, use your leadership skills and grow your empathy to identify who is not present in the room… and make room for that person.

It's something that every leader should practice. Making room for others is a leadership trait. Also just remembering a birthday or a milestone. Leaders may think the time spent on this is wasted. Why? Since, again, it cannot be measured. How the heck do you measure a nod, a smile, a couple of caring questions or a point of praise? These actions can make a world of difference to a colleague.

It's a glorious thing to be seen, even if it can't be measured. Children will crane their necks when performing on the stage or on the sports field to catch a glimpse of a parent or family figure watching them. People want to be seen for their talents. They want to be acknowledged. They want their ideas to be understood. Most importantly, people want to feel cared for. People don't care how much you know, until they know how much you care.

Care comes from being in fellowship. This means making time to listen and to reflect. It involves considering what lies beneath the spoken words. To lead is to be fully engaged in the well-being of the people in your care. It's the best market research you'll ever do.

Of course, business must get done. KPIs (key performance indicators) must be achieved. Balance sheets and income statements need attention. The *Harvard Business Review* ran an article entitled "Emotions Aren't the Enemy of Good Decision-Making."[35] If we have learned anything from the pandemic, it's that we are social beings. Close contact and communion with others brings meaning.

Even when it's hard, even when it's maddening, we are ultimately in this life to look after someone else.

Even if the time in the office is restricted, you might be tempted to only do that which is measurable. That which is felt, though, is just as important. This is a key message to leaders. The job carries a commitment to caring and the inherent responsibility for others. Sounds obvious, doesn't it? But it's easily forgotten in the pressures of a day.

Leaders can learn a lot from representative minorities because leadership itself is a minority. Minorities often prefer a more collaborative style of leadership for all the reasons stated previously. Not only is it more inclusive, effective, and respectful, but an authoritative style may create its own problems. Any minority is automatically aware that authority lies with the majority, so leadership does not need to emphasize it. If anything, it should do the opposite.

Emotionally intelligent leaders look at those around them with pragmatism yet through a lens of compassion. They empathize. They realize that everyone is vulnerable. Life and death are going on all around any community. You can never tell what the next person is living through. The death of a pet may sound trivial, but to lose a much-loved member of a family is a big moment. Everyone wants to be accepted and understood and this must include leaders themselves. Often, too many leaders ask more of themselves than they would consider reasonable from colleagues. Remember, compassion begins with self.

SUMMARY: CHAPTER 2

Deep divisions in society had existed prior to the pandemic; this global event simply widened what was already there. In education, a rationalist, conformity-based model abounds. Only a narrow aspect of intelligence is measured and rewarded. The production line model of education continues, with standardized test scores as the metric for success. Challenging that model to consider and value what can't be measured has become the task for leadership.

Leaders value collaboration, empathy, imagination, endurance, and humor. These are key qualities of the most talented people. The exponential growth and rise of social media has created more societal fractures. The power of the internet is far-reaching and has led to distortions. The struggle is to parse what is true, what is real and who decides.

The insulating nature of the internet can lead to confirmation bias. People are able to stay in online spaces where their own ideologies are reinforced. The politics of identity have become more pronounced. Classifications occur and individuals embrace their own seen and unseen identities. The debate around the concept of "woke" calls for both definition and examination. The split on woke is not based upon economic redress but on identity. The concept of a minority perspective matters. The future always arrives in the form of a minority. It is crucial to make room for new perspectives. Maximizing the best of all voices is profitable, effective, and forward thinking.

The next chapter examines what leadership actually is. Considering the elements that make up leadership provides the blueprint for effective change.

Aspirational Note

- As a result of having read this chapter, what might you do differently in terms of your own leadership style?
- What facts, stories, quotes, or points stood out for you?
- What might you explore further?

03

What Actually is Leadership?

What is the relationship between management and leadership?

Who are our first leaders?

What is the leadership attitude?

What is appreciative inquiry and how can it be used best?

What is the role of faith?

What is the essence of servant leadership?

What is the leader's relationship to the group?

What Matters in Leadership?

And so we find ourselves divided. There had already been growing divisions, then along came the pandemic which accelerated and deepened them. So now we have a choice. We can continue with the division and hatred, and we know where that path leads, or we can understand, think it through, and take action. We can also recognize that there is only one way out of this. It's leadership. We need to get back to where we should be.

If we're going to change leadership, however, we must first agree what leadership actually is. Sometimes, the examples that we're provided with through the media are not helpful. They feature the wealthy, the famous, the infamous, or the most notable. These are not necessarily helpful.

A powerful concept borrowed from post-apartheid South Africa is the notion of Ubuntu,[1] which is loosely defined as the notion of "humanity toward others." It is a leadership approach that centralizes care for one another. During the 1990s, the concept was adapted as an ideology to bring about harmony and cooperation from diverse racial and ethnic groups. The ethical values of Ubuntu include respect for others, helpfulness, community, sharing, caring, trust, and unselfishness. It underscores the importance of consensus and gives priority to the well-being of the community as a whole. Philosophically, it is a rich environment in which to develop one's leadership.

Let's start with the consultants. Perhaps they can help? The global management consultancy McKinsey & Company defines leadership as:

> ... a set of behaviors used to help people align their collective direction, to execute strategic plans, and to continually renew an organization.[2]

This sounds like organizational theory. Is a community an organization? Not really. Not any more than a family is. There are campaigning communities out there that have no organization at all. Some have one intermittently when they need it. Just Stop Oil describes itself as non-hierarchical, with activists in the group operating in autonomous groups that share resources, but it has no formal leadership. This is fine for a protest organization, but would this work where people needed protection or to work to a universal standard, e.g. with the police, health service, or education?

Individualism is now so rife that many potential leaders seek not to be involved. They don't want the responsibility, the profile, or, more frankly, the blame. Many online communities are simply moderated discussion groups. They have no organization. So, the definition above may be faulty because it focuses on what we do, not who we are.

How about this one from Warren Bennis[3] (also Peter Drucker)?:

> Management does things right. Leadership does the right things.

This is getting closer. Here, we're separating two terms that are often used interchangeably—management and leadership. Managers deal with a correct or standard operating procedure. Leaders deal with stuff that goes beyond the measurable. Under these terms, management can be measured. Any deviation from a regulation or a budget can be tracked. Management goals tend to be tangible. They're not a matter of opinion. You either hit them or you don't.

What people think and feel about the leader's behavior matters just as much. A leader is assessed on a range of characteristics. For instance, this might include how fair they are, how inspiring, or even just how well the team feels they are represented. Leaders may have a mandate to make decisions but does the leader make them feel proud and happy? Do they make any difference to how they feel?

Leadership and management, in reality, are overlapping Venn diagrams. They are just as important as each other. They have common elements, but they're not the same. Management goals, though, are measurable and tangible. Leadership goals are harder to pin down. For example, balance is one of the greatest leadership goals that is neither achievable, realistic, measurable, nor sustainable. Even if you did achieve it, you'd have to do it all again the next day. Can you achieve it? No. But is it an important goal? Undoubtedly.

To Be vs. To Do

If leadership is about doing the right thing, then what is the "right" thing? Who decides? Well, now we're into semantics. It all depends on who's asking. But stop and think for a minute. If you asked most people to define what is right, could we not agree that it means fair, honest, reliable, reasonable, respectful, ethical, considerate, thoughtful, maybe even unselfish? These words have something in common. An adjective describes a noun. These words are all adjectives. But there's something else. You cannot "do" any of these words. You can only "be" them. You can only be a leader. You can't "do" it.

This is our first clue that leadership needs more than just a "to-do" list. It must have a "to-be" list.

Here's an exercise:

- Describe your parents. Write down five words that summarize them.
- Now tell us about how you introduce yourself. Again, write down five words you use.

Chances are some of the words you used for your parents are below:

- Loving
- Inspirational
- Caring
- Funny
- Patient
- Quiet
- Social
- Strict
- Kind
- Thoughtful
- Ambitious
- Hard-working
- Mean
- Lazy
- Frustrating

What these words have in common is that none of them can be "done." You can only "be" them.

Now look at the words you use to introduce yourself. Chances are, you normally tell people what you do. What's more, you probably have a "to do" list.

Our parents are the first models of leadership we use. This is not so much in what they say to us or what they told us to do, but in who they *are* (or were). Or even what they seemed to be. If a parent's narrative is that they are a victim of circumstance, then this narrative can be learned. This matters because when someone is a victim, then they are relieved of responsibility for their own fate. The reason they are who they are is because of someone else. Someone else is to blame.

When these narratives become established, they can be difficult to shake. Optimism and pessimism can both be learned. This is good and bad—good in so far as it can be changed, bad in so far as you may have unconsciously learned something that might be damaging.

It's important for leaders to have both a "to be" list as well as a "to do" list. You should know what you're trying to do. Yet you should also know who you are and what values you hold. Being something is much harder to live with. Why? Because what you are needs to be done again and again. Tomorrow and the very next day. Let's say one of the "to be" list goals is honesty. This is an important goal but something that even if you did momentarily achieve it, then it would need to be repeated the next day. Because it can't easily be measured, however, it becomes a less important metric. It may be deemed a "soft" skill. It gets downgraded.

The Role of Attitude

Now it's getting a bit more interesting. Attitude and approach dictate outcome and not just in achievement terms. A faulty attitude can damage your health as well as your hopes.

Depression, for instance, is ten times more prevalent than it was fifty years ago. It affects women twice as much as men and it strikes a full ten years earlier than it did a generation ago. Until quite recently, depression was assessed on two main criteria: The psychoanalytical and the biomedical. Both create dependency on outside intervention whether it be clinical counsel or drugs. Yet what if depression occurs merely because we hold pessimistic beliefs? Further, what if this pessimism was part of an ingrained culture, learned from a parent?

This is where the notion of Appreciative Inquiry is useful. In the words of Professor of Social Entrepreneurship, David Cooperrider:

Appreciative inquiry is a radical departure from traditional deficit-based change to a positive, strengths-based change approach.[4]

The technique can be summarized by the phrase "Culture Eats Strategy." When leaders learn to be more positive, then achievement follows. The theory is that it fosters creativity through the art of positive inquiry. It builds skills, develops new leaders, encourages a culture of inquiry, and creates a vision of an organization's values and strengths.

One thing we know is that events can cause depression. Therefore, we know that it's not just brain chemistry alone that triggers or perpetuates depression. We also know that living in depressed communities can also trigger a similar response. What makes a community depressed? This can be as simple as economic depression, lack of employment opportunities and the resulting evils of drugs or drink. Worklessness, for instance, creates a profound change in attitude. The way we think changes us—especially about our health. The evidence suggests that optimists live longer.[5] Optimists experience fewer negative emotions. One report on aging even said:

The most optimistic women were also more likely to achieve exceptional longevity, defined as living over 90 years. These trends were consistent across all racial and ethnic groups.[6]

Any collective private or public team enterprise has a culture. And do you know what? Most people can tell you in detail what culture their team or place of work has. Just ask them what's it like to work there. They'll tell you because they know. Chances are, it's a different experience depending on what level they are. This is another clue. Humanity should be visible at all levels. Leadership can be shown at all levels. Leaders can change things with their attitude:

Because optimism is a modifiable characteristic that can be changed with interventions like writing exercises and therapy, improving optimism may be an effective strategy to improve health and extend lifespan across racial and ethnic groups.[7]

Good leaders that bring optimism as a routine don't just bring efficiency and wealth to their teams, they can also bring healthier outcomes as well.

And so, this brings us to purpose. And this is something that was illuminated by the experience of COVID-19. In this sort of crisis, how did we make life better for those around us?

What is this group here to do? What do we think it's supposed to do and what does it actually do? These may be different.

The Interplay of Vice and Virtue

A community, an organization, a club, a school, a hospital, a church, a team, a business, all have a common purpose. They are bound together by common goals, faith, and belief in what they are trying to do. What is faith? Richard Chartres, former Bishop of London, describes faith as "the opposite of sin." What does he mean? What does sin have to do with leadership? He says: "Sin is not something that just has a biblical or religious application. It is an activity solely focused upon the self." No wonder the word "sin" is at the heart of the word "business."

In the Christian tradition, the cardinal sins are pride/vanity, greed, wrath, envy, lust, gluttony, and sloth, which are contrary to the heavenly virtues of prudence, justice, temperance, and fortitude and the three theological virtues of faith, hope, and charity. Ah, that word faith again. Not logic. Not proof. *Faith*. Not measurable. But important, nonetheless. Christians might sum it up as Hebrews 11: "Faith is the substance of things hoped for—the evidence of things not seen."

And yet how often do we see examples of vanity in modern leadership? The biggest deal, the richest list,[8] the most influential,[9] many of whom, like Sam Bankman-Fried, Adam Neuman, and Elizabeth Holmes appeared on the cover of important magazines like *Time*, *Forbes*, and *Inc*. These pictures don't happen by accident. They happen only with the consent of the subjects.

The virtues are much harder to see. Why? They only manifest over time and, if done correctly, they're done in the name of service and love, expecting nothing in return.

In geology, there are two main ways rocks are formed—igneous, from volcanic activity, or sedimentary, laid down over years and then compressed. You can think of leadership virtues as being sedimentary. They build up over time. Leadership sins—or more accurately the focus on selfish needs—are igneous. They happen in a short period of time, and they come from within the leader. They can repeat and be chronic, but they are based on urge or impulse.

This explains why those who focus solely on their own careers rarely achieve great success. It's only when leaders focus on the careers of those around them that their careers take off. Real leaders exist to serve others.

Understanding Servant Leadership

This brings us to another definition, that of "Servant Leadership" as coined by Robert K. Greenleaf in his 1970 essay.[10] He got the idea from Hermann Hesse, a German writer and poet who told stories of something greater than just himself. He spent his time exploring an individual's search for authenticity, self-knowledge, and spirituality.

Servant leadership is practically embodied in the Four H's: Hungry, Happy, Honest, and Hard-working. These qualities can exist in isolation, but they only truly become animated when applied to a team. Leaders who exhibit these qualities are constantly adding value to their team. This need not be in tangible, measurable, "management" metrics. Sometimes these leaders add value through consistency, attention, recognition, even just giving of their time to show up.

This takes us to the philosophy of leadership. It's nothing new. People have been talking about it for a long time. The message of medieval philosophers such as St Augustine of Hippo and St Thomas Aquinas advanced theology into rational and practical argument.

What does this have to do with modern leaders? St Augustine pointed out the "God-shaped hole" at the center of all unhappiness. Put simply, a focus on the self can never be fulfilled. If the hole (or insecurity) is so great, then no amount of status, money, or importance will ever be enough to fill it. The hole can only be filled by the focus on something other than the self. The problem highlighted is selfishness. Thomas Aquinas was the first to talk about moral leadership as "a sense of duty" and the "universal good." You can still see this played out in the behavior of so many who pursue leadership. They do so for selfish ends.

This leads us then to another definition of leadership as "that which is focused on something other than the self." This can explain the poor performance of some inexperienced leaders where their actions are driven by vanity, greed, pride, envy, or any other of the self-centric sins. They are focused primarily on themselves.

So much for faith. You can't measure it or achieve it, but it remains massively important. Logically put, it's a sort of collective delusion that the future will be better if we defer gratification from the present. But it's powerful, nonetheless. Think of it as Tinker Bell's light in *Peter Pan*. Fairies only exist if people actually believe they do. As strange as it seems, this notion is fundamental to capitalism, too. If you don't believe that the system won't reward you more if you wait, then you don't invest. Without faith nothing works.

It's also fundamental to royalty and other institutions. For most of us, the need for something must be more than just what "is." There has to be hope. There has to be a sense of what "could be" or the things that bind us. This is what drives us forward and we are forever looking for allies in that cause.

How Does a Leader Shape the Collective Attitude?

Let's also talk here about vision. By its very nature, it's something invisible to others. It exists only in so far as the visionary can articulate it. And it's entirely reliant on the recipient's ability to comprehend it. This need not be complex.

Take this story. Three people are in a quarry. Each is breaking rocks. The first one tells you they're breaking rocks (which is obvious). The second one tells you they are breaking rocks because they are being punished. You might want to find out why, but you're not wanting to join in. The third and final one says they are building a cathedral. Now, you can see the bigger picture. You may not be religious, but you can see a plan. Maybe even a motive, too.

Is leadership dealing with stuff that's not real? Well, it's stuff that can't always be measured at least. That's why it's difficult to teach. It can only be learned. The mantle of leadership is diaphanous. You can tell people about it but it's better just to show it.

There's something important here about the leader's relationship with the group. A leader can certainly exist without a group. Displaying leadership is something anyone can do at any level. The group, though, provides the purpose for the leader. The leader is only ever a custodian of the group. The group is never the possession of the leader. The leader belongs to something bigger than just their team.

The leader, though, is responsible for the collective attitude. This is what we know as "culture," and it provides another definition of leadership. You could think of this type of leader as being the one who makes the biggest difference between success and failure. The relationship with failure is the most important one to study for anyone interested in success. We know it sounds paradoxical, but anyone can cope with success. Leadership psychology is all about dealing with failure. The leader needs to gain the permission of the team to try again after failure. Success is built on a pyramid of failure.

What Is the Interplay of Success and Failure?

To extend the paradox, continued success can also be the provenance of failure. Worse still, it can lead to depression and anxiety. Gold Medal Syndrome is a thing. Swimmer Michael Phelps, the most decorated Olympian of all time, has talked candidly about his downward spiral after the 2012 London games that led to a DUI arrest and time in rehab: "I still remember the days locked up in my room, not wanting to talk to anybody, not wanting to see anybody, really not wanting to live."[11]

Success may not be a spur to further improvement. Failure, on the other hand, provides that the belief in further improvement is there. The implication of this is also important. Failure is frequently a springboard to success. What matters is the will to continue.

The great management guru Peter Drucker described leaders as experts in marketing. In this world, the leader has one job. This is to figure out what the team needs and how to satisfy those requirements. Leadership, in this model, becomes a marketing job. Yet this is to ignore the needs of the wider community.

The leader is most famed for the success they can bring. Or appear to bring. Sometimes the leader's main product is their personality. This was referred to directly as being one of the reasons investors followed Adam Neumann, the tall, charismatic entrepreneur behind WeWork. At the peak of its value in October 2022, it was worth $47 billion. By January 2024, it had fallen to $14 million, a catastrophic fall in value over 18 months. It was a factor with Elizabeth Holmes from Theranos and Sam Bankman-Fried of FTX, both of whose companies collapsed into failure and scandal. The force of the personality, then, can act like a stock in its own right, apparently rising and falling subject to its own "random walk" methodology. In September 2022, Neumann's new company Flow received $350 million in new investment from Andreessen Horowitz.[12]

So, let's talk about investment in leaders. But to do this we also have to talk about business. So again, we need some definitions. The Harvard Business School defined business as: "The management of social relationships for profit, where profit may be financial." It's a good one because it addresses business in its wider context. It's not a financial, technical, or professional process; it's a social one. It's also vague about what profit means. It speaks of value. And this is important because it's not just value for its shareholders but for its customers, colleagues, communities, and collaborators. They all have a role. They can all benefit.

A profitable and successful organization is never the product of a leader alone. The provenance is always that of a successful culture. Some say that a profitable firm will always have a good culture. Simply not true. Some of the worst cultures exist within profitable companies. Organizations can make profits and still not be healthy, sustainable, or successful. This is very much a short-term position and again speaks to the leader as a long-term player. It is only when profits are made within a successful culture that they become sustainable.

What Leadership Is Not

When the orchestra conductor raises their baton in front of the players, they do not do so on the basis of their domain skill with any one instrument. The conductor is not a better violinist than anyone else. Nor are they likely to know more about a double bass than anyone in the string section. Management might be based on domain skill. Leadership is not.

Leadership establishes common purpose in a divided world. It's not involved in arguments about dividing the proceeds of success. This becomes harder in times of extreme inequality between rich and poor. This has been China's genius to this point. As long as living standards for the whole continue to rise, gaps and resentments don't boil over into conflict.[13] Or put another way, you don't fall off the bicycle as long as it keeps moving forward.

Do We Always Need Leaders?

Let's be clear. You can show leadership without being a leader. Leadership is something that everyone can display. You can be positive, supportive of others, come prepared, on time or early, and always do more than what you're asked. You act like a leader before you get confirmed in the role. Some will have come to this book wanting to know the secrets of leadership. There are none. It's a choice. No one can make it for you. You either decide the above or you don't. It's as easy as that. That's what makes it so hard.

How Important Is Leadership?

American businessman and, later, Bill Clinton's Chief of Staff, Erskine Bowles, once described leadership as "the key to 99 percent of all successful efforts."

But what does leadership actually do? Lots of things. The leader is there to improve communications and improve productivity. So far, so good. These are all things that can be measured. But they're also there to make people in the team feel good about who they are and what they're doing. They must feel motivated. They're there to stop, anticipate, and avoid mistakes. This takes imagination to see what might go wrong. But again, leaders don't normally get measured on what *doesn't* happen.

So, What Is Leadership Then?

Deep breath.

Leadership is that which makes other people more effective.

One of the great paradoxes about leadership is how few people use it to describe themselves, their roles, or their aspirations. Nor do people use the word "leader" to describe their boss.

There's especially a problem with the words used to describe the leader in a community project. Community leaders are the last to refer to themselves in that way. Joe Schipani, who runs the Flint Public Art Project (see Leadership Profile) says, "Don't talk to me about leadership!" He sees himself just as someone who gets stuff done. He just thinks of himself as an "ally." This is pretty low key. Yet he speaks for the projects and many of the artists.

Why do so many leaders feel uncomfortable with the title of "leader?" It could be that it is a political term. Most political parties refer to a "leader." Most famously, of course, Adolf Hitler, who was

Der Führer[14]—The Leader. It's the sort of thing that only aliens ask in sci-fi movies: Take me to your Leader!

LEADERSHIP PROFILE
Joe Schipani: Flint Public Art Project

Flint Public Art Project
Documentary

SOURCE TEAM LEWIS Foundation, https://youtu.be/9foez6ZAOm4?si=-DO1V33w7dlwC5LI
https://flintpublicartproject.com/

The Flint Public Art Project hosts events and workshops, and creates installations to inspire residents. It is responsible for over 300 temporary and permanent murals on the walls of buildings across Flint, Michigan. This is the city that was damaged by the effects of the General Motors reorganization in the 1990s. It also experienced a health crisis with toxic leaks into the city's water, particularly in communities of color. Subsequently, it suffered a decline in the quality of living, with many campaigning for more support. The project was identified by a TEAM LEWIS colleague, Zapporah Turner, who grew up in the community. The challenge was how to raise awareness for their work rebuilding the community.

Joe Schipani has served as the organization's executive director since 2015. His husky laughter opens the conversation as you enter his world. When considering leadership, he says the power is in the conversation. Using art to have discussions that lead to an exchange of ideas. He acknowledges that some have chosen to exploit the story of Flint rather than celebrate the strength of the community. He shares that words like "resilience" have become clichéd when discussing the community of Flint, but it is an accurate description.

We might think of identity as how we look, how we appear, our race, our gender, our height, our size, but these are just identity markers. They don't describe the soul or the spirit of a person or place. The soul of Flint is the spirit of the individuals who make up the community. While this is a community that has experienced trauma, the Flint Art Project is about healing.

Schipani's leadership is meaningful in that he is committed to both listening to the community and making sure that the works of public art truly allow people to see themselves. All the people. For him, success is measured by the impact of those experiencing the art and the ability to catalyze meaningful conversation.

Schipani says that there are barriers to accessing art that are rooted in race, age, and financial or social status:

> Not everyone feels comfortable going into a space, like a traditional art gallery or museum, where they feel they don't understand what they are seeing. Nor do they want to think they might be scrutinized differently because of who they are. Public art drops those barriers to access and allows everyone to participate.

To this end, the artwork represents the many different identities present in the community:

> Whether they're Black or White, gay or straight, rich or poor, it doesn't matter. Everybody can be represented. These are our community members, too. These are the things that are going to make us think and make us talk and have uncomfortable conversations that need to happen.

Change is made a lot less scary when those involved are allowed to discuss it. The breakdown in any organization or community comes when those involved stop talking to each other. Change becomes much more achievable where there is trust that comes from dialogue. This is where the art works as a catalyst. The nuance involved in the art provokes comment and exchange. Put simply, it gets people talking. This sounds simple but it's genius. The first part of healing divisions is getting people talking again. It wasn't easy:

> I chose art as the tool to have this conversation. We got a grant from the Warhol Foundation, and we had to do a public announcement. The amount

was a $70,000 grant for two years and people [were asking] why are you spending that money on art, when you could be spending that on the water crisis? But the grant was just for this purpose. If we were not going to use it for that purpose, then we would have had to give the money back.

Schipani cites a specific example of the North End of Flint. A significant amount of money and work went into developing a park. Yet, directly across the street from the park was an eyesore of an abandoned liquor store with images of cigarettes. The Flint Public Art Project "wrapped" a mural around that building to both enhance the view from the park and to add something beautiful to the community. What they do requires diplomacy and sensitivity:

We gotta make sure as curators and leaders that we're not pushing what we want on other people. We want to make sure that we're helping them get what they need and not what we want. We went into neighborhoods. We talked to neighborhood groups and one of my big things is if we're going to put a mural in your neighborhood, we want it to be something you want to see. Well, they're the ones that are going to have to look at it every day. I wanted to make sure it wasn't a gentrification project. If you notice, a lot of cities, they will put these murals in the Whitest, brightest area; what they think you should have whether you like it or not and they get tagged. They get destroyed. They get ruined. I had only two of my murals tagged out of over 300 because I want to make sure, when we do murals, it represents the population.

Schipani goes on to say that the participation and investment into the decision-making by the actual community members creates a sense of ownership:

Kids who engage in tagging don't want to have their butts whipped when they get home, when the mural matters to their mothers, fathers, cousins, aunties, and others in the community. Trying to get people to value street art has been a challenge because for many years, it has been considered vandalism.

An app was developed that tracked when people viewed the murals. Patterns emerged. It provided data to share with business owners about the time of day, which could allow them to time their opening hours. People congregated outside after a meal at an area restaurant to enjoy the art. During the pandemic, the murals were a way for people to get out and see something inspiring and lovely in their own neighborhood. Yet, Schipani notes that it is the immeasurable, intangible aspects of the positive effects of art on a community that matter most:

> We wanted to make the neighborhood almost like an outdoor classroom on Black history. We started off with Marcus Garvey; we moved over to Josephine Baker and then we have Martin Luther King, Jr., the March on Selma and then we have the Flint strike to end segregation in housing. The hardest thing to do is to get money to pay artists because people think art is a hobby. You don't go to a mechanic and say, "Well, you rebuild cars as a hobby, so will you change my oil for free and I'll buy you a sandwich?"

Humor is Schipani's hallmark, tempered with a deep sense of compassion for those around him. He jokes that sometimes in his role as a leader he felt like a professional beggar, asking almost every day for donations. He even quipped that the key to being a leader is having a lot of money. With a hearty chuckle, he shares that he is just kidding and goes on to speak of the joys and heartbreaks of leadership:

> I would tell anybody always to stand by your community and always stand by your artists because these are the people that you're helping, working with and working for. I've seen so many people throw artists under the bus because they don't want to take the blame. An example of this is the mayor who gave permission to do a Black Lives Matter mural on the street and then once he started getting complaints about it from a bunch of white people, he said you gotta stop. I told him, tell them you had nothing to do with it. You send them my way. This is what your community wants, and this is what your community needs to heal. If you're more worried about your pocketbook and your donors than you are your community, then you're in the wrong job.

The lesson is clear. The leader doesn't measure success by financial gains. Schipani worked a day job the whole time he worked for the public art project. This was because no one wanted to pay for an executive director. Nobody wanted to pay artists. So he did it for free, but:

I got paid in smiles on people's faces and their stories telling me about the impact the murals have in their neighborhood. It's just amazing to see the benefits to the community. All of a sudden, there's one corner of the earth that looks like a wasteland which is now becoming beautiful as a result of the people inside it, that are living in it. Those rewards are worth so much more than payment. You don't value what you're doing by how much money you're making. The impact alone is what it is and that's what you've got to remember.

SUMMARY: CHAPTER 3

There are myriad definitions of leadership, from those rooted in Ubuntu to organizational theory. Managers have a "to do" list. Leaders have a "to be" list. The attitude of a leader should lift others up. However, a profitable and successful organization is never the product of the leader alone. Culture is key. The positivity of the leader can build a workplace culture that eats strategy. Why? The leader is the custodian of the culture. The leader sets the tone for the collective attitude. Optimism is a powerful driver.

Communities, families, faith-based organizations, non-profits, schools, and teams are formed around a common purpose. They share goals, faith, vision, and belief in their collective enterprise. Real leaders exist to serve others. And the leader is in service of the group.

Leadership is that which makes others more effective. For many, the only certainty in life is change. Indeed, change is an area that most people struggle with. The next chapter examines what needs to change in leadership.

Aspirational note

- As a result of having read this chapter, what might you do differently in terms of your own leadership style?
- What facts, stories, quotes, or points stood out for you?
- What might you explore further?

04

How Does Leadership Need to Change?

Why don't leaders lead?

What is the paradox of leadership?

How does being obsessive create the foundation for leadership?

What can we learn from the leaders of causes?

How is leadership demonstrated?

How do leaders make change?

How does the leader scale the needs of the organization?

Who decides who gets to lead?

How can you demonstrate leadership?

What makes for psychologically effective leadership?

The Leader by Name

Think about it. We don't even use the job title "leader" to describe any of the jobs that involve leadership. Most often, individuals who lead use a job title that includes the word *chief*, as in Chief Executive Officer. We even have a "C Level" where everyone addressed is a "chief."

More non-profit organizations are using the title because of the perceived clout that goes with it. Obviously, there are other executive officers, but this one is the *chief*, the person highest in authority. This originates from the French word *chef*, which itself comes from the Latin word *caput* (head). This is where we get the word captain. History hands us many of our leadership terms. Take "Caesar" for instance. "Caesar" is the root word for the titles of czar, tsar, shah, and kaiser.

Some say the word "leader" itself comes from the Norse word *Leidar* or the North Star, Polaris. The Pole Star is reliable, constant, and guides the way. It has a practical role, but it is reassuring, consistent, and a bright spot in the darkness. This provides a model for what good leadership looks like with all the qualities of the modern leader.

Why Leaders Don't Lead

In a *Harvard Business Review* piece entitled "Why Capable People Are Reluctant to Lead," three specific risks were identified that deter people from stepping up to lead:[1]

1 **Interpersonal risk:** They were concerned that leadership might hurt relationships with their colleagues.

2 **Image risk:** That leading might make others think badly of them. This is almost a shyness, a reluctance to push forward.

3 **Risk of being blamed:** Finally, people were afraid that if they stepped up to lead, they would be held personally responsible if the group failed.

Being a leader is also a perilous place. Even starting out in an executive position, the odds are stacked against you. According to one survey, 50 percent to 70 percent of executives fail within 18 months of taking on a role. This is regardless of whether they were an external appointment or promoted from within. At the highest level, the turnover rates of CEOs of major North American corporations jumped by about 50 percent from the 1990s to 2000–2007,[2] and the average CEO tenure dropped 17 percent between 2013 and 2017.[3,4]

The average age for a C-suite leader is 56 years old and the average tenure is around five years, but it's been falling.[5] More CEOs are losing their jobs due to "ethical lapses" than ever before.[6] This rises as a percentage the bigger the company's value is. Or put another way, you're less likely to get fired as a leader of a smaller organization. This is not to say the behavior is necessarily worse but it may also be more visible and thus subject to scrutiny.

Worse still, the average retirement age is 61. So even if you do make it to the top, and you manage to avoid being fired, you won't be there into a ripe old age. Very seldom does this brutal reality get mentioned alongside the perks and packages of the position. And don't even think about doing it for self-esteem. Only 37 percent of people consider CEOs credible and this too has been falling.[7]

It looks like it will become increasingly difficult to attract leaders into key roles for any other reason than short-term money. This, though, has got to be the worst reason for anyone to want to become a leader—possibly a reason why leadership has become so degraded. So, this sets up a bizarre paradox.

Those who actually want to lead are often the ones you'd rather not have. And the ones who are reluctant are the ones who might do the better job. No wonder no one wants to talk about leadership!

Really, why should anyone want to lead? Well, there are some bona fide reasons. For instance, sometimes you can't achieve your vision without help. It may also be that, for some people, there is no alternative. No one else is stepping forward, so they feel a duty to do so. This is the case with so many of the social cause leaders we've profiled here. Perhaps, though, it's more about wanting to defend a set of values in a community. The latter reason is what can be seen in so many community causes. One person simply says, "This needs to be stopped and I will stop it." This is why the inspiration is so strong in these people. They're doing what they do for unselfish reasons.

LEADERSHIP PROFILE
Roy Tuscany: High Fives Foundation

Changing Lives with High Fives Documentary

SOURCE TEAM LEWIS Foundation https://youtu.be/WTOOvjSZORc?si=xwZfOjiu2gQCLp7u
https://highfivesfoundation.org/

When leaders operate from a space of empathy, they're unstoppable.

ROY TUSCANY

In 2006, Roy Tuscany was a professional skier who sustained a life-changing injury when he "went 130 feet on a 100-foot ski jump." He impacted the T12 vertebrae in his spine and rendered his lower body paralyzed. With the outpouring from those who donated funds toward his recovery, he realized that there were others who had no community of support and no infrastructure. He decided to create a foundation for those similarly affected by life-changing injuries. He has led the High Fives Foundation for 15 years.

His enthusiasm is palpable as he speaks with the verve and energy of a professional athlete. He is on the path of pain, insight, disruption, and change of identity that results from a life-altering injury:

> It can take us through the fire, but we need not burn up. It may not be the same, but it can still be awesome.

High Fives Foundation creates a universal shift in adventure sports that expands the possibilities for those with life-changing injuries. It also focuses on preventing injuries and provides immediate resources and hope if the worst happens. As a non-profit organization, it has helped countless athletes and veterans get back to doing what they love. The Foundation aims to be the leader in education and recovery of life-altering injuries in outdoor action sports. It takes resources, yes, but it takes experience and knowledge, too:

> It takes a team, an army, a village to get through life-changing injuries and I think that's a big takeaway from High Fives. We don't just show up with a handout. It's really a hand up to give people the opportunity to move forward but also know that what they have is an additional family around them to get them through.

Tuscany says acceptance is important because there's a tendency for people to waste time thinking regretfully and considering the "if only" aspects:

> When you can let go of trying to press rewind and figure out how to get back to where you were, and you actually start to hit play and move forward... [You] see where you might be able to get to, I think that's a big takeaway for a lot of people.

In Tuscany's estimation, the ability to let go of what was and the identity associated with that former self is the way through to the other side.

> I wanted to create an opportunity for those that don't have the same circle around them like I did. We could have created many different entities but when it comes down to it, I thought that the best thing was to extend the opportunity of hope and that comes through the work that we do as a non-profit.

He says it's been quite a learning process, on both the commercial and organizational sides:

> When I got hurt, I didn't know anything about non-profits and people helped me out of the kindness of their hearts. I think I have always had the kind of personality that attracts others so it's easy for me to create community and those that want to support me. So for all the people that don't have a voice or are afraid to use their voice, I just wanted to extend the opportunity of hope. Just because you're disabled doesn't mean you can't do something. You've just got to figure out how to adapt and move forward.

In this world, if you are truly thinking about leading, Tuscany says you need to decide if you are "the asshole" or "the inspiration." He reflects on the archetypal bosses that were depicted in the seventies, eighties, and early nineties who used either size or money to bully their way through leadership. Yet, for the modern leader, he says, there is another way:

> In your leadership, what if you could approach each relationship [by] being that missing entity in that individual's life? If you can become that person, for those groups that you're leading that they didn't have in their lives... maybe it's a father, maybe it's a mother, maybe it's an uncle, maybe it's a cousin or brother.

Tuscany challenges us to think about who we can be to others in their lives. And to seize that opportunity to help others, which ultimately helps ourselves.

Those with experience can and should share their wisdom freely with others:

> With your leadership position, within your company, why wouldn't you want people to really accept you as this key figure that can give them [creative] insight? Why wouldn't you want to share, if you've been doing something for many years?

There is a generational shift happening that Tuscany acknowledges, concerning the ways in which society views people with disabilities:

> Individuals with disabilities, with some modifications and adjustments, can live fulfilling lives. They can participate at high levels and can be even more impactful than an able-bodied person. There's a great generational shift that's starting to happen here.

There's an interesting point here. Most of us will encounter physical disability at some stage:

> O.L.D. [as in old age], it's coming for every single one of us and it comes in many different forms.

Aging is a metaphor for the accelerated process that a life-changing injury brings. The reality of injury slingshots the individual into a place where there is greater reliance on outside people and resources. This involves a need for technological aids and personal assistance. Adaptation to participate fully in the activities of daily living is needed.

Tuscany reflects that when people see a person with disabilities, it taps into a sense of fear of their own future in terms of aging. Changing the way people living with disabilities are seen is in the self-interest of everyone. It's an important point: "We are all only temporarily able-bodied."

In Tuscany's opinion, real leaders blend into the crowd. They know they're only as good as those that they surround themselves with:

> I don't think leadership looks like driving the fanciest car or wearing the most outrageous outfit. Neither is it showcasing how much more power you have due to the value of what surrounds you. I think what real leadership looks like is when you can be in a room of 100 people and the only thing that makes you stand out is the values that you have.

One final point here on inclusion. Few people think of this as "woke" but it is part of the diversity, equity, and inclusion idea:

> When I think of the word "woke," I really try to remember its origins, which is being enlightened and understanding the other person's position and point of view. We may not agree but that doesn't mean we have to hate.

What Other Qualities are Needed for Leadership?

Everyone knows about the fame and fortune associated with successful leaders. Behind everyone, though, lurks a set of qualities that people want to talk about less. Roy Tuscany's leadership illustrates the experience of many leaders. It's a victory won in silence and in pain away from the spotlight, where the drive is singular, unyielding, and relentless. It's hard to watch that. Hard, but inspiring. It's the stuff of the human spirit. That's the deceptive thing about humans. They all look similar. They're roughly the same size. There are lots of them, but some are very, very unusual. They are all the more unusual because of their "matter of fact" manner. Roy Tuscany is one of them. To others, what he has achieved is unusual. To him, he gets on with it every day, so it's just his normal. This is one of the qualities of great leadership; it just gets on with it day in and day out. It doesn't go around demanding attention. It commands it.

Obsessive Qualities and Leadership

These types of people aren't always easy to live with. All leaders have this to some extent. It's called obsession. An example of this is Pat Riley, a nine-time National Basketball Association champion. He pointed out that leadership can simply come down to being more obsessed than anyone else. In his case, with winning. As a player coach and executive, he is a nine-time NBA champion. He appeared in one quarter of all NBA Finals in history:

> To have long-term success as a coach or in any position of leadership, you have to be obsessed in some way.

Another obsessive who, believe it or not, wrote a research bulletin entitled "How to Grow the Peanut and 105 Ways of Preparing it For Human Consumption" was George Washington Carver. His extraordinary life is worthy of specific mention.[8] Born to enslaved people in 1864, his life began on a Missouri farm owned by Moses and Susan Carver. His father died and his mother was given her freedom by the Carvers and adopted their name. Before he was a year old, he and his mother were kidnapped by slave traders. His mother was never seen again, yet he survived. Despite this, he went on to become one of the most famous agricultural innovators in the United States. He summed up his determination in the depths of despair:

> Where there is no vision, there is no hope.

He also had something to say about the money and wealth his abilities gave him. He just wasn't interested in them:

> We have become money mad. The method of living at home modestly and within our income, laying a little by systematically for the

proverbial rainy day, which is due to come, can almost be listed among the lost arts.

Who the heck wants to be around obsessives? They can frequently be boring, monocultural, frugal, and unhappy. The obsessive is also likely to spend their time alone. Henry Kissinger, former US Secretary of State who died in late 2023, also noted this ability to tolerate isolation:

A leader does not deserve the name unless he is willing occasionally to stand alone.

Best-selling Christian author Max Lucado echoed this sentiment:

A man who wants to lead the orchestra must turn his back on the crowd.

Harnessing the Unifying Cause

In a *Harvard Business Review* piece entitled "9 Out of 10 People Are Willing to Earn Less Money to Do More-Meaningful Work,"[9] Shawn Achor, Andrew Reece, Gabriella Rosen Kellerman, and Alexi Robichaux explored the issues of motivation.

In every method of assessing talent, it's clear that while you can coach people to pass exams, the actual level of talent is relatively fixed. And it divides people by ranking them. The real variable in all performance is not talent, but attitude. There are two aspects to this. Yes, the individual has responsibility for their own approach. But the leader also needs to recognize that if talent is relatively fixed, the biggest variable is therefore the motivation of the group. This can be seen in every English Premier League match and every Major League Baseball game. An averagely talented group of players that work as a team is more powerful than one that doesn't. Its collective attitude can overcome the most talented group who are divided and not working together.

The lesson is clear from every leadership profile in the book. Whether it's food, music, art, sports, a location, or even one terrible event, it all starts with a shared experience. It's the most human quality of all. Life means nothing unless we share it. They all form up around something they all have in common.

Leaders don't climb mountains so they can be seen. They do it so they can see further and serve as a guide. With this vision, some key individuals can change the way people think, but it requires discipline to form new habits. You get good at the things you like. Things you like, you do most frequently. Excellence, therefore, is always a habit and it must be fun.

This is why Cause-Related Marketing (CRM) is becoming more widely accepted as an important part of motivation. Put simply, this is just a mutually beneficial collaboration between a community and a cause. It's powerful but it must be done right.

LEADERSHIP PROFILE
Alicia Altorfer-Ong, PhD: Ray of Hope

Count Me In: Ray of Hope ×
Clement Chow

SOURCE Ray of Hope https://www.youtube.com/watch?v=8yWkPxr6ics

Ray of Hope aims to build a stronger, more inclusive community in Singapore.

The organization began as Singapore's first and only crowdfunding charity, designed to help individuals and families in times of crisis and need, who may otherwise have no access to assistance. It incorporates casework and is a trusted platform for donors seeking to help those who have "fallen through the cracks." This positive giving experience continues to foster a greater sense of individual responsibility and stronger social cohesion.

In the past two years, Ray of Hope has broadened its mandate to address emerging and more complex needs in the community. It continues to mobilize financial capital (casework and crowdfunding), social capital (through partnerships and collaborations), and community capital (through volunteerism). With this broadened mandate, clients can be inducted into the Ray of Hope community, which includes a diverse array of partners from within the charity sector and beyond.

Most importantly, it recognizes that what someone is going through is not a reflection of who they are. The wider context is important, because every one of us is on the move. Dr. Alicia Altorfer-Ong, Deputy General Manager, shares:

> We see human potential before our very eyes. We meet clients at a low point in their lives, and it is only a snapshot in time. For example, sometimes we have a middle-income family who is at risk of being pushed into poverty because of a medical crisis.

Moving individuals and families from an unstable financial background to stabilization is the key. They are then able to participate in the community and contribute:

> We have clients who have since donated to other Ray of Hope crowdfunding campaigns.

Going a step further, former clients volunteering with the very organization that had previously helped them creates personal agency and social connectedness.

This includes a consciousness of the family's needs beyond the conventional. For example, to participate in holidays like Lunar New Year or Deepavali, families often need new clothes or to be able to offer guests festive treats. Financial distress can be isolating, and Ray of Hope helps break that. From goodie bags to tangible funds, it allows families to participate fully in the life of the community.

The strength of community transcends language. Ray of Hope has found strategies to bring together people through the universal language of sports and food. Altorfer-Ong says there's not a one-size-fits-all solution:

> There's no one model to do it. We just know that diversity and inclusion must be a part of our daily life, so we have to purposefully and meaningfully curate these activities. My great interest and strength converge in the people sector. I'm genuinely interested in people and in their development. We aren't static commodities.

Altorfer-Ong's approach is based on asking the right questions. She says getting to the root of any problem needs effective communication and a spirit of openness. She looks to solve problems in a collaborative setting. Cultural alignment is also a factor:

> I'm Chinese and from the majority race in Singapore. So I must be sensitive to unconscious bias.

Her constituency and team are highly diverse, ethnically, religiously, and generationally:

> We are more open to learning and trying something a little adventurous or new if we believe that those around us are supportive and have our best interests at heart.

Strengths-based problem-solving is a mindset shift that works.

Promoting volunteerism is a key pillar of the organization. Volunteers use their networks to assist the charity's cause and enable a broader outreach to unlock more community resources. Event-based volunteers can leverage their relationships and support Ray of Hope's activities; skilled volunteers often come aboard as mentors. Altorfer-Ong adds:

> My role then is to curate and match mentors to the team; there is a lot of learning and development that happens dynamically without my having to over-engineer and be too prescriptive.

The learning works both ways: reverse mentoring is another plus for the organization. Youths and young adults join Ray of Hope as interns and bring their skills and talents. The result is often mutually eye-opening and at times even transformative. Altorfer-Ong says:

> We learn from each other, also intergenerationally. There are a lot of things that I haven't come across, which they can share with me too.

This is especially helpful in keeping us agile in our communication with different partners and stakeholders. She says:

> There has to be openness and communication.

This builds the case for why diversity and inclusion are so crucial. When you have multiple voices, nothing gets overlooked. It is a more sustainable approach in the long run because it has buy-in. Concepts stand on multiple legs. More input means greater ownership.

Leadership is no longer the model of the solitary leader who carries the flag and charges the hill alone. The modern leader invites input. They are open to new ideas and create models where people feel invested in their community. Hope abounds!

How is Leadership Demonstrated?

Leadership is demonstrated by taking overall responsibility and by taking responsibility for yourself; you cannot take responsibility for others until you have done so. The next simple task is always to do more than is expected. People often wonder how they get paid more for doing less. The answer is simple. First you must do more than you are paid for. This is also the essence of those who take responsibility for themselves and others. This means setting high standards for yourself and meeting them. All sounds easy then? No. It doesn't. That's why so few people do it and those that do sometimes have no alternative.

One of the great ambiguities of leadership is also one of its strangest. If you are a leader, then when do you show leadership? Constant levels of intrusive leadership are construed as micromanagement and can be demotivating. The absence of leadership is just as damaging. Some say it should be present in crisis or celebration. Whenever there is something out of the ordinary. But this is to negate the ongoing involvement of leadership in training, development, and reassurance.

A good rule of thumb for leadership is to show up when there is a change in the air. Of course, during seismic change, leadership should always be present. But what about on a daily basis?

Leaders That Make Change

The relationship between change and leadership is a linear one. What is static cannot be steered. A way leaders can make change is by rotating leadership beneath them. Asking others to step up into a leadership role temporarily can do this. Or appointing leadership of a task force to investigate or oversee an area. In this way, the leader can allow others to demonstrate their capacity or readiness for leadership. This also breaks up cosy relationships which may need refreshing.

Leaders should be aware of the potential of liminal states. These occur wherever a threshold or boundary is passed. It comes from the Latin *limina,* which means "threshold." Traveling over thresholds is a hallmark of dynamic teams. These are full of potential, whether they be personal or collective.

A classic liminal state for the individual lies at the sleep/wake boundary. For instance, many report themselves as having their best ideas at this point. Another would be the dry/wet boundary when taking a shower (another place people report having ideas). Now of course, these are states that individuals pass through, but teams have this experience too, especially in times of change.

That's why many good leaders have a meeting at the beginning of a work session and at the end. Sometimes this will take the form of a morning assembly, as in a school. Sometimes at the end of the day at work, a team will head to the pub before heading home. This, for instance, is very common in London.

Leaders also take the opportunity to push their teams beyond their comfort zones. Again, this is a liminal state. Whenever anyone or a team is going through a liminal state there is uncertainty. And this is the time the leader needs to be present. A typical time of structural uncertainty might be a reorganization or redundancies when leadership should also be accessible, if not visible.

The rules for when leadership should show up are not hard and fast. Sometimes it's enough to be available. At other times it needs to be front and center. Even when leadership is present, it's not necessary for it to 'do' things. This can just get in the way of people who know how to do their job. Sometimes it's enough to praise and reassure the team. Of course, this isn't easy for those leaders who just can't let go. These are typically those with high levels of domain experience. Take for instance battlefield command. There are those new officers who find it hard to delegate tactical command to those who are still learning it.

What is Domain Skill?

Domain skill is held by the most accomplished person available with the most knowledge, experience, and talent. This would be the most skilled violinist in the orchestra, the most skilled soccer player on the pitch, the most talented surgeon in the operating theater.

This illustrates the problem with leadership. Who do you choose to lead? The one with the domain skill or the best at motivating the whole team? They may not be the same person. The most brilliant footballer may not be the person to get the best out of a team of brilliant players. Think of this as two ends of the spectrum. Domain skills and leadership skills. The latter could be where there is a minimal requirement for domain skills but an overwhelming one for team achievement. The hard-pressed football manager is a good example of this.

If you want domain expertise, you won't find it in leadership. The CEO will seldom know more about the actual detail of the work than the person doing it.

The problem with domain skill is that it can't scale. Leaders usually start out domain-skilled. Someone gets good at a job, so they typically get promoted and put in charge of others who are doing the job. This doesn't always work. The best salesperson is seldom the best sales manager. To lead requires not just the domain skills but also the psychological skills of leadership.

So how do leaders transition from domain-driven skills to being psychologically driven? This is especially difficult when they have a deep level of domain skills. Experts, by their very nature, will always be able to perform tasks better. But in collective enterprise, it's the volume of skills and not just the value that matters.

The point of leadership is that it allows you to scale. If you don't need scale, you don't need leadership. At least domain skill leaders have credibility. The worst type of leader is one who has neither domain nor psychological skills. You don't often need to look far. They often advertise themselves. If any of the following admissions apply to you, then don't become a leader because the results could be catastrophic for you and everyone else.

"I am insecure and I hate being the center of attention." Great. Be a reclusive artist.

"I am a bully and enjoy having power over people." Great. Take up martial arts.

"I am egocentric and hate other people getting attention." Great. Be a stand-up comedian.

"I want more money than anyone else." Great. Become a domain specialist and be the best in the world.

The problem with having these sorts of people in leadership positions is that they magnify the inefficiencies of poor leadership. The faults of an individual are amplified and multiplied in exactly the way good leadership makes a huge, positive difference.

Selecting candidates for leadership positions is therefore high risk, capable of achieving enormous swings in productivity for good or for ill. For these reasons, leadership selection requires multiple stages and interviews.

The Decision to Lead

The decision to lead is seldom a conscious one. Often it comes early in childhood. A natural instinct for leadership can sometimes be spotted at school. Sometimes this shows itself with domain expertise. The best runner becomes captain of the running team, for instance. A leader of a study group thus may be the most talented scholar.

The best type of enduring leader is one for whom there is almost no other choice. Roy Tuscany from High Fives Foundation (see leadership profile) is one such example. Tuscany sustained a burst fracture of his T-12 vertebrae, compromising 45 percent of his spinal cord, after going 130 feet on a 100-foot ski jump. The accident rendered his lower body paralyzed. After having high hopes of becoming a world-class professional skier, he then had to re-learn everything in life from the ground up. His organization provides hope and resources for athletes from all walks of life. It allows them to get back to their outdoor physical activity of choice, from snowboarding and skiing to surfing and mountain biking and beyond.

At times, fate intervenes and we are required to step up. Tuscany could have chosen not to step up, but he did. The experience of injury has altered his life course in such a way that rather than the personal glory he may have achieved as a solo athlete, he now is positioned to change the lives of others who have experienced a life-altering injury for the better. Furthermore, there is a deeper concept at work here. The nature of life is change. Learning to let go of what was and find joy in what is inspires everyone. He's a larger-than-life character who radiates hope, energy, and leadership.

Who Decides Who Gets to Lead?

Organizations and boards like to think that they're the ones who get to decide who leads. In reality, it's the team itself. All leadership contests require losers' consent. There must be at least some consensus that the leader is the best person for the job.

Often the best leaders are the ones who are the most difficult to convince of their leadership ability. "Imposter Syndrome" is a common emotion experienced by excellent leaders. Their doubt is their engine of improvement. For philosophers such as Descartes, the doubt was the key differentiating quality of mankind. He is remembered for his statement "*cogito ergo sum*" (I think therefore I am). However, when Descartes is read in the original Latin, the full phrasing becomes clear: "*dubito ergo cogito ergo sum*" (I doubt, therefore I think, therefore I am). Religion is based on certainty. Science is based on doubt.

Doubt is at the heart of leadership. To question why something is not done differently is the precursor to leadership. Leaders challenge the status quo, create disruption, and go beyond "what is" to "what could be."

How Can You Demonstrate Leadership?

Anyone who takes responsibility is showing leadership. Even the person who looks after their fitness is showing leadership. How so? Because it means they have the spare capacity to help others. In the same way, you can choose to be cheerful. Those who dump their negative emotions on others are not showing leadership. Try to leave people in a better state than you found them. All individual encounters are an opportunity to demonstrate this.

Any form of collective enterprise involves meetings. These can be platforms to show effective leadership. For instance, a good leader ensures that a meeting is properly organized. It should have:

- a chair (or chairs)
- an agenda, circulated in advance
- minutes of the previous meeting to discuss matters arising
- progress reports on key metrics
- discussion of problems
- minutes which record discussion and agreements
- equal time for all involved to participate
- the leader speaking first and last and seldom in between
- date and time of next meetings

What should not happen is that the loudest voice dominates, unless the group is under duress and has no time for discussion, such as when launching lifeboats. You probably don't want too much discussion of the best way of launching—this should have been agreed to before with multiple drills. The leader also prepares for the unexpected, even the unthinkable (but not unimaginable). For example, a school active shooter plan. No one wants to think about this, yet no one would want to have a debate at a crucial time.

What Makes for Psychologically Effective Leaders?

Psychologically effective leaders must strive to be happy. They must be operating of their own free will. They must be free. They must want to set others free. They must be articulate and capable of breathtaking vision. They must be of unbreakable will. Of course, they can curse and swear, but they never stop in pursuit of a goal. These people are so special, but they must not think themselves so. Do they go in for ostentatious displays of wealth? Not if they're smart. Do they wear a Rolex watch, drive a Lamborghini, or sail a yacht? They might, but the best of them do not. They believe it will just drive a bigger wedge between them and their team because no one likes a show-off. They are self-aware.

Who Can Lead?

Some will have picked this book up because they want to learn more about how to lead. Who doesn't want to learn more about leadership? But what's your motivation for doing so? Do you genuinely have an interest in how people are motivated? Do you have an over-arching vision of something you simply must achieve? Or is it because you want to make more money? If it's the latter, well the book can help you do that. At least it can help you earn more by increasing your skills and insights.

Leadership is a moral imperative or it is nothing. If it's just about money, then sure, you'll make some. Remember, though, that the ultimate scarcity is priceless. You've heard that word "priceless." Have you ever thought about what it means? It means it can't be bought or sold. The ultimate value is non-monetary. It's how you are seen. It's how you are spoken of when you are not around. It's how you're remembered. It's about legacy. This is not something that exists in the future to remember the past. The leadership legacy is visible whenever the leader leaves the room.

We can summarize all of the above with this simple graphic showing how leadership should change.

Leadership Style Guide

PRE-PANDEMIC STYLE	POST-PANDEMIC STYLE
RIGID	FLEXIBLE
MYOPIC	INFORMED
SELFISH	ALTRUISTIC
DIVISIVE	UNIFYING
RECKLESS	CAREFUL
CYNICAL	OPTIMISTIC
SHORT-TERM	LONG-TERM
HUMORLESS	CHEERFUL

SOURCE TEAM LEWIS

SUMMARY: CHAPTER 4

Choosing to lead can be fraught with difficulty. Leaders face criticism, loneliness, blame, and the risk of failure. The best leaders can identify and harness a unifying force to bring the group together. One of the key ways to demonstrate leadership is to take responsibility. Leaders must also occasionally stir things up to foster change. Press beyond the comfort zone. Be comfortable with discomfort. Domain skills equate to knowledge, experience, and proficiency. Yet, domain skills do not a leader make. Leadership is designed to scale talents. The leader is the conductor, not the lead violinist. Ask a cancer researcher what they do, and they will explain their domain skill. Yet ask them why they do it and you will unlock the motives that make a leader.

The leader prepares for the unexpected. They are also organized and ready for the expected to achieve results. Psychologically effective leaders care for themselves and others. They are self-aware. Leadership is also about the willingness to take on a role because the outcome matters.

Understanding the brain is a window into human behavior. How thoughts can impact behavior provides insight into the best ways to lead. Developing self-awareness is key to becoming an effective modern leader. The next chapter examines the leader's thinking.

Aspirational Note

- As a result of having read this chapter, what might you do differently in terms of your own leadership style?

- What facts, stories, quotes, or points stood out for you?

- What might you explore further?

05

Understanding the Leader's Thinking

How can leaders change the way they analyze and think?

How does understanding brain function help leaders?

Why does sleep matter?

From where do our best ideas "flow?"

What is the psychology of persuasion?

How do empathy, rapport, and control operate in leadership?

Why is experience truly the best teacher?

Thought Into Action

We know how leadership needs to change in a post-pandemic world. It must try to bring people together when everything else is driving them apart.

The hard bit is changing the way leaders think. This is because many leaders are academically educated in the same way. All their lives they've been told they're smart. The evidence of their success is all around them so why should they think anything is wrong?

The vast majority of our institutional leaders are university or college educated. Their peer group is also similar.[1] They mix in similar circles. According to a survey of age diversity by the AARP (formerly the American Association of Retired Persons):

> *Most people don't have much age diversity in their friendships. A 2023 study found that, for a group of young adults ages 21 to 30, more than 80 percent of the people in their social circles, not counting relatives, were born within five years of them. Even looking at a broader age range, nearly 63 percent of adults don't have any close friends who are at least 15 years older or younger than them. We should all make more friends of different generations.*

According to The American Economic Association, 98 percent of the S&P 500 CEOs have at least a bachelor's degree;[2] 52 percent of North American CEOs have obtained at least a master's degree;[3] 10 percent of them will have a doctorate. There's not much diversity by education either. Nor by gender. Most of them are men.

In his book *Why Do So Many Incompetent Men Become Leaders?*, organizational psychologist Tomas Chamorro-Premuzic points out that one way of convincing others of the supremacy of your skills is to believe it.[4] This book is important because it points out that overconfidence in men is a real problem. His research shows that when applying for jobs, men will do so with a lot fewer qualifications for the role. Women will only apply when they have nearly all the qualifications required.

There are other problems as well. He points out that it's not enough to focus on gender underrepresentation in leadership. We need to understand much more about why this happens. He also points out that the majority of leaders are incompetent because those selecting them are unable to distinguish between confidence (how good people think they are) and competence (how good they actually are).

He says there is a surplus of leaders who lack empathy or self-control, who are unaware of their limitations and who are unjustifiably pleased with themselves. This leads them to be reckless, impulsive, and ignorant of what's happening around them.

Self-Awareness is Key

The lack of self-awareness is the key factor here. This could also be said to be a lack of self-doubt. Many leaders believe in themselves to the exclusion of all else.

It doesn't help either that competent people tend to be boring. They work hard. They are considerate. They listen to others. They act with integrity. There are no scandals. There are no fascinating charismatic dark sides. No one talks about them. No one will want to make a film or tell their story. They make for poor reality television ratings.

Narcissists, on the other hand, are alluring. People being famous for just being famous has been a growing trend for many years. They are outspoken. They are opinionated. They are controversial. They indulge in ostentatious displays of wealth. They are arrogant, rude, and operate at the boundaries of what is acceptable. The fact that their behavior is marginal makes them newsworthy.

Chamorro-Premuzic says this is not helped by those who encourage self-belief at all costs, as if it's the only thing that matters. The ideology purports, "Believe in yourself and show a sense of entitlement." Win at all costs.

These are some of the things Chamorro-Premuzic says:

Men are more typically more deceived about their talents than women are.

In general, we are unable to differentiate between confidence and competence.

Being unaware of your limitations increases your probability of being a boss.

The best leaders tend to be humble, even boring.

If we were to promote on the traits of competence, humility, and integrity this would also lead to a higher proportion of female leaders. All the scientific evidence shows that women score higher on these qualities. The point here is not to focus on representation but on improving the quality of leaders.

The solution is not to lower our standards when selecting women, but to elevate them when selecting men. Not asking women to behave more like incompetent men.

There's more on this here:

Why do so many incompetent men become leaders?
Dr. Tomas Chamorro-Premuzic,
TEDx University of Nevada

SOURCE TEDx Talks, https://www.youtube.com/watch?v=zeAEFEXvcBg

The Constraints of Academic Education

Let's be clear, there's no problem with confident, educated, or experienced leaders, nor with having a similar type of cohort. Education should be welcomed, but a key part of being educated is understanding its limitations.

Academic education has a specific methodology. College graduates are very good at analyzing problems to come up with solutions. They are skilled in the process of what's called Western Reductionism. It's scientific, measurable, tangible. We touched on this previously. Academic achievers get scores for individual achievement, not collaboration or empathy. Put simply, this is the way academic intelligence works. It breaks things down and compares, contrasts, and analyzes.

Below is the introduction to a paper on "Reductionism in Social Science." It is a particularly good (problematic) example of the genre:

Broadly speaking, "reductionism" is used in philosophy to refer to doctrines according to which one can explain some object by reducing it to a different, usually more simple level—for example, the

meaningful to the physical as in behaviorism, knowledge to sense data as in phenomenalism, the social to the biological as in sociobiology. The reductions are not made merely as a way of simplifying complexity, but of locating what their advocates believe to be the causes or sources of the explananda. Anti-reductionists argue that the explananda are irreducible, that even though they may depend on the things to which reductionists appeal—thought on brain cell activity, for example—they have emergent properties or powers which cannot be reduced to those of their constituents without residue. Anti-reductionists therefore argue for a stratified ontology, in which any higher stratum presupposes lower strata but not vice versa—as in the asymmetric relation of the biological to the physical. The strata usually cited are the physical, the chemical, the biological and the social, but further strata may be invoked within each of these. The plausibility of the idea that the world is stratified arguably provides a warrant for the existence of different disciplines: the physical, the chemical, the biological and the social deal with different strata of reality. However, as we shall see, the subdivision of social science into disciplines has a much less clear relation to stratification. In part, the rise of different social sciences seems to correspond to the differentiation of spheres in modernity—politics, law and economics, for example—rather than to different strata, though some might argue that psychology is an exception. A third group argues against both these positions, arguing that all objects and processes are on the same level within a relational field, and that what eventuates are products of interaction rather than emergence.[5]

And that's just the "introduction."

Sorry for that, but it illustrates several points. You'll notice that the sentences are long. There are many strange, multi-syllabic words. It is not concise. It is not simplified. It is not summarized. It is designed to be complicated and only accessible to other academically qualified people. It's almost written in code. It is typical of an academic style and approach. It almost rejoices in complexity. It's unnecessarily verbose. Most would skip over it because it is impenetrable. Did you? It represents the apogee of Western Reductionist thinking. The academic world is full of text like this. Nowhere in the business world would this be acceptable. It is a measure of how far removed from the "real world" academia has become.

Professor Peter Checkland, now retired from Lancaster University in the UK, was a pioneer of a different type of thinking. He was a chemistry student. His doctoral thesis was on measuring the distance between two atoms of prussic acid (hydrogen cyanide). At his viva, he was asked how many people around the world would be interested in his findings. He could only think of four. It was a Damascene moment. He realized that Western Reductionism had led him down a path to this point. He went away and wrote a book that stood scientific reductionism on its head[6] and then spent the rest of his life teaching it.

This is revolutionary stuff. You need a lot of courage to challenge the system. You also have to admire the humility of this type of thinking. Of course, Checkland was a brilliant chemist, but he ended up rethinking the process of thinking itself. The Emeritus Professor of Lancaster Business School, David Brown, keeps this memory alive. He suffered the gross misfortune of tutoring one of the authors of this book, Chris Lewis.

How Do You Analyze a Problem Effectively?

You analyze a problem by breaking it down. Then you analyze those sub-units and so on. College graduates are typically very good at this. In reductionist thinking, there is a right answer and it's at the back of the book. It looks like this: we drill down into a subject to understand it. Yet what if we also had a "look across?"

This is, by and large, the way that we separate and order our leaders. If you can think in this way, you're much more likely to become a leader.

Yet there is a completely different methodology available. It's easy to understand and it does the opposite of that above. This is called holistic thinking or parenthetic rather than analytic thinking. It looks at related systems or moves upwards to see to what the

Real Thinking Is About Depth as Well as Breadth

NOT JUST ANALYSIS

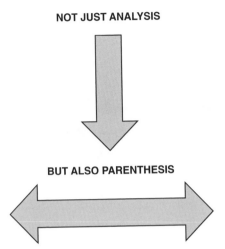

BUT ALSO PARENTHESIS

SOURCE TEAM LEWIS

system belongs. In this way, an equal meaning is derived which will be different to a reductionist approach.

Let's try an example. If we apply a reductionist approach to define what a car is, we break it down into engine, transmission, steering wheel, and seats and deduce that the car is a transportation device; it's a utility and benefit for humans.

However, when we start treating the car as a whole and relate it to other systems, then a new picture emerges. We introduce fresh air to the front, if it's not an electric vehicle, and we get dirty air out of the back. We introduce humans in through one door, and we can get damaged humans out of another. Now we can surmise that the car is a danger to humanity. It pollutes the air and kills its passengers; it's a liability and a danger to humans.

These are two completely opposite conclusions arrived at from two different approaches to thinking. Neither is perfect for understanding, but both are useful tools. The problem with the latter is that it's not used enough. Reframing and widening the analysis is the key to more effective problem-solving.

LEADERSHIP PROFILE
Donna Schoenherr: Move Into Wellbeing®

Move Into Wellbeing Documentary

SOURCE TEAM LEWIS Foundation, https://www.youtube.com/watch?v=G3AaWDXFcpQ

Move Into Wellbeing® was conceived and founded by Donna Schoenherr in 2014. This was her inspired response after her father was diagnosed with Parkinson's disease. She is a professional dancer who created the organization specifically to help people with movement disorders. She explains, "The idea is that, at any age, we should have a chance to move."

In essence, Move Into Wellbeing provides opportunities for movement, regardless of physical or mental ability. It speaks to the importance and inherent need of humans for mobility. Like many of the causes, she taps into something in common between people. Humans, wherever they are, respond to music. In the classes, Schoenherr sees toes tapping, heads bobbing, and hands waving, even with those who have extremely limited mobility. The social component helps alleviate isolation for seniors. Depression is reduced and moods are raised.

The movement and the music give the participants something that they just can't get on their own—confidence in fellowship. It creates joy and happiness. There are smiles shared and interaction with those around them.

Having a place to go and something to look forward to is vital to quality of life. It's also a setting where seniors are treated respectfully. There is a structured curriculum of dance and movement but it's also a chance to play. When a senior has dementia or a neurological disorder, there's a tendency to pathologize their behavior. Sometimes, seniors just want to be silly and there's nothing wrong with that. They just want to laugh and have fun in a non-judgmental setting. Schoenherr says:

> You're sitting in a circle, and you pass something around like we used to do at birthday parties. Where you'd say something to someone and then it comes around. We do that with movement. It's just lovely you know because they can just do that and feel free.

It's a place where the clients are known. Staff, volunteers, and teachers ask about everything from grandchildren to changes in health status. Creating a familial environment is a high priority. Schoenherr reflects:

> The image I use of my work environment is of a healthy ecosystem—every living being is an important part. All must work together to create the healthy sustainable atmosphere. When I'm in that studio, everyone is a colleague there. I care for them like they're family. I know their names. I know about their families. I know about their health situations.

Schoenherr says that movement is a primal experience. People are born to move. Scientists have found the correlation between music and movement positively impacts parts of the brain. Seniors often come in with a walking stick. After listening and moving to the music, some find they're less dependent on their walking aides.

Schoenherr acknowledges that she is uniquely sensitive to a son or daughter seeking a safe environment for their parent. Their worries and questions are many, right down to what their loved ones should wear. Many have a concern that their relative has no dance experience, but no one needs to. They are invited to move. In some cases, these are individuals who can't walk or talk. They are vulnerable and need a compassionate setting.

It's not always easy. The stress and the needs of clients can be wearing on the staff and volunteers. Burnout is a real issue because they need lots of emotional energy. As the leader, Schoenherr ensures that her team take breaks, are paid well and pace themselves.

A poignant story from Move Into Wellbeing features an elderly woman who always wanted to dance. Yet in her country of origin, Persia, now known as Iran, women were not allowed to do so. She joined the group and fulfilled a life-long dream. At her funeral, her family shared that the experience at Move Into Wellbeing had meant everything to their mother. A dream was fulfilled. "Those things mean a lot to me," Schoenherr says.

Move Into Wellbeing continued online throughout the pandemic. Isolation was acute. With the help of technology, it proved to be a lifeline for many people living with Parkinson's and other conditions such as dementia. There is a burgeoning awareness of what music and movement can do for seniors. It builds physical as well as social benefits where adult children can have a member of their family participate in a community of their own. Schoenherr believes that creativity through movement is such a powerful tool that connects and empowers people.

On being a leader, Schoenherr is frank. She remembers having many "horrible" bosses. From outright degradation, misogyny, and disrespect, she learned what she would never do in a leadership position. As a dancer in the 1980s, it was common for her to have contracts that required her to maintain a certain weight. People would be weighed in front of their colleagues, body-shamed, and fined for being over their contracted weight.

Today, in her leadership meetings, she has everyone seated around a circular table. Listening to the team is her priority. But whether she's setting up chairs for a class or dealing with a more complicated client issue, she is present, she is hands-on, and working closely with her clients and her team.

She seeks ways to match the ethos of the organization with fundraising. The latter is a constant need. Costs are always increasing. Schoenherr has created innovative ways to raise funds as well as visibility for the organization. With the help of her nephew, who is a classical pianist, they have managed to raise funds whilst showcasing performances at a local hall:

> I do artwork and I did an exhibition. I had an open studio, and it was accessible to all of West London. Proceeds from the show were directly donated to Move Into Wellbeing.

Schoenherr believes that success should always be tied to a sense of duty to the community:

> Try volunteering a few hours a week to a cause that matters to you. Whatever you do, engagement with those around you is the key to success.

How Does the Brain Process Information?

When we talk about the two sides of the brain, we're not saying that processing for one type of thinking is done exclusively on one side. For most of the processes we've discussed, you need both sides of the physical brain. Yet there is no doubt about the nature of the two processes, which are clear and distinct.

This has been described best in a video by the extraordinary brain expert and psychiatrist Iain McGilchrist:

RSA ANIMATE: The Divided Brain—Iain McGilchrist

SOURCE RSA, https://www.youtube.com/watch?v=dFs9WO2B8uI

McGilchrist argues that the left hemisphere has evolved to focus attention on detail. The right hemisphere, on the other hand, has a broad and flexible attention that is open to possibilities, and it sees things in their wider context. If the activity in the two hemispheres is reflexive—activity in one stretches activity in the other—then the right hemisphere could be vital. The argument is that the left hemisphere should not dominate the right. It's a good servant, but an evil master. He says:

> ...the brain's left hemisphere helps us ap-prehend—and thus manipulate—the world; the right hemisphere to com-prehend—see it all for what it is.
>
> The left brain seeks the satisfaction of getting things done, whereas the right brain sees the big picture and seeks meaning and fulfillment. In this way, we do what is important, not just what is urgent, and complete tasks with satisfaction, but according to a higher purpose. This decreases burnout and increases the quality of the final product, not to mention increasing our own personal fulfillment.

McGilchrist says the Western world throughout history has alternated between left-brain and right-brain function focus, with some periods of balance. During certain times, such as the Renaissance, there was a movement toward right-brain dominance. Whereas since the Scientific Revolution and the Age of Enlightenment, with exceptions such as the Romantic movement, it has become increasingly left-brain dominant. McGilchrist is concerned about the many cultural and global crises that are happening as a result of this.

There are many things that could be said about his exceptional work. Suffice to say he lives on the Isle of Skye, off the coast of Northwest Scotland. He embodies the power of his thinking here:

> Our talent for division, for seeing the parts, is of staggering importance—second only to our capacity to transcend it, in order to see the whole.

What's Sleep Got to Do with It?

We all know how we feel when we've been working for hours without a break. The brain becomes fatigued, and we need to get outside and stretch our legs. There's a reason we do this, according to brain biologist Russell Foster:

> The brain is homeostatically defended. The more we do in one area, the more the brain recoils into the other.

Foster is an expert on sleep and what the lack of it does to us. What his research points to is a growing problem with sleeplessness. He points out some basic problems with sleep hygiene. For instance, people brush their teeth in a brightly lit room just before going to bed. The light can stimulate the brain and push back the onset of deep sleep. Furthermore, he adds that people sleep better in cooler bedrooms. The only problem with this is that many bedrooms are upstairs in a house and therefore grow warm as heat rises. He also says that when people live together, they also sleep in the same room. This disturbs the other sleeper and also adds further heat.

Chronic lack of sleep is deeply implicated in raised levels of cancer and diabetes. This is due to the stress being interpreted by the body as a threat. This stimulates the body to produce a hunger hormone called ghrelin. This is why jet-lagged people want to eat high-fat, high-sugar products.

Anyone familiar with political high office knows that sleep deprivation is a major problem around national leaders. There are lots of tired people and burn-out is common.

More from Russell Foster here:

Life Time: The New Science of the Body Clock with Russell Foster— WIRED Health

SOURCE WIRED Events, https://www.youtube.com/watch?v=B6EwbOaJf_s

Tired minds are quite often stuck in left-brain mode because they are trying hard to stay focused.

The brain detects imbalance and wants to rectify it. More about this later in this chapter. Yet it gives some insight into how mathematicians can be brilliant musicians and scientists love art so much. One of the authors of this book, Chris Lewis, first met Russell Foster at an art exhibition when he described the effect of a painting on the frontal lobe, which is in a part of the brain called the cerebrum.

How to Optimize Brain Balance

This explains why knowledge workers seek to get out of the office for a walk as well as exercise regularly. Or go to a concert or art gallery. Let's try another test. Where are you and what are you doing when you get your best ideas?

Chances are you responded with one of the following:

- driving
- walking
- commuting on public transport
- taking a shower
- falling asleep
- waking up
- playing with a pet
- working out in the gym or running
- talking with friends

The factors these things all have in common is that more often than not, your best ideas come when you're a) not in the office, b) sometimes on your own, and c) not trying.

The authors, Inez Odom and Chris Lewis, would take lengthy brisk walks together to discuss the content for the book, synthesize ideas, and catalyze their thinking.

This again cuts against the approach of the left-brain achievers. Most of them have spent their entire lives trying very hard indeed. Yet this is one of those areas where less is more. The looser grip holds more effectively.

Golfers may also have had this experience. One mistake in golf is to try to hit the ball too hard. Golf pros will often ask someone to relax and hit the ball only half as hard as normal. In so doing, they end up hitting the ball further. Why? The golf swing is about timing, not outright force. A brilliant metaphor for leadership.

Knowing what induces your right brain or suggestible mode is important. First, it allows leaders to go to that space or trigger when actively seeking new ideas. Second, if the leader knows how to induce this state in themselves, then they will also realize how to bring others into that state. It's for this reason that many leaders will take their teams off-site.

This is why it is worth understanding what activities drive the left and right brain states. Things that drive left-brain awareness are interruptions such as email or social media alerts. They force the recipient into a *who, where, what, when, why, how* mode of thinking, all of which are left-brain process questions.

These are hallmarks of not being in a "left-brain mode." You can't bring forward or switch on the "right-brain mode," you can only switch off the left-brain process side.

What's the Benefit of Being "In the Zone" or "In Flow"?

Runners will be familiar with the experience of being "in the zone." You start by being fully aware, at the start of the run, with left-brain acuity. Yet after the initial phase, the left brain switches off and then you go into "the zone." This is where the right brain is dominant. Runners sometimes report that they can sometimes run quite a distance in this altered state. Many elite athletes talk about using flow. For instance, Olympic Gold medal winner Mo Farah said:

When I run, I just go out there, go in the zone and just block everything.

The same is also true of car drivers on a habitual route. They can set off, only to arrive later at a destination with little recollection of the journey. They can describe this as "being on autopilot" or in "flow." This is a sense of fluidity between body and mind. It is the experience of being absorbed by and focused on something, beyond the point of distraction. Under these circumstances, time feels like it has slowed down. The senses are heightened. Action and awareness synchronize to create an effortless momentum. This is the flow state and it's accessible to everyone, whether you're engaged in a physical activity, a creative pursuit, or even a simple day-to-day task. Time is experienced differently and can often feel as if it has flown by.

Flow experiences can occur in different ways for different people. It most often happens with something enjoyable in which they are skilled. For example, it happens when painting, sculpting, singing, drawing, or writing and can also occur when skiing, biking, swimming, dancing, or running.

There is evidence of physiological changes to the brain when in this state.[7] A flow state is associated with a decrease in activity in the prefrontal cortex. This is the area of the brain responsible for higher cognitive functions, including memory and self-consciousness. This may explain why people experience a distorted sense of time and loss of self-consciousness. According to this theory, flow allows other regions of the brain to communicate with one another more effectively. While in a flow state, an increase in activity in the frontal cortex contributes to increased higher thinking.

Other research suggests that there's also an increase in dopamine, a brain chemical involved in pleasure and motivation, when people are experiencing flow.[8]

There's much more written on this subject. At this point, the authors solemnly promise that they haven't gone out of their way to cite those with unusual surnames. There have been many books written on the subject. Yet it is Mihaly Csikszentmihalyi, in his book *Finding Flow: The psychology of engagement with everyday life,*[9] where he believes the obsessive left-brain focus has led us astray:

> *Work fills our days with anxiety and pressure, so that during our free time, we tend to live in boredom, absorbed by our screens.*

Flow, the Secret to Happiness—
Mihaly Csikszentmihalyi

SOURCE TED, https://www.ted.com/talks/mihaly_csikszentmihalyi_flow_the_secret_to_happiness?language=en

Csikszentmihalyi studied thousands of people. His conclusion?

Flow happens when a person's skills are fully involved in overcoming a challenge that is just about manageable, so it acts as a magnet for learning new skills and increasing challenges. If challenges are too low, one gets back to flow by increasing them. If challenges are too great, one can return to the flow state by learning new skills.

The corollary of this is also true. Flow is a dynamic and ever-changing state. As your skill increases, the level of challenge that is needed to help initiate a state of flow must increase. This explains why some people can fall out of love with a task. They have stopped challenging themselves.

Importantly, part of this theory is that you can't achieve flow with something you dislike. This is because the left-brain focus is awake, comparing, contrasting, and analyzing, telling you something specific. Namely, that you don't like it. Competence can only follow preference. You can't get good at something you hate. Nor can you get there whilst distracted or whilst something is competing for your attention. You have to focus fully on the task at hand.

Not only do people often perform better when they are in this state of flow, but they may also be able to improve their skills. Like anything else, you can achieve it with practice. However, you've got to like it.

In this alpha or flow state, the brain becomes highly receptive to ideas that simply "pop into the head." Understanding this innate ability is critical to real leadership. There is little that most leaders can learn from this text about analytical, reductionist thinking. They already have huge experience in that realm. Learning how to release the subconscious and applying the right brain, that's another matter.

As Einstein put it:

The rational mind is a faithful servant. The intuitive mind is a sacred gift. We honour the servant but have forgotten the gift.

Einstein himself was a devotee of long walks on the Ostend seafront, where he worked as a patent clerk. All the time he was walking, ostensibly doing nothing, he was actually doing a great deal.

What Does the Left Side of the Brain Do?

The left-hand side of the brain controls logic-related tasks, such as science and mathematics. It is also involved in language processing, like grammar, vocabulary, and fact-based thinking. It manages analytical abilities and sequential processing.

Nevertheless, the notion of each brain hemisphere controlling distinct tasks is a simplification; in reality, both hemispheres collaborate for most activities:

- language
- logic
- critical thinking
- numbers
- reasoning
- aligning
- symbol
- details
- descriptives

Things That Make You Go Leftwards

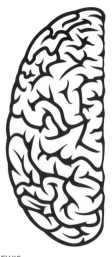

INTERRUPTIONS

CONCENTRATION

REVISION

FOCUS

HOMEWORK

POWERPOINT DECKS

SOURCE TEAM LEWIS

What Does the Right Side of the Brain Do?

The right-hand side of the brain primarily controls spatial abilities, facial recognition, visual imagery, musical awareness, and artistic skills. It's also linked to creativity, imagination, and intuition. However, as mentioned previously, the concept of each hemisphere controlling distinct functions is an oversimplification. Both work together for most tasks.

The leaders of our organizations are intelligent. Indeed, many have undergone decades of education in schools, universities, and professional institutes. Yet our leaders have had a narrow education focused on this particular type of thinking which resolves problems by analysis. This leads to a "drill-down" philosophy that is used for everything. When you only have a hammer, every problem is a nail.

This is having catastrophic effects on collective endeavor. Organizations that have been set up as logical structures suddenly find themselves unable to adapt. They are too siloed by the divisions they imposed upon themselves as part of their structure. Organizations and brands are suffering and so are the stakeholders

Things That Make You Go Rightwards

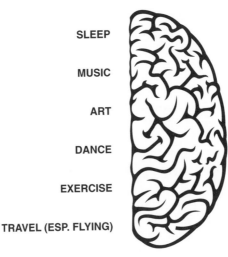

SLEEP

MUSIC

ART

DANCE

EXERCISE

TRAVEL (ESP. FLYING)

SOURCE TEAM LEWIS

Left and Right Brain Deployment

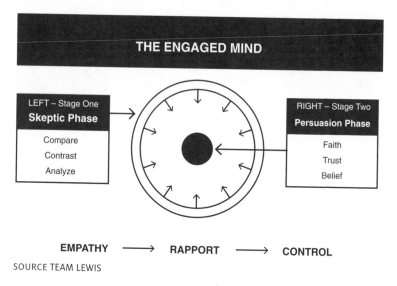

SOURCE TEAM LEWIS

and the environment itself.[10] Organizational structures have fossilized thought.

Everything is reduced into an atomized group of parts. The divisions described in Chapter 1 have already been maximized and accelerated by the pandemic. To add to this with further reductionist thinking compounds problem on problem.

To understand these two types of thinking is straightforward. To understand how they deploy is not. This brings us to the subject of persuasion. All leaders need to persuade people. We'll talk about how the leader sounds and looks in the next chapter. For now, it's important to understand the psychology of persuasion.

The Psychology of Persuasion

In any interaction with people, the opening phase—even with people you know well—is conducted in the left brain. The recipient is scanning for new information to be aware of what's changed. Its main method is to compare, contrast, and analyze. It fiercely protects access to the right brain qualities of faith, trust, and belief.

Many of you will recognize this as the format for many an exam question. The left brain is good at noticing variation. You may have experienced this when conducting an interview. In the initial phase, your left brain will be looking for difference.

Let's ask some questions.

The candidate in front of you is sweating profusely. The sweat is soaking through their shirt. Would you notice?

The sweat is not just visual but, unfortunately, the person has an offensive smell. Would you notice?

The candidate has a tattoo on the top of their right hand clearly in view. It is a swastika. Would you notice?

Please try not to make any value judgments about the above. The main question to answer is "would you notice?" If the answer is "yes," then the next question is how long would it take for you to notice? If the answer to that is "within the first five minutes," then we're already deep into left-brain territory. We're locked on to difference. The brain has noticed these features and then goes looking for other behaviors and cues that are consistent with the initial findings. This is called confirmation bias and it's really difficult to get away from.

And that's just the first five minutes...

Many people report having made up their mind early in an interview, then having to sit through the rest to be polite.

This is why the first five to fifteen minutes of any interaction, whether a presentation, interview, or pitch, is vital. You have to get them on your side and not excite the left brain. After the skeptic phase is completed, chances of persuading the person go up.

Think of the left brain as being like a sleeping dragon. For those looking to persuade, the initial phase is the most dangerous. You're trying to get past it, without waking it up. For this reason, good presenters tend to start slowly and get the audience on their side.

Always remember that highly educated people have very developed critical faculties. It's how they've achieved in their careers and found success. This hypercriticality, though, does have a personal drawback. Often, the first place this hypercriticism is used is on the self. This excoriating self-critique can undermine confidence and can especially be a problem with women, as discussed earlier. All the research shows that male leaders have a tendency toward higher levels of confidence over competence. We should not confuse the two.

Hypnotherapists have different techniques for persuasion. However, broadly they describe the stages of their process as "Empathy, Rapport, and Control."

The "Empathy" stage is tiptoeing past the dragon. This then involves phrases such as, "make yourself comfortable and close your eyes. Relax."

The "Rapport" stage begins with phrases such as, "as you hear my words, I'd like you to concentrate on the gaps between the words. As you hear this, you're feeling warm and comfortable."

The "Control" stage begins with "you're now very relaxed and feeling very comfortable."

The hypnotherapist may then ask the person to go back into their childhood and describe a situation when they were happy. All that's going on here is the process of taking someone out of their left brain. Or alternatively, a temporary suspension of one's critical faculties.

Jill Bolte-Taylor is a Harvard-trained neuroscientist. In 1996, she experienced a severe hemorrhage in the left hemisphere of her brain, causing her to lose the ability to walk, talk, read, write, or recall any of her life. Her story is here:

My Stroke of Insight—
Dr. Jill Bolte Taylor

SOURCE TED, https://www.ted.com/talks/jill_bolte_taylor_my_stroke_of_insight?language=en

Applying Left- and Right-Brain Thinking

A speech might begin with neutral statements such as:

- It's an honor to have been invited here...
- Don't worry, I'm not trying to sell anything to you...
- I'm thrilled and pleased to be asked to address such an expert group...

This is the Empathy stage. And then it moves into the Rapport stage:

- Now, if you're anything like me, you'll want to...
- I know what you're thinking; here comes a lecture...
- The data appears to suggest this course of action...

Then we move into the Control stage:

- So, if this makes sense, I hope you'll support this...
- This is as logical as we can make it. I hope you agree...
- If the data is right, there's really only one solution...

Here are two speeches on providing better public transport in your local neighborhood. Which is more persuasive?

Speech one:

Hello everyone. Sorry I'm late. The parking here is terrible. Couldn't find anywhere to park my BMW. There's no doubt, you need better public transport. No wonder everyone drives a car like me. I can understand how you feel. Back me and I will get it done.

Speech two:

Hello everyone, thanks for making the time to come out this evening. It really is a struggle to get here. I was nearly late, I had to change buses twice from the train station. There's no doubt, we need better public transport. I hope you will join me in solving this problem. I can understand how you feel. Back me and I will get it done.

In terms of persuasion, speech two clearly invites empathy, with courtesy playing an important role. Further rapport is established through the identification of the problem, coupled with an expression of empathy. Control stems from the invitation to partner to solve the problem.

The more powerfully left-brained people are, the more skeptical and judgmental they will be. They will be convinced that what they see is "the truth."

Let's learn more about the other side of persuasion, which is perception. Time for some more tests.

Why Perception Matters

Silhouette Illusion
(Spinning Dancer)

SOURCE Nobuyuki Kayahara, https://upload.wikimedia.org/wikipedia/commons/2/21/Spinning_Dancer.gif

Which direction is the woman turning in?

Profoundly left-brained people will only be able to see it spinning in one direction. Stare at it long enough and it should change direction.

There is a classic drawing that speaks to perception. In one view, the observer sees an older woman with a prominent nose. When perception shifts, the observer sees a young, well-dressed woman in a long dress. Very left-brained people may struggle to see the alternative image.

Our perception can create the story that we tell ourselves. The leader must consider how perception may differ within a team.

Revisiting the problem or challenge may help solidify a team's perception of what needs to be done.

Look at this picture. What do you see? What sort of *boy* is it?

SOURCE Facebook. Posted by Savannah Root from Lamar, Missouri, 2016

Follow the Arrow:
Hidden Designs
In Famous Logos

SOURCE Jacopo Prisco, CNN, https://www.cnn.com/style/article/hidden-designs-famous-logos/index.html

In which direction does the FedEx logo above want you to move? You should be able to see a hidden arrow featured in the article.

What we're demonstrating here is that not everyone sees things in the same way. People literally see the same thing in completely different ways. Or they don't see it at all. This is why we need to understand that different perspectives exist which are valid to the observer. Leaders understand these variations in perception and recognize that they may need to adapt their approach accordingly.

How Ideas Find Form

We can use the understanding of left- and right-brain techniques to make our creative processes more effective. The diagram below suggests four stages of the creative process. If these were days of the week, you might spend Monday and Tuesday researching a problem. Then you may choose to rest on Wednesday and Thursday. By Friday and Saturday, the ideas are forming. Then by Sunday, they are complete. Research suggests that the subconscious right brain is absorbing information about a problem all the time. But it must wait for the left brain to be switched off before it can bring forward the solution. This is why so many ideas come outside of work and during the weekend when we are outside and active. It's also why so many leaders refer to the importance of solitude.

The Rise Four I's Creative Cycle

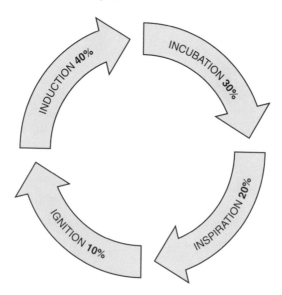

SOURCE LEWIS Rise Academy. First published by Kogan Page Ltd in 2016 in *Too Fast to Think: How to reclaim your creativity in a hyper-connected work culture* by Chris Lewis

The Power of Solitude

Aldous Huxley said:

> *The more powerful and original a mind, the more it will incline*
> *towards the religion of solitude.*

Solitude is also a good litmus test for whether you're an introvert or extrovert. The test of this is how people recover their energy. Extroverts do so with other people. Introverts are on their own. You'd think that a star like Audrey Hepburn would be extrovert, but:

> *I have to be alone very often. I'd be quite happy if I spent from*
> *Saturday night until Monday morning alone in my apartment. That's*
> *how I refuel.*

Lord Byron said:

> *In solitude, where we are* least *alone…*

Even Aristotle saw the importance of it:

> *Whosoever is delighted in solitude, is either a wild beast or a god.*

Reading the Room

Educated people are easily recognizable. They're the ones sitting with their arms folded, legs crossed, or otherwise with hands clasped together. The position of the thumbs on the hands or the arm over arm indicates the brain dominance. The body will always protect its strongest side. Don't believe it? Try switching thumbs or arms and see how comfortable you feel.

The majority of people are right-handed. The right hand is controlled by the left brain. Damage to this side of the brain results in paralysis on the right-hand side of the body. The Latin words for left and right are *sinister* and *dexter*. Dexterous is skilled and clever. Sinister is evil and suspicious. Historically, the left side and even left-handed people have been viewed with suspicion.[11] There was a time when left-handed people would have their left hand bound to force them to use their right. The word left comes from the Anglo-Saxon *lyft* or weak. In French, left is *gauche* or clumsy.

In many parts of the world, the left hand is even considered unclean or rude to use. If you're left-handed and visiting places like India, Pakistan, Bangladesh, Indonesia, Nepal, and the Middle East, it's thought of as rude behavior to eat, pick up, or hand over things with your left hand. This is the hand used for, well, ablutions.

Though left-handers make up a small percentage of the population, many are in prominent positions. Several US presidents have been left-handed, including Bill Clinton and Barack Obama. Former UK prime minister David Cameron and Prince William are left-handed, as was Winston Churchill. Singer Justin Bieber is left-handed, as are Oprah Winfrey, Sir Paul McCartney, Lady Gaga, and actress Jennifer Lawrence.

The British even drive on the left to keep their sword hand free for people passing on their right. The traditional right-grasp handshake came about to demonstrate that you were not carrying a weapon. Even the Vikings were right-handed. They steered their boats on the side with their right hand. This is called the steerboard or starboard side. You'd never dock your boat against the rudder, so the other side became known as the port (harbor) side. All boats are still docked on their left-hand (port) side.

The "Eyes" Have It

Eye deflection may also indicate brain activity. You can see this when people are thinking. Where do their eyes deflect? Upwards and some say the brain is accessing the visual cortex and memories. Those who are "upward deflectors" may even use phrases like:

- I see what you mean.
- That looks good to me.

They may even look well-dressed or have office and home space which looks highly ordered.

"Downward deflectors" are predominately sonic. This is the brain accessing sonic memories. They may even use phrases like:

- That sounds good to me.
- I hear what you're saying.

They may have partners with a specific tone of voice. They may even feel uncomfortable in noisy places or react to "trigger" sounds.

"Side-to-side deflectors" are kinesthetic people. They may even use phrases like:

- I feel that's the right thing to do.
- I sense that this is wrong.

They may feel uncomfortable in spaces that are too hot or too cold.

The experienced persuader is trying to get through the skeptic phase. They will read the person and try to align their approach to the thinking in the room.

Pivoting and Reframing

It's important to be aware of the way you think because leaders are just not wired the same way as others. Astute leaders realize that the test of intellectual ability is not how much you know, nor is it how fast you can come up with the right answer. It's the ability to move rapidly between the skills of the left and right brain. It's the ability to parenthesize as well as analyze.

Ironically, it all starts with doubt. This is the ability to remain flexible that whatever the right answer currently is, it may change. It was Goethe who said "Doubt grows with knowledge."

The provenance of certainty can only be mediocrity.

This is not to say that leaders are far better if they radiate doubt—far from it. There's a difference, though, between how leaders think and how they communicate. So many of them are reframing situations to provide a different perspective. Take this for example.

George Blacklock is former Dean of Chelsea College of Arts in London. Although a talented artist in his own right, he was tasked with working out how to get the best creativity out of others. He was finding himself constantly on the receiving end of students asking him what he thought of their work. Art students are notoriously sensitive. It's a very fine line. You have to be able to praise and critique in the right measure, often depending on the person. It seems like an impossible task. He made it look easy. How does he respond to students?

> *Well, it's pretty straightforward, I can use several forms, but it usually comes down to asking: Why have you decided to do this in such a conventional manner?*

At one level, it's an inquiry into decision-making. At another, it's asking about the process. At another level, it's an assumption. At yet another, it's an encouragement to go beyond. Leaders ask powerful questions.

The author, Chris Lewis, once asked him how he knew when a painting was finished. There is always a tendency for artists to "over-egg the pudding." Just one more change, but then you run the risk of it being ruined. Another genius answer reframing the subject of the process:

> *You're finished with a painting when it's finished with you.*

This represents a level of trust in your own ability. Obviously, there is no evidence that a painting can give you instructions. It has no opinions but treating it as if it has is liberating. It removes the pressure from the creator and encourages trust. Good leaders create perspectives that grant permission or embolden.

Of all the chapters in our book, this may be the most difficult to grasp. Why? Unless you've had the experience of an idea popping into your head for no apparent reason, it makes no sense. For instance, how could you ever understand grief or love if you'd only read a book about them? You have to experience them to understand properly.

For those that do grasp this, nothing is more important. It's central to their existence to tap into their creativity. They feel like they would burst without being able to experience the flow state. Among many great leaders, it dictates that they simply must express themselves. This is the case among writers, dancers, musicians, artists, businesspeople, just about anyone who is pre-eminent. They just have no alternative. It's dangerous to deny this. It can lead to a lifetime of denial. Listen to this case as related by the late, great Sir Ken Robinson:

How a Famous Dancer
Escaped Traditional School—
Sir Ken Robinson

SOURCE Education Options TV, https://youtu.be/a2XhfGNGhNk?si=4OmjBF1cjZkxRl7g
(adapted from TED "Do Schools Kill Creativity?")

In this example, Gillian Lynne wasn't sick. She was, at her core, a dancer. She joined the Royal Ballet. She went on to choreograph the musical *Cats*. There are some people who are just born to dance. There are so many people forced into a career by an education system that's designed to put square pegs in square holes. The point of this chapter is to understand you might not be a peg at all.

Your job as leader is to understand your own potential. Thereafter, your job changes into a duty to help everyone else reach theirs.

SUMMARY: CHAPTER 5

The majority of traditional leaders are university or college educated. Ironically, the language of academia can impede leadership. Rather than right and wrong answers, effective leaders are open to ambiguity. They don't simply analyze... they parenthesize. Understanding the function of the right- and left-brain hemispheres provides a roadmap to human behavior. This lends insight into decision-making, mastering domain skills, persuasion, building empathy, fostering creativity, and "reading the room."

Often, the best ideas do not occur in the workplace. They happen when in a liminal state such as transitioning from sleeping to waking. Or when walking the dog, driving on the highway, or exercising at the gym. A "flow" state is entered. Flow is dynamic and ever-changing.

The ability to pivot between the skills of the right and left brain is present in the best leaders. In the next chapter, the importance of communication is examined. Exploring the look and sound of leadership provides the blueprint for optimal ways to lead.

Aspirational Note

- As a result of having read this chapter, what might you do differently in terms of your own leadership style?

- What facts, stories, quotes, or points stood out for you?

- What might you explore further?

06

What Does Leadership Look and Sound Like?

What is the look and sound of modern leadership?

What does the modern leader say and do?

Is there any such thing as a good leader or only what looks like one?

Why is communication key?

Why does simplicity matter?

What is the way to deliver a great presentation?

- Audience
- Medium
- Message
- Form
- Eye contact
- Attire
- On camera
- Questions (everything you ever wanted to know...)
- Lecterns
- PowerPoint
- Room arrangement
- Rehearsal and reconnaissance
- Lighting
- Memorization
- Reducing nerves

How Does Appearance Factor into Modern Leadership?

We need to evolve leadership thinking but we also need to ask some questions. What does leadership look like? And does this perception stop people from wanting to be leaders?

We know that leaders are now much more visible from both inside as well as outside the organization. With more emphasis on communication, leaders can't avoid the spotlight. First, leaders are in the public eye and, with social media, they can be subject to constant levels of criticism. This is frequently anonymous and can spill over into comments about family and friends. Leaders need a thick skin. The public scrutiny puts some off a leadership role. There are a number of other reasons worth exploring.

They may also believe that the time in the public eye necessarily involves less time spent on their own domain expertise. Some would rather remain an expert in one field than become a generalist and be responsible for other experts. Many turn down leadership because of the effect on their work/life balance.

There are also leaders—and we talk about some in the leadership profiles—who simply think they don't fit the "model" for leadership. They may think they just don't look and sound like leadership is supposed to. This notion will put a lot of people off wanting to become a leader. However, it's not surprising that a set idea of what leadership looks like is out there.

This is Malcolm Gladwell in his book *Blink*:

> *In the US population, about 14.5 percent of all men are six feet or taller. Among CEOs of Fortune 500 companies, that number is 58 percent. Even more striking, in the general American population, 3.9 percent of adult men are six foot two or taller. Among my CEO sample, almost a third were six foot two or taller.*[1]

We expect our leaders to be tall. This is something that militates against women, who tend to be shorter. For this reason, female leaders should always consider standing up when presenting to a room. Height is often correlated with authority. Voice matters as well because research shows that loudness is correlated with confidence. Again, this is another issue that works against women because they tend to have quieter voices. The tall, loud person looks and sounds like the stereotypical image of a confident and authoritative leader.

The New Look of Leadership

In an increasingly diverse environment, the stereotypical notion of what looks and sounds like a leader is becoming outdated. Perhaps we need to do for leadership what the brand "Dove" did to the notion of beauty and recognize that modern leaders come in many different shapes, sizes, ages, and colors.

According to one US survey:[2]

- There are over 98,183 entrepreneurs currently employed in the US.
- 42 percent are women and 58 percent are men.
- The average entrepreneur age is 44 years old.
- The most common ethnicity of entrepreneurs is White (67.1 percent), followed by Hispanic or Latino (15.4 percent), Asian (6.4 percent) and Black or African American (6.3 percent).
- 10 percent of all entrepreneurs are LGBT+.

A third of all entrepreneurs are people of color. Specifically Black women are the fastest-growing group of entrepreneurs in the United States.[3] That's often because Black women simply cannot get the access, flexibility, or opportunities working in a corporate setting. Female-owned businesses are growing twice as fast as the average.[4] These may be single-person businesses like many at start-up. Perhaps we must rethink our idea of what an entrepreneur is?

It's conceivable the reality of leadership is quite different to that usually projected to us. Maybe it's not about image and more about what leaders say and do. Maybe the stereotypical image we have simply represents the loudest group of entrepreneurs and the largest.

A lot of these "loud" leaders are vocal about their vision. Yet sometimes leaders are just trying to do something better. This could be returning something to normality, fixing a problem, or just making daily life more viable, as in, say, a food bank.

Even at this scale, we do need to be able to win people over to the cause. If you are a leader, they need to be able to trust you. If we're going to do something on a bigger scale, though, then we need a bigger vision.

Communication Is Key

How do leaders do this? You can't articulate a vision without an ability to communicate. Let's look at communications ability. This is especially important given that trust is in decline, especially among leaders in general and CEOs in particular.

Why do communications skills matter so much? If people can understand what you're trying to do, they're more likely to follow you. The better you tell your story, the more people will engage. The more they engage, the more they will trust you. This soon becomes a virtuous circle. With trust, you're more likely to radiate confidence, which should in turn build more trust.

If there's one transcendent quality of leadership, it's the ability to communicate clearly. Leaders must learn to simplify. Leaders do not agonize on the horns of a dilemma, at least not publicly. Communication skills are at the heart of this.

In the communications industry, whether it be advertising, PR, internal comms, public affairs, brand or general marketing, there is one central equation that dictates whether a message is remembered:

$$\text{Recall} = \text{Frequency} \times \text{Duration}$$

People will recall what you say depending on the frequency and the length of time they hear the message.

This is apparent in all sorts of slogans, whether they be political or commercial. For instance, *Make America Great Again* or *I'm Loving It* or *Just Do It*.

In the words of American Catholic priest and academic Theodore Hesburgh:

> *It's got to be a vision you articulate clearly and forcefully on every occasion. You can't blow an uncertain trumpet.*

This point about an uncertain trumpet is important. Confidence—even overconfidence—is a hallmark among many leaders.

Communications ability was identified by James C. Humes, an extraordinary speechwriter for many US presidents across politics including Eisenhower, Nixon, Ford, and Reagan. This was when American politics were less partisan:

> *The art of communication is the language of leadership.*

That involves knowing when not to communicate, too. Warren Buffett, chairman and CEO of Berkshire Hathaway, once said that really effective leaders are discerning about what they get involved in:

> *They say no to opportunities and things that don't excite them, speak to their values, or further their mission in life. They say no to spending time with uninspiring, critical, or negative people who drag them down. They say no to overworking and neglecting self-care and family. They recognize that everything else suffers if they can't take care of themselves.*[5]

Let's be clear. The physical form of the leader is fixed. There's not much you can do about how tall you are or even how loud your voice is. There is a lot you can do, however, about the way you present. Let's look at some of the common ways you can improve how you present.

First, let's talk about the message.

Message Content... What To Consider

We've already mentioned that "An eight-word sentence is easy to understand." Leaders must simplify the message. Yet, ideally, it should also be an identifiable story. In a Judeo-Christian society, many of these stories originated in the Bible, such as David and Goliath, Judas, the Prodigal Son, and the Resurrection.

Joseph Campbell's book *The Hero's Journey* is an excellent resource to learn about themes and story structure.[6]

Core to the leader's message is hope. We'll talk much more about this is in Chapter 8 but suffice it to say that leaders must bring *hope*. This is the very essence of the leadership message.

Thomas Coombes is the Head of Brand and Deputy Communications Director, Amnesty International.[7] This is his advice:

> *It's not about finding a hopeful story; it's about finding the hope in every story.*

Consider:

- What is your message of hope?
- What does it mean?
- How is it relevant? Most people will want to know what it means for them.
- What change will be involved?
- What is the destination?
- How will we know when we are successful?
- When will we get there?
- What happens if we don't get there?
- What is the *community good* here?
- What role will your suppliers play?
- Is this something that is easy to understand?

- What is it like?
- Could it be seen as a threat?
- Are there any metaphors or similes that can make it more understandable?
- If it were a picture, what would it look like?
- What does it sound like?
- How do you want the audience to feel at the end of your message?
- What questions will they want to ask?
- How will the perception of this change by level within the group?
- How will you test it?
- What will you give people to allow them to tell the story to their friends, family, and colleagues?

When people are given the input and the materials to advocate for an idea, it increases the chance that they may engage with it.

The leader's message will need to be sustained as part of an ongoing campaign. This will contain many different types of messages.

For instance, news, from North, East, West, South—the reporter's beat—always needs six specific components. Who, why, what, where, when, how, and (one more) how much? The most important part of the story comes at the top, then it's supporting components. The shape of a news story is a pyramid.

There are two types of news content. Hard news is political journalism, business journalism, and watchdog journalism. Soft news includes sports journalism, entertainment journalism, and celebrity coverage.

The other type of general content, apart from news is a feature story. This is something that may broadly be relevant to what's going on, such as having a news peg or hook. Yet it may also just be an in-depth exploration of a particular subject. The content story normally starts in one place and then is finished there. The shape of a feature story is a circle.

LEADERSHIP PROFILE
Jo Roberts: Wilderness Foundation UK

Wilderness Foundation UK
Documentary

SOURCE TEAM LEWIS Foundation, https://www.youtube.com/watch?v=zLxRIOXld7k

The Wilderness Foundation environmental education and outdoor therapy courses help young people and adults reconnect to society through outdoor experiences. Their programs highlight the positive impact of wild nature on personal, social, and mental well-being. Developing stewardship for nature and wild places is imbued through the teaching of "Leave No Trace Ethics" alongside conservation volunteering opportunities.

This is embodied in the personal philosophy of Jo Roberts, Chief Executive Officer of the organization:

> *By destroying wilderness, we are destroying the cathedrals of our own healing because there is evidence that the more connected we are to the natural world, the better we function and find meaning as human beings.*

The mission is to preserve wild places and change lives through outreach that educates, inspires, and reconnects people and nature. The Wilderness Foundation creates opportunities for those wishing to learn more about their relationship with the natural world and what they can do to protect it. They equip and enable people to acquire skills and develop strengths from within themselves to navigate their futures safely and successfully. They are working to keep people healthy and the planet wild. Roberts says:

> *Actually, at the end of the day, sometimes we just need to freaking go sit under a tree, put our back against it, look at an ant for 15 minutes and just breathe. It is amazing how healing that can be.*

Many of the people that the Wilderness Foundation serves are in need of healing. Whether they are survivors of domestic violence, at-risk youth or traumatized children, opportunities to be in the wilderness build confidence and resilience:

> You've got one life and how do you make that one life really matter? What do I need in order to get there?

From social anxiety to excessive amounts of screen time to depression, engaging with the wilderness can heal the ills of modern society through building connections. Our world has spun away from the very programming in our DNA that allows us to access peace and respite in wild spaces, and experience deep belonging to something bigger than us.

Based on "likes" and "clicks," young people believe they have massive friendship groups. They spend hours online gaming, texting, and using technology. In reality, they simply have online experiences that are ultimately isolated and isolating.

Roberts purports there is evidence that the more connected people are to the natural world, the better they function as human beings. She wonders:

> If we lose that natural world, where do [we] then go for [our] healing as human beings and for survival of the non-human world with whom we share the planet?

She says that lives are transformed when people are taken into the wilderness in a curated, simple fashion:

> The ability to share space with time on your side, to put an arm around someone, to look them in the eyes and listen deeply to the earth and each other is the path to healing.

The Wilderness Foundation is located on a 400-acre working farm outside London. Thirty-six outdoor therapists mix being extraordinary role models with the wonders of nature. Skilled outdoor facilitators lead with compassion, patience, and kindness. They draw attention to the web of life and share the awe of wildlife, birds, and beetles. Roberts shares:

The participants draw on their internal strengths and they learn to understand where they are. This is done through curiosity in the wild, where they learn to make things work for themselves. They pitch a tent; they build a fire; they cook; they talk; they laugh from their bellies and cry cleansing tears. With skilled facilitation, confidence is developed. The participants draw on their creativity in an environment that is often far outside of their comfort zone.

Part of Roberts' inspiration for creating the Foundation came from reading *Zululand Wilderness: Shadow and soul.*[8] In this book, Ian Player speaks about bringing people back into relationship with the land. This was in the context of Black people in South Africa, due to their disenfranchisement as a result of apartheid. As a South African herself, Roberts was excited about a model that brought people in touch with their ecological heritage.

Roberts grew up going into the bush and game reserves with her father, who was a doctor. Her parents were particularly concerned with those who struggled with malnutrition or were marginalized due to race or poverty. Covered only by an old mohair blanket, Roberts would spend the night camping in a game reserve with her dad, who believed simplicity was the way forward. From an early age, Roberts learned to care about people and appreciate the beauty of the natural world.

During the organization's tenure to date, they have had thousands of participants go through their programs, with over 8,500 children just in 2023 alone. Their accredited wilderness therapy programs and environmental education include a Board of Directors with strategic oversight.

Having just raised $750,000 to buy woodlands to demonstrate non-invasive forest management and home therapy programs, this represents the single largest donation ever received. The Wilderness Foundation maintains a very professional organizational structure. Yet, Roberts says it's important to her to run the organization as a family. The team mirrors the values she holds for clients and has a sense of belonging and connection. They feel heard and are actively listened to. She shares:

It's about making sure that together, as a team, all of our culture and values permeate up and down through the organization. In terms of the leadership perspective, our office is all about kindness.

Roberts' academic background in anthropology and research led her to partner with the University of Essex in the early 2000s. They use peer-reviewed research methodology to measure outcomes. Those outcomes are tied to the experiences of those who participate. The more connected a participant feels to nature, the more confident, resilient, and hopeful they are. The effect is lasting and meaningful. Even wayward youngsters find their smiles.

They routinely take before and after photos when beginning and ending a wilderness experience. Roberts notes the visible physical changes that take effect:

> When we start a wilderness program and I have a photograph of a group of young people we're working with, there's a sort of tightness or toughness. There's no eye contact. There's a body presentation that shows tension and darkness. Ten days later we'll do a photograph of the group and ourselves. We'd be dirty and smelly. We've been kayaking and wild camping. And we look so different. Faces have softened and they've softened.

Young people who said they didn't think they could talk to anybody now feel they can open up and respect themselves more fully. The Wilderness Foundation is giving them a platform to be perfectly human, with all its foibles, successes, and failures. Roberts declares:

> My purpose each day is that I just want to feel that I've made use of my brain and my opportunity and my right of being alive. And then being sure to use that to leave a positive legacy for people and nature in whatever small ways possible.

What Audience? What Medium?

The message will also vary by who is receiving it. Bear in mind your audience may cross generations and may be both inside as well as outside the organization. The media used may need to be across many channels. The message will therefore need to be told in different ways. Younger audiences may appreciate a video format. Some will want Instagram. Others may prefer to use Facebook. Almost all of your organizational colleagues will want to use LinkedIn. Whatever channel is chosen has different implications for the message. It may also change from whom the message needs to come.

Who Should Deliver the Message?

Above all else, the leader must avoid the biggest mistake of leadership communication. This is that the leader alone needs to be front and center of any message. Leaders decide on the message. It's important that message is delivered clearly. Yet the leader also needs to decide exactly how much of that message should be delivered by them. Sometimes, leadership messages need to be delivered by the whole leadership team, even by other stakeholders like unions or suppliers. It helps if everyone is on board.

The importance of this is implicit—the whole leadership team is behind this. It's important to have a vision but it's not enough just for the leader to have it. Remember, Jesus had 12 disciples. Most leadership teams are bigger than that (or should be).

The more people that share in conveying the message, the more will own and advocate for it. It also helps if they are allowed to shape the message and the way it rolls out. Remember that leaders can tell people what to do, but how to do it requires a colleague's domain expertise and input.

The first principle of any presentation is that the vast majority of the message is visual. Yes, people will listen to your words in any format, but how you appear matters more. Let's look at the reasons why.

The Importance of Eye Contact

In a discussion of eye contact, it is vital to acknowledge that there are cultural aspects to be considered. In some cultures, eye contact relates to the individual's relationship to the other person. In some circumstances, direct eye contact can be seen as a challenge. At other times, indirect eye contact can be a form of deference and a means of indicating respect. The advice shared relates primarily to both a British and American framework.

Perhaps at school or at university you had a teacher that looked at the floor, out of the window, or at the back wall when speaking to the class? How did that make them look? Bored? Distracted? Arrogant? Most of the time when people are not making eye contact it's none of those things. It's because they're shy and that's quite common. They may feel shy. Yet, they look rude. This illustrates a common problem. How people feel when presenting is not how they look. You may feel quite comfortable not making eye contact, but your behavior might be interpreted in many different ways, none of them helpful.

Strong eye contact is normally considered to be four to five seconds locked on. Now, you can't make eye contact when addressing an audience, so you do a "box scan." Divide the room into six sections. Front center, middle center, back center, left front, left center, left back and so forth. Four to five seconds staring at each section will look like strong eye contact.

Some report that keeping their eyes locked on to someone or something for four to five seconds feels awkward. However, as we've established, that's not how it looks. Eye contact engagement feels reassuring and attentive to the viewer. One of the tricks to making steady eye contact on a one-on-one basis is to ensure you don't look at the other person's eyes. Look at the bridge of their nose or their forehead and the other person won't notice the difference. It might make you feel more comfortable, though, because a forehead and nose are inanimate. A nose cannot give you information back as you're talking. Eyes, though, can be very distracting while you're talking. Making sustained eye contact feels awkward at first but it will help you look more confident.

Speakers with glasses do need to be aware that it's much harder to make eye contact when you're wearing them, depending on the lighting conditions. For high-trust presentations, this can be a factor.

Why does this matter? Wherever the eyes go, the voice goes. If you're trying to fill a room with sound, you don't want to be projecting your voice into the ground.

A word of warning. If you're trying to give praise to people when you're not making eye contact, it can appear disingenuous. Similarly, if you keep eye contact locked on while giving negative feedback, it can give an emphasis which accelerates the negativity. Eye contact needs to be used carefully.

Consider Attire When Appearing On-Air

Clothing also really matters but often not in the way that people think. The key piece of advice here is to be appropriate to the audience. If you're addressing a funeral or a formal event, you should be dressed well. This shows your respect for the gathering.

There are also some basic rules. Darker colors diminish people, brighter ones expand them. For instance, if you're in a brightly lit TV studio, avoid colors that will bulk you out, unless you are particularly slight. People should avoid brilliant white shirts. These can make studio lights *kick* so it looks like the person is shiny or sweating. If offered powder to dampen your face down, take it. Trust the make-up artist. If in doubt about the studio, then wear a pink shirt. This is "TV white" and will look white under bright lights.

Remember also that TV studios can be hotter places than normal. If you want to avoid sweat patches, keep your jacket on or wear a t-shirt or vest underneath.

Other Considerations When Being Recorded

Most often during TV interviews, you will be sitting down. If so, then make sure you are sitting upright. Ideally, adjust the chair so it is on its highest setting. Sit tall. Sometimes, sitting in a chair that has been adjusted for someone much shorter can diminish presence.

Essential items for studio visits are tissues and throat lozenges. These will help keep your throat clear and boost your blood sugar.

Most studios will have green rooms that will have water and refreshments.

Ideally, avoid alcohol before any appearance on TV, especially if it's live. TV lights, heat, and adrenaline have the same effect that altitude has on alcohol—they magnify it. It sounds stupid but it's been done and it's usually, unfortunately, memorable.

Remember that television often features close-ups. This means that you should try to keep your head still. Using stage techniques such as exaggerated movements can be difficult for TV. The movement can take you out of shot. Think of it as the difference between movies and theater. On a stage, the whole body needs to move to illustrate a point. The very business of drama means exaggeration. Film and TV are the opposite. The slightest facial expression change will be noticed in a way that would be impossible on stage. This is why there are great film actors and great stage actors, but not necessarily those who are great in both.

Anything that moves gets attention. For this reason, try to avoid pendant earrings for TV presentation. They sparkle, move, and catch the light. This can distract from the main message carried in the eye contact. You want the audience looking at your face and your gestures. Pay attention to shoes as well. Presenters may be standing for a long time in heels. Going up stairs onto the stage can also cause hemlines to catch edges of heels and cause a fall. Chamfering the inside of the heel can reduce this.

Think of clothes in terms of the effect they can have. Sometimes clothes can elongate, such as pinstripes. Bright block colors can shorten people. This rule applies across genders. Shorter people should avoid double-breasted suits, for instance. These tend to widen and shorten stature.

It's alright if you want to wear something eye-catching as long as you're happy for it to take a large amount of the visual message. If you're a comedian, then being dressed as a banana is fine. It may not work quite so well with an audience of shareholders at the Annual General Meeting.

Managing Responses to Questions

You may be asked several questions at interview. Like most presentation areas, there is a golden rule:

The question is just an invitation to speak.

Remember, you don't have to answer. Sometimes it's a lot better if you don't. In fact, it's vital for message discipline. We'll come on to that in a bit.

When you are asked questions, divide these up into *green, amber,* and *red* questions. Green questions are ones you can go ahead and answer. These include:

- How are you?

- How did you get here?

- What's your favorite color?

- Do you like kittens?

Red questions are those that are unhelpful to your message, should you decide to answer them. If they are red, then you should not answer under any circumstances.

These include questions in the vein of:

- Describe a person you hate.

- Describe a time when you broke the law.

- What were your predecessor's main mistakes?

- Given a choice between theft and larceny which would you choose?

- Who do you plan to fire first?

- Will you be cutting costs?

Unless you plan to fire people and cut costs, answering these questions may be unhelpful to your message. Answering a question such as "Will you be firing people?" may lead to an unfortunate headline or take away such as "X denies plan to fire people" or "X says no plan to fire people."

An amber question is one where you're not sure. These include:

- How will you be changing things?
- How long will it be before we see success?
- What changes are you bringing?

When it comes to answering questions, let's be clear, there are no right answers. There are only answers that support your message and ones that don't. Under any circumstances, you want to be able to transmit your message.

If you really can't think of a question to ask back, go to your "point of refuge." This is your core message. For instance:

Q: How many do you plan to fire?

A: I'm a people person. I want to create a happy, sustainable place to work.

or

Q: What budgets will you be cutting?

A: I'm a people person. Before I do anything, I'll want to speak to as many people as I can to hear their views.

It's an answer to the question that is not an answer because it's a red question. Remember: "The question is just an invitation to speak." You don't have to answer, but anything you do say may be taken down in evidence and used against you in a court of law. This is why the US Constitution has the Fifth Amendment. It's the right to say nothing just in case the defendant incriminates themselves.

If a journalist calls you and you have nothing to say, then do not call them back to tell them you have nothing to say to them. Sounds stupid, we know, but people do it. There are many times when it's perfectly legitimate to say nothing; for instance, when criminal or court proceedings are pending. Or when there's a danger you might divulge market-leading information. Equally, there are some public offices where it is a legal requirement to talk to the press. In these cases, it's normally a requirement to hold a press conference, where all journalists are told the news at once.

A word of warning. Nothing is ever "off the record." In theory the ethical thing to do is not report or even repeat off-the-record information. There are exceptions to every rule. Yet if it's off the record then it's probably on the record in some way. "Just on background" is another tricky phrase. Typically, it means a source shares information that a journalist is free to use with one caveat: that the information cannot be attributed to a named person.

If you want to transmit a message effectively, then it must be consistent. What can make it inconsistent is when you are talking about things that are unhelpful to the message. This is why it matters how you respond to questions. If you try to answer red questions, you'll end up off-message.

How do you deal with red and amber questions? Two primary ways:

1. Consider answering the question with a question.

Q: How many people do you plan to fire?

A: Why should I be firing people?

Q: What's your opinion of your predecessor?

A: In what respect? Her business record? Her approach with customers?

Having the ability to respond with a question allows you to demonstrate that you won't be pushed into a position where you blurt something out. Second, it allows you to buy time to think.

2. Always keep your answers to questions short.

This is especially important at the beginning of any interview. There's another important reason for this. It minimizes the amount of time your interviewer has to come up with another question. Keeping the answers short keeps the pressure on the interviewer. The shortest answer of all is, of course, a question.

Incidentally, questions are also a good way of transmitting a message without saying something explicitly. How you ask something can be as important as what you ask—for instance, when your partner shows you something they're wearing and asks you what you think. A question back might be more diplomatic, such as: When are you planning to wear it? Is this part of a wider make-over? Have you seen someone wearing this? If yes, "Then do you want to look like them?" If not, then this could be, "Do you really want to look like them?"

Under these rules:

- Why isn't this done yet? becomes...
  - Can you give me an ETA for completion?
- Why is this so badly done? becomes...
  - How might you improve this?
- Why are you late? becomes...
  - How was the traffic this morning?

Answering a question with a question isn't as evasive as it sounds. It's much more frequent than you think. An example would be responding to, "Would you like some tea?" with "Do you have any coffee?" It's an answer to the question but the message is clear.

Question With a Question

Answering a question with a question is also an excellent way of warming up before any major presentations. Play it with your teams and your colleagues. The person who makes a statement loses. You can only answer a question with a question. It's surprisingly diffi-cult and it also illustrates perfectly how we've been taught to answer questions all our lives. This is the central process to how the left brain works. Answering questions with questions feels almost the wrong thing to do. This is because for so long we've been trained to answer questions and not leave them hanging. The sort of graduates in senior positions only know how to answer questions. That's often the way they put people on the spot. That's why so many interview questions can have lethal consequences if you give a "wrong" answer.

For so many questions in leadership, there is no right answer:

- How hard should I be working all the time?
- What's the right balance between home and work?
- What are the right criteria to assess people on: qualitative or quantitative?
- What matters more, people or getting things done?

The answer to all these questions is "it depends." Depending upon the time and circumstances, the answer may change. A leader's judgment is a crucial tool.

There are instances when a leader needs to say nothing, and they need to ignore the person that's asking the question. This should always apply to "doorsteps." These are questions often shouted out by journalists who are catching someone moving from one location to another. These questions occur outside a formal press conference. This should be avoided unless, of course, you really want to do an interview walking down the street.

Responding with "no comment" is a comment and it's only made by people who have no media training. "No comment" is clear acknowledgment that the person heard the question, understood it, and chose not to answer in an unnatural and suspicious way. If you've got nothing to say, then say nothing.

If there's a camera or a microphone present, assume they are live. This applies no matter what you are told. There is such a thing as the "two-tape trick." This is where a recording device is placed in front of the subject. They are then told the device is switched off. Then the questions come in: What do you really think about…? Then there's another recording device that's still on. We know it sounds unscrupulous, but it's been done.

Lecterns

A word about lecterns. If at all possible, avoid them! Those using a lectern tend to read their speeches from a piece of paper. This means their eyes are down on the lectern and the voice is projected down, too. Lecterns also encourage people to grab hold of them and stand still, which means they can't move around on a stage. Grabbing a lectern also restricts the use of the arms in illustrating a story. Bear in mind that most lecterns are also of the non-adjustable type. This penalizes women because they tend to be shorter. People of shorter stature can have the problem of having to peer over the lectern to make eye contact with the room. A tall lectern can make a short person look shorter.

Lecterns also tend to be accompanied by fixed lighting and proximity microphones. This illuminates the lectern and records the area but leaves the rest of the stage in darkness. It will also stop the presenter from moving around because they will need to move into darkness and away from the microphone. It can also stop you engaging with the audience if there's a spotlight focused solely on it. This will prevent you from actually seeing the audience with the light shining into your face.

PowerPoint

PowerPoint is a visual aid. It is supposed to help you augment your message. It should not *be* the message. For an average presentation of, say, 30 minutes, your deck should not be longer than 15 slides. Minimize the text and make the majority of the slides into images.

"You need to add more text to that PowerPoint slide," said no one ever, to anyone, about any presentation.

One of the great problems with PowerPoint is the complete lack of spontaneity. The best presentations are where nobody knows what's going to happen next.

If you're using PowerPoint at all, be prepared for it not to work. Anticipate that your laptop may not connect, the projector may fail, or the screen may not work. Have a fallback plan. Better still, don't use PowerPoint. When was the last time you went to the theater and saw the players using PowerPoint? Quite.

Rehearsing movement and other visual stunts can be much more entertaining. Why? Because it looks more human. Anything that is more human is more entertaining and engaging.

If you're engaged in sales, then remember: people buy from people, they don't buy from PowerPoint.

Room Arrangement

Leaders spend a lot of time in rooms making presentations. Quite frequently these are with teams on both sides. One team is attempting to persuade the other. It's important to understand room dynamics. Leaders should always allow their teams to speak. They should only take on the most decisive or important of points. Ideally, the two most senior leaders on each side should be the furthest apart. If two leaders are placed adjacent or opposite, they will marginalize the extremes of the room and exclude them. Typically, this rule is ignored in political meetings where a bilateral meeting will have the two leaders opposite each other. This tends to be more confrontational and less collegial.

Always be aware of posture when you are sitting down. Quite a few people will slump. Some sit sideways. A good tip is to try to ensure that your eyes are the closest part of your body to the person you're communicating with. This means that you will be upright, leaning slightly forward with your back against the chair.

Rehearsal and Reconnaissance

Always be sure about the room in which you're presenting. Find out:

- Does it have a stage?
- Does it have a raked floor?
- If it's a flat floor, then you need to know the layout of the chairs.

There are many different layouts:

- It could be theater style (row on row).
- It could be cocktail style (high-level "poseur" table).
- It could be boardroom style (one giant table with everyone sitting around it).
- It could be banquet style (in circles, normally 10 to a table).

Banquet style means that some people may have their back to you. This is typically what you might find at a wedding reception. The room may be laid out in a U or even a square. Sometimes, speakers will even be "in the round," completely surrounded by the audience. This format makes it especially difficult to use speaking aids like autocue and teleprompt.

Autocue is used for political speeches and big set pieces. This is where two flat screens are reflected upwards and through 90 degrees, so the speaker can read the text off two transparent plates. Teleprompters are screens at low level that the speaker can see. These can be used to show slides or to help the speaker cue the next guest. Making eye contact professionally while using a teleprompter is challenging.

Sound can also be a problem here because as the head is tilted down to look at the teleprompt, it may move the voice away from the microphone. This turns the presentation into a series of sound waves.

It's fine to have too many people in a room. That creates an air of excitement. Having too few people can kill the atmosphere. Sometimes presentations fail simply because no one has thought about that detail.

Details to Consider

- Is it too warm? If it's too warm some will fall asleep, others will be unsettled.
- Does the audio-visual equipment work?

- What are the acoustics like? Rooms with hard flat surfaces will likely reverberate the sound. This means that speakers need to speak more slowly and allow the room to calm down acoustically before continuing.

- Can you rehearse? There's a saying in presentations that "time spent on reconnaissance is seldom wasted."

- Try to spend time walking the course of your presentation in as realistic conditions as possible.

- Who is introducing you?

- Who is following you?

- Will you have reviewed their material so you can be sure to fit in with the overall messaging?

Cameras are another increasingly important consideration. Your live crowd is likely to be a fraction of the online or on-demand audience. You want your presentation recorded so as to maximize the audience. This means that how your presentation is seen is as much about you as it is about the production.

For instance, you may want to have certain parts of your communication delivered into one camera. This is why you may want to reconnoiter which camera angles can get the best shots for specific parts of the message.

For instance, a jib camera can give a better venue overview than a cut-away shot. Speak to the director of photography (DP) if you can. They control lighting and manage the cameras. You can tell the DP how you want a shot to look. They will then choose cameras, lenses, filters, shot composition, light design, and setup to get it right.

Lighting can make a huge difference to how you appear. This video shows how a person's face can change according to the lighting angle:

How a Face Changes With Light

SOURCE bestvideo05, https://youtu.be/xQHyLKz-oxc?si=6sEyjfMI_RWmEjwP
Adapted from Opale, "Sparkles and Wine"
Noisey, https://www.youtube.com/watch?v=AdsYpi_1Zc4

This can mean a close-up, high-angle shot, a low-angle shot, a bird's-eye view, a worm's-eye view, and why your shoes need to be clean...

The more you have thought through your presentation as an overall concept, the better. The best way to do this is to watch other people's presentations and films. It can give you lots of ideas of how you want the message to look.

Final Considerations

- Always be sure that when you get on stage, you know your way off it.
- Where will you go after your presentation?
- How will the audience know you are finished?
- Where will you go to remove the microphone if you have one?

Another word of warning. After speaking for forty minutes, with a lot of adrenalin, you may be in need of the facilities. Remember to remove the microphone first.

Techniques for Speaking Without Notes

When speaking, how will you remember what you have to say?

Some people use prompt or index cards. This is quite common, especially in military circles. However, it can make the presentation look overly formal and unnatural. This is because it makes it harder to make eye contact or use your hands easily. This makes the person look less animated and hence less relaxed. It's also easy to get cards mixed up.

In instances where the content of the speech doesn't have to be a precise description of policy and has latitude, colored disks or stickers can be used on the floor of a stage. This is especially the case on a large stage where the speaker can move around. Sections of the speech can be color-coded and correlated to positions on the stage.

The speaker walks to the green disk and talks about environmentalism. Then goes to the red disk and talks about emotions. The blue disk correlates to finances. The yellow disk is about the future and so on. Provided the emphasis is more about the speaker than the content, this can look impressive.

This technique uses spatial memory as a basis for recall. This is where the presentation's impact can become almost magical. Where the detail needs to be much more precise and ordered, then the techniques need to become more visual. This involves programming against a familiar journey. For instance, this could be a sequence of objects the person sees on arrival at home. The precise list of items to be remembered is then programmed against this list and visualized. This allows complex, long lists to be remembered in detail in a relatively short period of time.

The standard at this highest level of a precision speech is demanding. When the authors train at this level, the subject needs to commit to an hour of preparation for every minute on stage. If you're going to make it look really easy, then the training has to be detailed. Train hard. Speak easily.

Techniques for Reducing Nerves

Nerves are a big problem for many presenters. The reason for this tracks back to what we discussed about the left brain. The first place you learn to use your hyper-criticism is on yourself. This can lead to speakers becoming paralyzed or freezing on stage.

White circle technique is a psychological displacement methodology. It involves the speaker imagining a white circle around them. The circle protects them and all the time they're inside it, they're safe. The point here is not whether the circle keeps them safe, it's that their left brain is focused on it. This means it can't be active in self-critique.

Inner child technique is another psychological displacement methodology. This involves the speaker applying their own critique as if it were coming from their nine-year-old self to their adult self. The conversation runs something like this:

Nine-year-old: "I'll never be any good as a presenter."

Adult: "Nonsense. You'll get better. Besides, you're only nine!"

Depersonalization technique is another way of coaching better delivery. This involves asking the speaker to name a person they admire as a presenter. Then ask them to imagine how they speak, walk, and act on stage. Then ask them if they can act like this person. The reason this works is because the presentation is then just an act. It's not you personally. Your critique is not of yourself, but of you performing a role. This makes it easier to see the performance objectively.

Ultimately, for big speeches, leaders will be nervous and there's nothing wrong with this if it makes the performance better.

Whatever leadership looks like today, it will look different tomorrow. It might just look like you.

SUMMARY: CHAPTER 6

There are characteristics that have been traditionally associated with leadership. The mold has been broken. Leaders come in every possible form. It is critical not to mistake the loudest voices with the most competent. Often, true leadership conducts itself quietly, with no need for self-aggrandizement. A key element rests in communication skills. Leaders who can share their vision are apt to find success. Simplification, telling the story clearly, and sharing the vision are key.

In the world of communication, recall equals frequency multiplied by the duration of the message. The way a message is constructed can define its impact. To be effective, being self-aware is crucial. Presentation skills equip the modern leader to maximize communication. The components of presenting include audience, medium, messenger, message, form, eye contact, attire, appearing on camera, questions, lecterns, PowerPoint, room arrangement, rehearsal and reconnaissance, lighting, memorization, and managing nerves. With conscious attention, practice, and commitment, presenting well can be within everyone's grasp.

In the next chapter, the roles of the leader are examined. From therapist to judge to coach, the modern leader wears many hats. The secret is to know which hat to don for the situation.

Aspirational Note

- As a result of having read this chapter, what might you do differently in terms of your own leadership style?
- What facts, stories, quotes, or points stood out for you?
- What might you explore further?

07

The Unexpected Roles of the Leader

What unexpected roles might a leader assume?

- Entertainer
- Therapist
- Politician
- Midwife to the future
- Parent
- Judge
- Convener
- Coach

What Do We Need to Understand about the Generations to Lead?

There's no doubt that leadership has become more complex and multifaceted. It has the potential to make or break teams. It's simply not enough to have a vision or the ability to carry it out. It requires a leader who can pivot and adopt various roles to support their team.

The Leader as Entertainer

We live in a world overloaded with data. If we want to cut through this then we can use the battering ram of "Recall = Frequency × Duration." Or we can create an entertaining story. The problem is that competent leadership is not always the most exciting. Yet this need not be a problem. Remember that the leader needs to tell a compelling story. It doesn't need to be *their* story. Leaders must know what will stimulate and motivate their team, their client, or their audience.

The Leader as Therapist

Understanding mental health issues might have ranked fairly low several decades ago in leadership skills. With the changing generations, understanding the role of mental health and the effect on the team is critical. This is something that cannot always be seen and measured. There are clues such as absenteeism and mistakes. Indicators can sometimes come out in conversations. There are individual manifestations of mental health problems. These could include loss of interest, insomnia, loss of appetite, slow or sluggish thinking, poor concentration, and loss of energy. Four or five of these experienced together could be an indication of a severe depressive episode.

If mental health was less of a pressing issue before COVID-19, it certainly is now. According to the UK Health and Safety Executive:

> *Stress, depression or anxiety and musculoskeletal disorders accounted for the majority of days lost due to work-related ill health in 2022/23, 17.1 million and 6.6 million respectively. On average, each person took around two weeks off. Prior to the pandemic, working days lost had been broadly flat. The current rate is some 30 percent higher than the 2018/19 pre-coronavirus level.[1]*

It's worth understanding a little bit more about the facts relating to this. For instance, the onset of depression happens a decade earlier than it did a generation ago. It affects twice as many women as men. On top of this, almost 20 percent of children and young people aged 3–17 in the United States have a mental, emotional, developmental, or behavioral disorder. Suicidal behaviors among high school students increased by more than 40 percent in the decade before 2019.

COVID-19 itself increased mental health issues by 25 percent, according to the World Health Organization.[2] Mental health issues in children start early. According to the organization, one in seven 10–19-year-olds experience a mental disorder. Depression, anxiety, and behavioral disorders are among the leading causes of illness and disability among adolescents. Suicide is the fourth leading cause of death among 15–29-year-olds. Many of these health conditions extend into adulthood, limiting opportunities as adults.

The issue of mental health, especially among children, has been discussed for quite some time. This is the children's TV host Fred Rogers (Mr. Rogers) talking about it in 1969:

Mister Rogers' Message for Mental Health

SOURCE Health Policy Politics, https://www.youtube.com/watch?v=wkJHiCsC2cE

As we've seen elsewhere in this book, this is a different generation. The levels of stress, depression, and anxiety reported are much higher in those under age 50, where the majority of the workforce is concentrated. The understanding of essential humanity is a real advantage to managing this group. Further, understanding the way they communicate with each other is vital.

Percentage of Individuals Worldwide Reporting Moderate to Severe Symptoms of Stress, Depression, and Anxiety in 2022, by Age Group

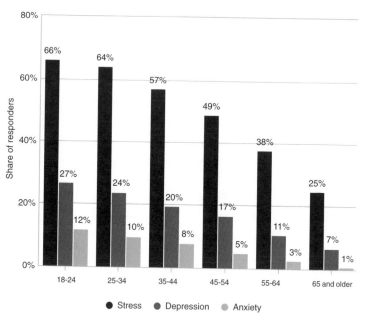

Additional Information:
Worldwide; AXA; Ipsos; September 5 to October 5 2022;
30,636 respondents; 18-74 years; self-reported data; Online survey

SOURCES AXA, Ipsos. In Statista, https://www.statista.com/statistics/1400861/percentage-of-individuals-reporting-symptoms-of-stress-depression-anxiety-by-age-group-worldwide/

The extent to which people congregate not by location but by feeling and interest is difficult for older generations to understand. The internet has facilitated this connection. However, like a frequency wave, sometimes it amplifies the emotion and at other times mitigates it.

The leaders of all Western countries are worried about the three D's: Depression, Dementia, and Diabetes. To some extent, each of the problems affects the others.

An understanding of what causes depression is important for any leader. Until recently the two main approaches have been either through psychological counsel or biomedical. However, in recent years a behavioral approach has become more common.

How to Release Potential

Leaders should be concerned with how to release potential, enhance performance, and develop talent. It's why you have leaders. They develop the people around them and in so doing develop themselves and their teams.

The behavioral domain is especially important for leaders to understand because, to some extent, it can be quantified. Once the condition or situation is assessed, it can be systematically treated.

In the book *Learned Optimism* by Martin Seligman, he puts forward many tests that can be taken on an individual and collective basis. The results of these allow some characterization of what Seligman calls the *Explanatory Narrative*. This is effectively how the person speaks to themselves. Understanding this internal dialogue is important to understanding how optimism and pessimism contribute to depression. Those scoring highly in terms of pessimism are far more likely to experience depression. This doesn't just have implications for well-being, it affects performance and achievement of goals. Those suffering from depression tend to shorten their lifespan by 5 percent, or four to five years, based upon an average life span.[3]

The fact that depression afflicts twice as many women as men is worthy of further discussion. COVID-19 affected women disproportionately not just in terms of employment but also in terms of mental health.[4] In what Seligman describes as "*rumination*," women develop a passive and repetitive style of responding to negative mood that prolongs it and increases the likelihood for depressive symptoms. Further experiments have revealed four types of rumination: brooding, reflection, intrusive, and deliberate, in a sample of those who had experienced a highly stressful event.[5]

This pessimism can be addressed through training the internal dialogue to work in terms of a temporary rather than permanent conversation. Known as cognitive behavioral therapy, this is the difference between a narrative of failure that says, "I've failed because I always fail," and one that says, "I've failed on this occasion, and I can improve this facet." Those thinking in the former way often display a quality Seligman calls *learned helplessness*. This is where failure is experienced which then programs the person's subsequent behavior, even when circumstances have changed.

In-Person, Remote, and Hybrid Work: Harnessing Potential

The whole person comes to work. The personal reward for helping those suffering with depression is life-affirming. This is where the leader and indeed the physical office comes into play.

This may yet become the overwhelming narrative for teams returning to a collective, in-person workspace. The argument for flexible working is based on work-life balance. What happens, though, when the flexible working is itself a cause of mental stress? There's considerable evidence that social isolation caused by working from home contributes to depression.[6]

The leader doesn't have to perform the role of well-being coach themselves. They should, however, have an understanding of how to liberate potential in those affected. The leader should be the catalyst for ensuring well-being, even if it is only to ensure optimal performance.

The notion of the workplace as a place that ensures well-being and mental health protection would be new. And welcome. And needed. Stranger still is the idea that workplace leadership could be the antidote for mental stress rather than the cause of it.

The purpose of the collective enterprise can then become internal and external. Internal, as in a true commitment to the sustainability and well-being of the team. External, as in having a beneficial impact on the community. Both walk hand in hand to create any truly effective team.

This opens up new horizons where the evolution of the nature of the office is only equaled by that of the development of effective leadership. It is only fitting that these new challenges should be met by a new generation of leaders.

The Leader as Politician

The leader's job is to unify. This could be for a common goal. It could be to defend a set of common values. It could be both. It usually is, because the leader's job is to articulate the values to be defended and a vision of the road ahead.

There can be nothing more toxic to this task than modern party politics in a social media age. It sticks simplistic labels on people. From that point, they are no longer trying to solve a problem. They are following an agenda.

Expressing a party-political point of view immediately divides a team into three groups:

• There are those who support the party of government.

• There are those who support the party of the opposition.

• There are those, usually in leadership positions, who are trying to avoid division within the team.

Incidentally, it's not just politics that does this. Religion and money are other subjects of which leaders should steer clear.

Another reason for steering clear of politicians is their age relative to the workforce. For instance, in the UK, the average age of MPs in Parliament is 50. The average age for the House of Lords is 71. They may seem out of touch or irrelevant to the majority of the team.[7]

Why seek to lead in the political realm? The best possible motive is their personal desire to make a positive change. However, politicians have no real power. Any policy change takes years. Any allocation of government funding is closely scrutinized by administrators. There are strict rules.

One reason is a leader's vanity. Politicians have institutional or official recognition. There is a halo effect, albeit temporary. They have a public profile. They also have convening power. They can bring people together to focus on specific problems. They can also draw attention to a specific issue. They are accompanied by media. They can provide patronage, which elevates leaders. They get to meet interesting people by virtue of their position. They get to do interesting things like visit other countries.

Politicians themselves also want to be seen with other high-profile leaders like those from the worlds of sport, business, and mainstream media.

The nature of adversarial political systems is that the conflict is out front and in public. No one wants to look like they don't understand an issue. This requires people to have an opinion. We know that everyone is overwhelmed with information. Many in politics know this as well, so they advance a simple solution that is easy to grasp and sounds plausible. This is quite frequently oversimplified and even more frequently false.

In this respect, the internet and social media remains influential in whipping up emotions on "wedge" issues. As discussed, speed and truth are inversely proportional. This can lead to rapid polarization.

Let's try this. Listed below are some "wedge" issues. Go through the list below as fast as you can deciding if you are "for" (yes) or "against" (no):

- Same-sex restrooms
- Trans rights to use single-sex spaces
- Same-sex marriage
- Working from home
- Lower taxes
- Free university education
- Controlled rents
- Better public services
- Six-month notice periods for employment
- Affirmative action in favor of minorities or a minority perspective
- Blind recruitment[8]
- Mandatory DEI training
- Cheaper fuel

- Cancel culture on unacceptable views
- Defunding the police
- Stopping immigration
- Compulsory Catholic church tax
- Designated mothers' rooms
- Designated lactation spaces
- A strong military
- Immediate full employment rights on joining
- Office dress codes
- Mandatory screens on Zoom calls
- Gender-balanced boards
- Net Zero carbon footprint
- Mandatory drug testing
- Refusing tobacco or vaping clients
- Refusing pharmaceutical clients
- Refusing legacy energy clients
- Mandatory employment of those with disabilities
- Accommodation of those with disabilities to perform their work

All of the listed issues are either mandatory or discretionary in many markets and jurisdictions around the world. Your stance on the above issues can label you as belonging to one political camp or another. And if your response to the above is "it depends" then you're saying judgment is required. This means that there may be an exception to a hard and fast rule. This means nuance, grey areas, and ambiguity. In the binary world of instant judgment, this is problematic.

The Importance of Alignment

The only general rule that should apply in leadership should be that the rules are made for the obedience of fools and the guidance of wise people. To decide is to divide. This is why so many of these complex areas are delegated or outsourced to middle management specialists. From a leader's point of view, pragmatism is far more important than politics. Where politics takes over, the usual result is mutual distrust, suspicion, and division.

You cannot be "for" and "against" all of these things. Every one of these issues is complex. Every one of them has someone that opposes it. Chances are that your parents would not have had to cope with anywhere near as many of these issues. However, the point is that for each of these issues, there is a political dimension. This can then lead you into an "us" and "them" situation, and is why leadership tries to avoid these areas.

Again, this is different from the leadership models seen by some "celebrity" leaders who espouse an "I win, you lose" or "I go looking for confrontation" ideology. Becoming a successful modern leader is all about alignment.

In politics, though, nothing is ever as easy or as simple as it seems. It involves compromise and dialogue. The great irony of divisive politicians is that they sound good but achieve little because all politics is about compromise. It's one of the safety valves in a democratic system. It relies upon the consent of the minority. If they feel abused or ignored or worse, then they're far less likely to give their consent to the majority.

Why do politics matter? Simply because the world is a transparent place. What is said and done in leadership is visible and shareable. This is even more the case with the advent of the smartphone and remote working. It cannot be seen in isolation because leadership no longer exists in isolation. Social media is watching and feeds on any controversy.

How Perception Matters

This means that wrongdoing is visible, if not immediately, then at some point. Even those trying to do the right thing must be aware of the potential for the *perception* of wrongdoing. So, it's not

The Generations Defined

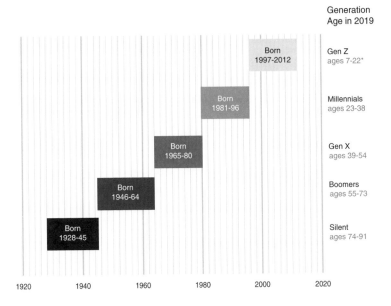

*No chronological endpoint has been set for this group.
For this analysis, Generation Z is defined as those ages 7 to 22 in 2019

SOURCE Pew Research Center

enough for leaders to police the actuality of wrongdoing but also the perception of it. This includes the way that leadership actions might be misinterpreted or represented in an unfavorable way by any hostile group. Social media influencers do not gain followers on the basis of the truth of the statements but because they are entertaining.

This is why it's important to understand the difference between the generations. For instance, a leader working in the same company for many years may be considered foolish by Gen Z and wise by Gen X. Similarly, someone from Gen Z moving from job to job frequently may be seen by Gen X as unstable (see below).[9]

We must be careful with generalizations. The leader has to be careful to focus on the trends present in generations, not generalizations about people. Would you want your attitude and behavior to be subsumed into a generalization about your generation? Of course not.

If we want to understand the future environment for leaders, then we need to understand characteristics that may be different about Gen Z. This is the second-youngest generation, with Millennials before and Gen Alpha after.

The Leader as Midwife to the Future

Why do the Gen Z and Millennial groups matter so much? For three reasons:

COVID-19 accelerated the exit of the older groups from the workforce. These were the Baby Boomers and Gen Xers. Many could not cope with remote working practices. They either retired early or temporarily left and have still yet to return. Also, this group was the richest of all of the cohorts to date. Put simply, they could afford not to work. Incidentally, as this group dies off, they will be responsible for something important. This will be the largest-ever transfer of wealth from one generation to another.[10] Consequently, more than 61 percent of today's workforce is younger than Generation X. As the Second Wave Boomers begin retiring, Gen Xers will be subject to increasing pressure as the gap in experienced leadership grows in organizations of every size, in all industries.[11]

The first Gen Zers were born when the internet had just achieved widespread use. They were the first "digital natives." They grew up with the internet as a part of daily life. The generation spans a wide range. The oldest have jobs and mortgages, while the youngest are still preteens. Importantly, the latter part of the generation also grew up with the iPhone launch (2007). This technically splits the group into two, with different approaches in terms of usage: those who grew up with a desktop computer and those with mobile internet. Roughly 75 percent of all transactions are now handled on a smartphone.[12] Gen Z is entirely comfortable with all digital technologies and remote working in particular.

What to Know about the Generations... Especially Gen Z

Gen Z experience brands at every moment as they move through their digital and physical worlds. This has especially important implications for commerce. They appreciate a good bricks-and-mortar environment, yet the online experience, especially on mobile devices, has to be excellent. Companies often have Gen X or Boomers handling online recruitment. An enlightened leader in this environment might create a good online experience when seen from a desktop. However, this is of limited value because most of Gen Z will be experiencing a company's site on a smartphone.

In a McKinsey Report on Gen Z, one of the paradoxes is that they are generally more pragmatic.[13] Strangely, though, this sits alongside a complicated idealism and anxieties for the future. For instance, an example of this complicated idealism is related to fashion. Gen Z wants to stand out rather than fit in and has a rapidly changing style. Fast-fashion, low-price retailers like Chinese giants Temu and Shein are popular with Gen Z. This despite both having been criticized for their commercial practices on environmental and copyright issues. Shein adds 6,000 new products to its website per day. This might seem at odds with the values of sustainability.

Even within these fashion trends Gen Z also loves thrifting and vintage styles. Sites like Vinted.com and Depop.com cater to this, which is more in line with sustainability. Retro clothes have also become popular, especially from the 1970s. It's normal for a Gen Z wardrobe to be a mix of cheap fast fashion and treasured vintage pieces.

Gen Z see the accomplishments of their parents. They dream of personal career fulfillment but expect economic challenges. They're right to do so, incidentally. They are much less likely to be able to support a whole family on one salary or to be able to buy a house than their parents were at a similar age.

Unsurprisingly, then, they have fewer positive views, with lower levels of emotional and social well-being than previous generations. Again, it's no surprise that they express interest in belonging to a more inclusive, supportive community. Despite this, they're more individualistic, with a stronger urge to express personal opinions.

This makes them more politically and socially active, advocating on social media. These views are quite frequently strongly in favor of racial justice and sustainability. Climate change is also one of the key issues and they expect sustainability commitments from companies and organizations. They often choose brands that have a strong story or purpose, as well as those committed to green practices.

In another McKinsey study, 73 percent of Gen Z expressed a preference to only source from companies they consider ethical.[14] The vast majority believe that companies have a responsibility to address environmental and social issues.

The Environmental, Social, and Governance factor

In fairness the drive towards greater Environmental, Social, and Governance (ESG) is wider than just Gen Z. For example, investment companies have been paying close attention to the ecological/environmental, social, and green aspects of businesses they invest in. BlackRock, for instance, mandates at least two women on the board of any company in which it invests.[15]

Businesses large and small have also taken notice of the rising popularity of ESG, and more countries are adopting it in their development policies. This emphasis is highlighting the poor business and leadership practices followed by corporations in the blind pursuit of profit. Most investors and leaders understand that they cannot ignore ESG and have started changing how their businesses are run.

There are dangers here. Gen Z can tell when a brand is just paying lip service and isn't backing up diversity or sustainability claims with real change.[16] There is a growing skepticism for companies "washing" their products. This can include "greenwashing," "pinkwashing," and "bluewashing."

Italian oil giant, Eni, was fined €5 million for greenwashing by Italy's Competition Regulator.[17] BP, Chevron, Total, and Royal Dutch Shell are also known for similar practices. Museums have found themselves in the firing line, too.[18]

In a pinkwashing case, H&M and Levi's brought out exclusive, colorful ranges as part of their Pride collections to promote solidarity with LGBTQ+ communities.[19]

Blue is the symbol of the United Nations. Bluewashing was first used in relation to the UN and their July 2000 Global Compact. Research found that 40 percent of corporate members who volunteered for the scheme did not use its 10 principles to make any policy reforms.

It looks cynical. How can this be combated? The answer lies in empowering others to become leaders. As the saying goes, people will work for money, but they'll die for a cause.

How can you know what people are passionate about? You can give them money and see what they donate it to. This is what happens in the TEAM LEWIS Foundation. Every employee receives a minimum of $1,000 to spend on a local charity of their choice. As they do, they receive a bonus of $1,000. Surprisingly, perhaps, 16 percent donate this amount as well. This, of course, is ethical behavior but it's entirely optional. There's no pressure on anyone to do this. It's entirely spontaneous.

One different approach between generations relates to access rather than ownership. Again, this is paradoxical. Sales of vinyl records have just overtaken sales of CDs for the first time in decades.[20] However, subscriptions to streaming platforms instead of buying music also seem to prevail. This extends even to services like car shares or luxury clothing rentals.[21]

It's not a completely different world, but the differences are significant, and they are growing. The final important point is that Gen Z and Millennials will rise to about 58 percent of the global workforce by 2030. They are already at approximately 38 percent.[22] This consequently will bring an increased and accelerated dependence on the labor of Gen Z and Millennials. This again is a direct result of COVID-19. It also resulted in wage inflation and a shortage of staff during the pandemic due to staff shortages. US interest rates, for instance, have been held high to cope with the inflationary labor market overheating.

What this means is that most workers today assume their work relationships will be short and transactional. Workers of all ages are under more pressure as work becomes more demanding. As the pressure increases, work-life balance becomes an increasingly powerful countertrend.

The Leader as Parent

Typically, leadership comes to people around the same time as parenting. There are useful parallels: There's no official instruction manual, there's no perfect parent, all you can be is the best version of yourself. Yet understanding as a parent is a complex business. So many children find themselves as vicarious projects of their parents' ambitions. That's not to say that they won't turn out to be ambitious, but not necessarily in the way you think. Children are far more likely to be influenced by who you are, not what you tell them to do.

In the same way that all children are different, so is each generation. Each is shaped by what was going on as they grew up. Gen Z has come of age in the shadow of climate doom, pandemic lockdowns, and fear of economic collapse.

Think of Greta Thunberg. She was born in 2003. She first came to prominence when she protested outside the Swedish parliament. She called for stronger action on climate change by holding up a *Skolstrejk för klimatet* (School Strike for Climate) sign and handing out informational flyers.

It's worth hearing her in her own words because it's an authentic Gen Z voice:

> *When I was about eight years old, I first heard about something called climate change or global warming. Apparently, that was something humans had created by our way of living. I was told to turn off the lights to save energy and to recycle paper to save resources. I remember thinking that it was very strange that humans who are an animal species among others could be capable of changing the*

earth's climate. Because if we were and if it was really happening, we wouldn't be talking about anything else. As soon as you turn on the TV, everything would be about that: headlines, radio, newspapers. You would never read or hear about anything else as if there was a world war going on. But no one ever talked about it. If burning fossil fuels was so bad that it threatened our very existence, how could we just continue like before? Why were there no restrictions? Why wasn't it made illegal? To me that did not add up. It was too unreal. So, when I was 11, I became ill. I fell into depression. I stopped talking and I stopped eating.

To me it is black or white. There are no gray areas when it comes to survival. Either we go on as a civilization or we don't. We have to change... we are in the midst of the sixth mass extinction with up to 200 species going extinct every single day.

So why are we not reducing our emissions? Why are they in fact still increasing? Are we knowingly causing a mass extinction? Are we evil? No, of course not. People keep doing what they do because the vast majority don't have a clue about the actual consequences of our everyday life, and they don't know what rapid changes are required. We will think we know, and we will think everybody knows, but we don't because how could we? If there really was a crisis, and if this crisis was caused by our emissions, you would at least see some signs, not just flooded cities, tens of thousands of dead people, whole nations levelled to piles of torn-down buildings. You would see some restrictions, but no, and no one talks about it.

Thunberg's profile has grown subsequently as she has become more vocal in criticizing global leaders. Interestingly, she fits the pattern of depression outlined earlier. She struggled with her mental health for almost four years as a teenager and was diagnosed with Asperger's syndrome, obsessive-compulsive disorder (OCD), and selective mutism.[23] She described this as meaning she "only speaks when necessary."[24]

Gen Xers and Baby Boomers may struggle to empathize. They lived through the legacy of World War II, rationing, the Vietnam War, and the Cold War. Gen Xers and Baby Boomers prioritize such qualities as patriotism and frugality. They have a strong value system characterized by loyalty and perseverance. They are also quite socially conservative. It was the Gen Xers that brought social liberalism to the forefront.

Around the world, the dependence on Gen Z is growing fast. They will make up a quarter of the population of the Asia-Pacific region by 2025. This generation missed out on the hands-on mentoring, training, orientation, and assimilation that in-person work provides. As a result of the cataclysmic change they have experienced, they have some advantages. For instance, they have qualities that make them well-suited to dynamic, fast-changing environments, opportunities, and challenges. They value workplace flexibility as the number one employee benefit. However, this draws them into direct conflict with office-based Boomers and their loyalty and perseverance thinking.

LEADERSHIP PROFILE
Jacqui Campbell: The Julian Campbell Foundation

 Julian Campbell Foundation Documentary

SOURCE TEAM LEWIS Foundation, https://www.youtube.com/watch?v=THrZJk-8ax8

The mission of the Julian Campbell Foundation is to help young people who have undiagnosed mental distress such as stress, anxiety, or depression. The foundation provides practical and emotional support to them and their families through befriending and mentoring.

Jacqui Campbell is the founder. She has a radiance and warmth that captivates when you meet her. Tragically, her brother chose to end his life. His death was a critical turning point in Campbell's life. After his death, her profession as a lifelong educator seemed to no longer make sense to her as a way to serve young people. Her call to action was providing early intervention to support mental health and prevent young people from considering suicide.

Campbell says that teachers are under pressure to have students achieve test scores and produce prestigious academic results. She feels that needs to be balanced with the true job of teaching: developing our children in their emotional intelligence. Information is so readily available and at their fingertips. Teaching young people how to self-regulate and engage with others is not so easily done. She points out that during lockdown at Cambridge University in one 18-month period there were 10 suicides.

Campbell believes we cannot divorce the emotional from the intellectual. Mental health support is vitally needed and must take precedence. How can we care about test scores when young people feel desperate enough to take their own lives? We need to pay attention.

After months of reflection, she concluded that if her brother, Julian, had a mentor at the critical juncture from adolescence to adulthood, it would have made a difference. She says:

> If he'd have had that intervention in those teenage years, he'd not only be alive, but he'd be the best version of himself. The good thing about having to deal with a death is that I wasn't afraid of anything else because the worst thing that could happen, had already happened.

While there were mental health services provided by other organizations, Campbell did not find a group that directly addressed young people aged 12–20. So, she created one. Ongoing, caring intervention to let young people know that they're not alone and that suicide is not an option. Early intervention and working with young people who may be experiencing even mild anxiety and stress matters.

Helping to make certain that other families don't experience the pain of a loss from suicide drives Campbell:

> I use my brother and his life as a springboard to decide what kind of services we are going to provide.

The mentor relationships forged and the coaching that occurs change lives for the better. Mentors are volunteers who want to help. From Facebook to LinkedIn, volunteers reach out. Also, young people use Instagram to request services and to ask for help. Mentors work with students locally and from various parts of the globe. Given the pandemic, the foundation was willing and able to have vetted and trained mentors who could work with young people remotely.

Campbell remembers a mentor who owned an app development company. Not only did he actively coach a young boy in the program, he also introduced him to his business. In addition to mentoring around mental health, this young man got involved with his mentor's company. The young man wrote an article for the company's magazine and became interested in app design. He later went on to university to study app design. This was a significant development on top of the coaching experience. Particularly for boys, it's not only about getting mental health support, but also life lessons. This can allow them to grow up into manhood and understand what that looks like and means in the 21st century.

A child or young person can think that they're the only one experiencing a certain feeling of distress. They can believe that trouble will last, rather than realizing that it dissipates over time. Just as the good times don't last, neither do the bad times.

Campbell acknowledges that many parents look after the material aspects of life for their children. They give their children direction and instruction. They make sure the bills are paid, the homework gets done. Yet, the conversations she advises are to simply ask how they are and provide space for listening. As adults, we need to be willing to share our own struggles with mental wellness to allow young people to see that it is normal.

Campbell's relationship with God and her faith are central to her ability to lead:

It was my brother's death that really shifted things for me, where I really started stepping into my purpose. The organization is something that I've started but I'm an instrument for God. In my time, I want to be able to make a difference to thousands of young people's lives. It's not about me, but it's about the team. It's about us working together to stamp out teen suicide. To live in a world where it's just not an option.

Faith to me is like a muscle that's built up over the years. When I first started praying to God, I had little faith. Then, as I weathered storms, my faith was like a muscle. It got bigger and bigger and bigger.

Her determination and commitment are inspiring.

Social and Psychological Considerations Concerning Gen Z

According to a PWC report, Gen Z:

... may not readily cultivate meaningful in-person relationships or respond to feedback the way that other generations do. Their responses to stress and anxiety may include low morale and absenteeism, contributing ultimately to attrition. Individually, their behavior can be greatly influenced by their peers—some of whom they may never have met in person.[25]

Jon Haidt and Zach Rausch address the mental health issues of Gen Z in their piece entitled "What We Learned in 2023 About Gen Z's Mental Health Crisis."[26] Their conclusion? Social media is a major cause of the Gen Z mental illness epidemic.

They cite the US CDC's bi-annual Youth Risk Behavior Survey,[27] which showed that the majority of teenage girls (57 percent) now say that they "experience persistent sadness and 30 percent have seriously considered suicide." The rates of depression and anxiety among boys are not as high and their increases since 2011 are smaller. This was backed up by another study that analyzed data from 19,000 British children born around the year 2000. It produced these comments on the data:

We have shown that there is an adolescent mental health crisis, and it was caused primarily by the rapid rewiring of childhood in the early 2010s, from play-based to phone-based. It hit many countries at the same time, and it is hitting boys as well as girls, although with substantial gender differences.[28]

This was backed up by Senator Lindsey Graham's comment to META CEO Mark Zuckerberg at a Senate Judiciary Committee hearing in January 2024. This was specifically about the company's content moderation policies, regarding children and teenagers:

> *Mr. Zuckerberg, you and the companies before us, I know you don't mean it to be so, but you have blood on your hands. You have a product that's killing people.*

Several other social media companies were represented besides Zuckerberg; Twitter/X CEO Linda Yaccarino, TikTok CEO Shou Chew, Snap CEO Evan Spiegel, and Discord CEO Jason Citron all appeared before the panel during its hearing titled "Big Tech and the Online Child Sexual Exploitation Crisis."

Percent of UK Teens Depressed as a Function of Hours per Weekday on Social Media

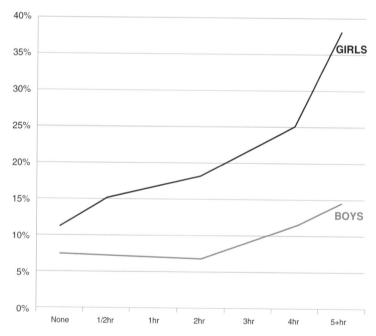

SOURCE Jonathan Haidt, in After Babel, February 22 2023, https://www.afterbabel.com/p/social-media-mental-illness-epidemic

"It is now time to repeal section 230," Graham said, referring to a federal law that allows online operators and publishers to moderate content on their platforms as they wish.

It may not help if you take an adolescent off social media:

> *If all of her friends continued to spend five hours a day on the various platforms then she'd find it difficult to stay in touch with them. She'd be out of the loop and socially isolated. If the isolation effect is larger than the dose-response effect, then her mental health might even get worse.*[29]

It seems that there might be a Goldilocks position between too much and too little. This cohort effectively points to something else. All girls would be better off if everyone quit. But taking it away from one child may make it worse.

There's something else here. Older generations may not be able to recognize the problems in Gen Z:

> *Gen Z's manage stress proactively. Gen Z's may not exhibit the same signals or cues demonstrating that they need help—but that does not mean they aren't struggling.*[30]

This illustrates the importance of intergenerational mentorships between younger and more senior employees. This can not only help Gen Z to adjust, but to modernize Boomer thinking.

A Final Point About Generation Alpha

It would be nice if generational change would slow down, but it isn't. In fact, it's speeding up dramatically. Generation Alpha (Gen A), born approximately between 2010 and 2024, will be the largest ever in global history at more than two billion people. This is principally due to the numbers of young in Africa and the Middle East.

It's important to point out that this generation is still being born, so to some extent, it's still a work in progress.

Some trends, though, are already visible. This large cohort has already had to deal with a climate crisis and the pandemic, which necessitated more reliance on digital media. Their media-centric environment was exaggerated by the pandemic. It was their "normal" and they grew up with virtual schooling and parents working from home.

Consequently, it is the most media-centric generation ever, specifically with respect to video. TikTok is the platform of choice, and exposes users to anyone and everyone, rather than just networks of friends and family. In this respect, it's very different to Facebook, the choice of Gen X and Millennials, which only directed them as far as friends and family.

Gen A's use of social media starts very young. For instance, the use of TikTok is restricted to 13-year-olds, but there's evidence that users are much younger. This is possibly through the help of siblings or even the consent and supervision of parents.[31] This generation's use of AI has also been there from the start, having grown up with Siri and Alexa and other voice commands, for instance in the car.

Due to living large parts of their lives to date online, they are the least socially adept generation ever. This is caused mainly because they haven't had the experience of making friends and being exposed to different opinions. If you've been brought up in a bubble of consistent algorithmically curated views, the first exposure to a view from outside can be traumatic. This is what drives the outrage and cancel culture. They are recoiling from views that are beyond those they have known as the norm.

Many of this generation have grown up with virtual friends, but with no guarantee that they graduate into in-person relationships. They are sensitive to face-to-face interactions, maybe even suspicious of them simply due to unfamiliarity. They can find in-person communications confrontational.

Why Does Understanding the Individual Matter?

Although it's important to understand the different generations, it's important not to rely too much on generalizations. It's important to treat everyone as individuals. One-size-fits-all doesn't work. Most will think of the differences between generations as a diversity issue. The main point here is that we need to rethink leadership. The generations are more alike than they are different. They like active, caring leadership that adds skills and brings humor. They like praise, interesting work and fun colleagues. They also like an overwhelming cause that goes beyond just their need to earn money.

This is where the notion of the universal good comes in. Most people want to help in their local community. In the UK, over 70 percent of people are involved regularly in charitable work.

Leaders must work across generations and political views. To move between these groups a leader needs to be reliable, honest, and polite. You cannot achieve anything by abusing those with whom you disagree. To abuse your opponents only motivates them to diminish you, in turn, when they are able. If you really want to weaken your opposition, you listen to them and include their views and wishes where you are able. You can lose battles, as long as you win the war.

The paradox of leadership is that everyone wants certainty. If you seek certainty, however, then leadership is no place for you. Leadership is an ocean of ambiguity. The only place there is certainty is in middle management. This is where either a task is performed satisfactorily to a standard or it is not.

The Leader as Judge

In many respects, the difference between leadership and management is the difference between the police and the courts. While the police are able to use their judgment to a certain extent, changing the law can only be done by the courts.

If you think about leadership, it reflects a world of judicial principle. There are statutes. Then there are trials. A judge in a trial may interpret the rules in a different way. Judges, however, must never be seen as pressing political points of view. It undermines their authority. The UK judicial authorities describe the qualities as the three I's: Independence, Impartiality, and Integrity. It's a good model.[32]

Dr Ian Cole has served for over 10 years as a magistrate in London:

All sorts of people come before me. I see all aspects of human nature. You do need to know the law, but you also need to have a strong sense of community. This applies both to the protection of its values and the advancement of them.

The Leader as Convener

There are seldom times where the leader alone needs to make a decision. This is especially the case in detailed policy/compliance issues as discussed above. As well as the decision itself, the way it is arrived at is just as important. Meetings are often the place where decisions get made, but *how* they get made is interesting in its own right.

The leader's role here is that of convener. Individuals must be allowed opportunities to talk. This can either be done in time allocated or in turns or both. The allocation of time to develop ideas or to talk them through is vital. The loudest voice must not prevail. If the leader speaks at all they should speak last. The leader's job is to ensure the process is properly executed. Groups that have been involved in decision-making are far more likely to be able to implement the decisions made. This also allows credit to be given in different areas, including the research, the operational aspects, the detailed considerations, the communications, and the contingencies. If the leader is the smartest person in the room, they're in the wrong room. The leader should make everyone else feel like they're the smartest person in the room.

The Leader as the Point of Culpability

Leaders all too easily accept credit for things that go well. They do this more easily than for when things go badly. This matters, especially in public office. Where colleagues sense that the leader will politically maneuvre the blame onto someone else, the whole organization becomes political and risk-averse.

Leaders who accept the blame or responsibility then create more open structures where communications flow. This is called minimizing the downside for colleagues. If they feel that there is more praise on offer than criticism, they're far more likely to take risks. They have to feel like the leader has "got their backs."

In a *Harvard Business Review* piece entitled "Why Good Leaders Pass the Credit and Take the Blame" by Tobias Fredberg, he discusses the difference between leaders in US, UK, and European firms:[33]

> ... *the American and British CEOs, in general, tended to talk about themselves more than the team—they used* me *much more than* we *(or related words). This seemed to reinforce the European CEO's stereotype. The opposite was generally true for the CEOs from the rest of Europe and India, who tended to use* we *more than* me.

The best leaders took personal responsibility when things went wrong and did not hesitate to share the credit with their teams when things went right:

> *They see the willingness to accept personal responsibility—especially during tough times—as critical to winning the trust of employees and other stakeholders. Leaders, in their view, need the endurance and stamina to lead their organizations through thick and thin. They also need to contain the anxiety of their employees. A leader who spreads the blame, who fails to accept that he or she is ultimately the one in charge, increases the insecurity of their people and lessens the likelihood that they'll take ownership of initiatives.*

Another *Harvard Business Review* article also looked at how to combat blame culture. Citing a report from The Gottman Institute, it highlighted the "Magic Ratio" research which showed why relationships endure.[34,35]

The Balance of Good and Bad

The research showed that the brain responds more strongly to bad experiences than good—and memory retains them longer. The researchers concluded that "Good can only match or overcome bad by strength of numbers."

Put another way, for every single negative experience in a relationship, there need to be five positive ones to offset it. The Gottman research measured employees' moods at work and found that when they reported a negative event, it "affected their mood five times as much than if a positive event had occurred."

Some leaders think that one good act can offset one bad one. The difficult truth is that it takes five positive experiences to offset one bad one. It means leaders have to work much harder on positivity and optimism.

Gottman reported that there were many destructive behaviors in relationships, such as criticism, contempt, and defensiveness. The most lethal behavior of all was blame.

There are two big challenges to overcoming blame.

One is how the brain processes good and bad news. The former is processed by the prefrontal cortex; this is the part of the brain that deals with impulse control, decision-making, and planning. It tends to conclude that good things happen by serendipity. Bad events though are processed by the amygdala; this is responsible for emotions such as anger, fear, and sadness, as well as the controlling of aggression. The amygdala helps to store memories of events and emotions so that similar events can be recognized for the future. It usually concludes that bad things happen on purpose, and someone is responsible.

Second, blame is not just a biomedical process; it is also a habit. It needs a conscious effort to control it.

The brain interprets blame in the same way as a physical attack. Nobody will accept accountability for problems if they think they'll be punished for doing so.

Now that we better understand the psychology behind blame, here are two simple changes you can adopt to promote a blame-free culture on your team, especially as a leader. This is done with a change in language used and a change in outlook.

If we accept that all success is based on failure, then there's a way through this. Mistakes can be used as teaching moments, provided there is a learning culture in the team. This is the leader's direct responsibility. It can come through in modified language.

For instance, "Who's to blame?" becomes "Where did the process break down?" Problems are more likely to be found looking at the systems rather than the employees. Eradicating blame might not fix processes, but it certainly will improve morale and well-being. Now, this might sound like an ideal solution to be used in the cold light of day. Yet how would it work in the heat of the pressurized day? This again is a matter for the leader. One thing is for sure, processes are hard enough to get right without the blame culture. With it, they become almost impossible.

The Leader as Coach

In the *Manager as Coach: The new way to get results*,[36] Jenny Rogers explains the OSCAR model. The book includes a step-by-step approach to using the model, which stands for: Outcome, Situation, Choices and Consequences, Action, and Review.

This is a simple framework for any coaching conversation with colleagues who have performance problems as well as with those who are high-flyers. The important part of this methodology is that it doesn't involve the leader "telling" the colleagues anything. It asks them to concentrate on what the colleague is trying to achieve:

- What is the *Outcome* they wish for?
- Then it asks them to describe the *Situation* where they are now.
- It asks them what *Choices* they need to make to get from where they are now to their chosen destination. Then it asks the person what the *Consequences* are of the choices.
- It then asks how they are putting the steps into *Action.*
- Finally, the steps are *Reviewed.*

It is a brilliant model and has won Jenny Rogers a reputation as one of the foremost coaches.

Providing coaching for members of an organization can be transformative. The primary investment that most organizations make is in personnel. Helping to upskill and develop employees is both sound business practice and a valuable investment. Understanding the expectations of what coaching can and cannot achieve is crucial.

Doug Silsbee, in *Presence-Based Coaching*, defines it as:

> ... *intended to support others in developing competence in behaviors that are effective and authentic and produce results.*[37]

Similar to hiring, match and fit between coach and client is important. The best coaches can work across industries. There is a universality of challenges found in any workplace:

- How can I earn a promotion?
- Why can't I get my team to collaborate with me?
- Why does my manager over/underestimate me?
- Why is this client so difficult?
- How do I build a better rapport with my direct reports? With my superiors? With my colleagues?
- When and how should I ask for a pay increase?

Sound familiar? The human condition transcends profession and industry. In the words of philosopher, physician, and all-round polymath Albert Schweitzer:

> *Success is not the key to happiness. Happiness is the key to success. If you love what you are doing, you will be successful.*

SUMMARY: CHAPTER 7

Leaders assume many roles. The role of leadership will demand different skills at different times. Being able to tell a good story is a crucial skill. Understanding the perspective and mental well-being of the people who are being led is vital. Appreciating how to release potential and enhance performance occurs when people are understood. An atmosphere of optimism can help the team be most effective. The leader's role is to unify. Many issues are divisive.

Having an appreciation for how the different generations respond is crucial to lead. Studying the various generations and what motivates them provides a leader with insight. The first leaders most people experience are their parents. Similar to parenting, what a leader does means more than what they say. Technology's influence on humanity is felt acutely. Understanding its impact and depth on the various generations equips the modern leader. Gen Z and Gen Alpha have a unique experience with technology which will change their engagement as employees in years to come.

To decide is to divide. Leaders must bring people together to make decisions. Those decisions may not always be popular nor universally accepted. It is the leader's job to tend to those who may feel excluded based upon the decision, even to the point of accepting blame. The best leaders share credit and assume blame. They understand that failure and success are closely related. Using mistakes as learning moments from which growth and redirection can occur is the hallmark of a leader. The power of developmental coaching can be another valuable tool for the modern leader to employ.

In the final chapter, the role of hope is examined for the modern leader. Hope is an essential and necessary part of becoming a modern leader.

Aspirational Note

- As a result of having read this chapter, what might you do differently in terms of your own leadership style?
- What facts, stories, quotes, or points stood out for you?
- What might you explore further?

08

The Future and Hope

Why do we hold onto hope?

Why does hope matter?

How has the landscape of mental health changed and what must the leader know?

What's love got to do with it?

"Hope" is the thing with feathers –
That perches in the soul –
And sings the tune without the words –
And never stops – at all –

And sweetest – in the Gale – is heard –
And sore must be the storm –
That could abash the little Bird
That kept so many warm –

I've heard it in the chillest land –
And on the strangest Sea –
Yet – never – in Extremity,
It asked a crumb – of me.

EMILY DICKINSON

Hope and the Modern Leader

What will this book change? Who knows? You might ask why anyone would bother reading it, let alone bother writing it. The answer is simple—hope. There's a reason that this word is mentioned more than 30 times in this text. There's nothing simpler. There's nothing more important. There's nothing more inspiring. Hope is the light of humanity. It's what keeps us going. That's why there are so many leadership profiles in this book. They are all about hope. That's why this subject has a chapter to itself. Hope is the key to the door of possibility. Hope is the springboard for action. Hope is the beginning of the attempt. Hope is the precondition for trying something. Without hope there is no endurance. Hope is a choice we make every day. It is a discipline for those who aspire. It is a habit for those who achieve.

At times, we use the word casually as a throwaway—we live in hope, we hope beyond hope, there is the hope that springs eternal, we have a forlorn hope. There is a body of religious and philosophical work going back thousands of years covering hope. It's in the Agama traditions of Hinduism, the Bhagavad Gita, the Bible, the Puranas, the Tao Te Ching, the Talmud, the Tanakh, the Tripitaka, the Upanishads, the Veda, and the Qur'an. Every religion refers to hope.

Hope is not a new idea. Commentary on the concept of hope can be found throughout the history of philosophy and across all philosophical traditions. It was discussed by St Augustine and St Thomas Aquinas amongst many others like Plato and Aristotle, who described hope as "a waking dream." Almost all major philosophers acknowledge that hope plays a role in regard to motivation. In earlier chapters, there was a discussion about "sin." This was described as the concentration on the self, the seven deadly sins being an illustration of this. The opposite of sin are the three theological virtues of faith, hope, and charity. They form the basis for Paul's Epistle to the Corinthians:

> *When I was a child, I spake as a child, I understood as a child, I thought as a child: but when I became a man, I put away childish things. For now we see through a glass, darkly; but then face to face: now I know in part; but then shall I know even as also I am known. And now abideth faith, hope, charity, these three; but the greatest of these is charity.*

Some of the discussion in this book has focused upon charity and faith. That's why we also need to look in detail at hope. Perhaps the greatest religious manifestation of it is the hope for life after death.

Hope is our everyday culture. Our musicians sing about it. Our poets compose on it.[1] Our painters and artists use it every day. No one goes near a blank canvas without it. No sunrise happens without it. It's not taught in schools, colleges, universities, or business schools. And yet all leaders must have it.

The first duty of leadership is to bring hope. It always has been. It has been central to so many political and military leaders. That's why we need to distill the history and learnings here to show how integral it is to leadership. Hope reduces feelings of helplessness, increases happiness, reduces stress, and improves our quality of life.

What Does Hope Really Mean Though?

Rest assured, you can't hope for the past. Hope is about the future. Leadership needs to maintain a permanent future orientation. This means anticipating what might happen and trying to bring together trends. Leaders challenge the orthodoxy. Challengers need change.

Yet what is hope? It is defined as an expectation or desire that something will happen. It is also defined as an experience of trust. When hope is applied to mental health issues, there are often improved treatment outcomes and the mitigation of symptoms. After all, when a situation is "hope"-less, then what is the rationale for carrying on? Hopelessness is a feeling that things will not and cannot change and it can create a certainty that there is no solution to a problem. Dostoyevsky said, "To live without hope is to cease to live." This thinking is often behind some of the worst cases of depression—a sort of inner cynicism made worse by intimate knowledge.

These same cynical voices will also say that "Hope is not a strategy."

This is what the US Army War College says about hope:

*At the end of the Cold War, President George H. W. Bush foresaw
a "new world of hope and possibilities and hope for our children,"
and he set American strategy accordingly, charting a cautious but
resolute path toward opening up formerly repressed regions. President
Clinton extended this course of hopeful engagement; his final National
Security Strategy called for the US to "bring our country's strengths
directly to international publics, governments, and militaries, with
the hope that this exposure may inspire others to promote democracy
and the free market." President George W. Bush came into office
advocating a more cautious approach, but he soon mirrored many of
President Clinton's policies by actively involving the US in the Middle
East, in the belief that, "The best hope for peace in our world is the
expansion of freedom in all the world." The long-term wisdom of these
administrations' engagement strategies may still be up for debate, but
the fact remains that hope has long been a unifying theme of American
national security strategy.[2]*

They summarized this by saying:

*Hope is not "a" strategy: It's the only strategy. Hope as a strategy
builds trust, inspires solutions to wicked problems, and helps us learn
from our failures.*

Why does hope matter so much? Why has it been given such a
prominent place in the ultimate chapter of this book? Because one
of the biggest problems leaders will face is a loss of hope.

In *We Hunt the Flame*, Hafsah Faizal said:

...a person without hope is a body without a soul.[3]

There are two ways to gain back hope. From without and from
within. Either way needs space. A lack of hope only normally
happens when someone is overwhelmed. It could be with grief, it
could be with tiredness, it could be with work. The fortunate thing
about the human body is that it has enormous capacity to heal and
rebalance itself. Each person is different in what they find inspiring,
restorative, and reinvigorating. The two biggest differences are

those who do so with others and those who do so alone—see the discussion in Chapter 5 about introverts and extroverts.

There are times when even the leader will lose hope. There will always be setbacks, even catastrophes. No stranger to this was British Prime Minister Winston Churchill. When invited to address his old school (Harrow), he said this:

> *You cannot tell from appearances how things will go. Sometimes imagination makes things out far worse than they are; yet without imagination not much can be done. Those people who are imaginative see many more dangers than perhaps exist; certainly many more than will happen; but then they must also pray to be given that extra courage to carry this far-reaching imagination... this is the lesson: never give in, never give in, never, never, never, never—in nothing, great or small, large or petty—never give in except to convictions of honour and good sense. Never yield to force; never yield to the apparently overwhelming might of the enemy.[4]*

This tenacity and determination are also linked with hope. This is Churchill on the meaning of success:

> *Success consists of going from failure to failure without loss of enthusiasm.*

The generations most in need of hope are the youngest ones. This is why leaders need the capacity to access hope.

What Is the Next Frontier of Leadership?

The frontier of leadership is not a physical but a spiritual one. It's in the mind and the attitude of the leader and the team. The leader must be sure of those in the team. They, in turn, need to have confidence in the leader. Collectively, they both also need to understand the ethos of leadership. There must be hope for the team unconditionally. The team must be united. This is not about individual talent. Team culture and attitude eat strategy and talent every day of the week.

Most companies are run from a boardroom, not a dressing room, and this is part of the problem. Boardrooms are dominated by financial and legal interests. Dressing rooms are dominated by emotional and spiritual ones. Dressing rooms are all about the team. They can be crucibles of fire. They are places of pride and passion and performance. Talent counts only if it exists to serve the team, then it is to be welcomed. Talent for its own selfish ends is poisonous.

Why does the team matter so much? The team is everything. History remembers individual leaders who would have been nothing without a team. This matters even more now because people have never been so isolated. The technology was already well on the way to doing this even before COVID-19. During the pandemic, people were separated like never before. We're still only just recovering.

Just about all psychological techniques geared around breaking people down begin with isolation or "solitary confinement." This is because individuals alone can be crushed by circumstance and pressure. They quickly lose their terms of reference when isolated from others. On social media, the disinhibited behavior is nothing like you might find offline. People say and do things on social media that they would never dream of doing in person. You can lose your bearings easily when living in an online world. This is how radicalization happens online; it's a natural environment for it.

The Role of Psychological Safety

Psychiatrist Cynthia Nguyen, Adjunct Professor at Stanford Medical School, explains some of the mental effects of COVID-19:

> First, it was anticipatory dread at the beginning in 2020 because we thought we were going to all die. Now, there's so much depression and there's so much anxiety. This is our "Long COVID-19." A lot of people who weren't affected before, now it's come back to really haunt them. Psychiatrists have never had this much business.

Nguyen expresses that in a post-pandemic world, people are asking, what's the point? There are wars around the world. The world is burning, melting, and erupting. The earth, the seas, the skies are polluted:

> *This generation is questioning having children in a way that is unprecedented.*

She shares that the days are gone when we valued being the last one out of the office just to demonstrate our worth and commitment. That is seen as a ridiculous model destined for burnout. Instead, workers value setting their own pace and rhythm with the work. They don't want to punch a clock, metaphorical or otherwise.

Something else interesting Nguyen says is:

> *You can't regret stuff in the past that you can't change. But predicting stuff in the future is useless too. So, the only thing you have is living for the moment.*

It is her belief that what is valued by employees in a post-pandemic business setting consists of the following:

- Providing work/life balance
- Planning for elder and childcare for those who are managing aging parents and children—crèches for elders and children
- Finding meaning in their work
- Helping the earth survive
- Building culture in the virtual space along with the in-person workplace
- Providing in-person work opportunities to combat isolation
- Supporting mental health and providing wellness benefits and support
- Reducing a toxic work environment
- Operating at their own pace

This approach will have a big impact on the current generation as to what they consider to be "normal." Bear in mind that by 2030 more than 25 percent of US citizens are going to be elders.[5] Younger workers will be the majority of the workforce.

2030 marks a key demographic turning point for the United States. Beginning that year, all boomers will be older than 65. This will expand the size of the older population so that one in every five Americans is projected to be retirement age. Later that decade, by 2034, older adults will outnumber children for the first time in US history. The year 2030 marks another demographic first. Beginning that year, because of the US population aging, immigration is projected to overtake natural increase (the excess of births over deaths) as the primary driver of population growth for the country.

As the population ages, the number of deaths is projected to rise substantially, which will slow the country's natural growth. As a result, net international migration is projected to overtake natural increase, even as levels of migration are projected to remain relatively flat. These three demographic milestones are expected to make the 2030s a transformative decade for the US population. Beyond 2030, the US population is projected to grow slowly, to age considerably and to become more racially and ethnically diverse.

Despite slowing population growth, particularly after 2030, the US population is still expected to grow by 79 million people by 2060, crossing the 400-million threshold in 2058. This continued growth sets the US apart from other developed countries, whose populations are expected to barely increase or actually contract in coming decades.

Understanding Team Dynamics and Change is Key

Team dynamics are not something that leaders ever get right. This matters for leaders because teams can bear much more pressure than any single person. That's why leadership teams need to be bonded socially as well as professionally. They are up against a cynical world.

Hope matters so much that US President Bill Clinton campaigned on the notion of *hope*. Hope was actually the name of the town in

Arkansas where he was from. Hope powers English Premier League football fans.[6] This is the league table published by *The Athletic*:

The Premier League Hope-o-meter: How followers of *The Athletic* feel about their club's chances in the 2023–24 season

SOURCE X/Twitter https://twitter.com/TheAthleticFC/status/1689875541711798272, August 11 2023

At the time of writing, the league leaders are Liverpool. West Ham United are sixth. You might conclude that hope is a bad leading indicator. Hope, however, doesn't necessarily deliver results, but its presence ensures that the crowds keep turning up. What matters is that the reality is better than what was expected. On this basis alone, West Ham United should be delighted that they are still in the running.

Hope is really an aspirational feeling that circumstances can improve. It transmits that we'll be able to get through. It reassures you that there is at least as much good in the world as bad. This can be a chaotic world, especially for younger people who are more depressed than ever before. There's a feeling that we're living through catastrophic times. Bad news is reported from all over the world.

Hope is written off by cynics as naive or delusional thinking. It's possible, however, to be both cynical and optimistic at the same time. Generally, people can have a cynical view of certain aspects of life or society while remaining optimistic about others. Take the football fans referenced. They might be cynical about a club owner's motives but ever hopeful about their team. These attitudes are not mutually exclusive and can coexist within a person's thinking.

This is what Harvard University said about hope:

> *Among young adults with chronic illnesses, greater degrees of hope are associated with improved coping, well-being, and engagement in healthy behaviors. It also protects against depression and suicide. Among teens, hope is linked with health, quality of life, self-esteem, and a sense of purpose. It is an essential factor for developing both maturity and resilience.[7]*

Hope is a powerful protector against dread and dread is everywhere. Hope is rocket fuel. Hope and success are also reflexive. They feed on each other.

Hope needs to be grounded in realism. When that's the case, it serves many positive functions. When it's based on delusional thinking, it can work counterproductively. This is especially the case when hope exceeds reality. Good leaders always manage expectations.

LEADERSHIP PROFILE
Teresa Silva: Fundación También

Fundación También Website

SOURCE tambien.org

Every day you have to be in action. You have to be happy. You have to be thankful. It's very important to be a thankful person.

Teresa Silva is the founder and president of Fundación También. She is an athlete who suffered a life-changing accident during training for the World Championships in Austria. She was planning to compete as a member of the Spanish Paragliding Team. The accident left her in a wheelchair for life. This caused her to see first-hand the difficulties involved in practicing sports for a person with a disability:

> I discovered I was strong. You know why I was strong? Because I practiced sports since I was a child.

Her goal is to help people living with disabilities with their personal growth, self-improvement, and socialization. Silva wants to see people with disabilities doing something uplifting and healthy instead of staying at home isolated. She views sports as important for a mentally and physically healthy person.

In April 1998, Teresa Silva started adapted alpine skiing and began to collaborate with organizations related to the world of disability. In January 2000, she created an Adapted Alpine Skiing Exhibition and Competition Team with the aim of creating access to the sport.

Given the success of the experience, she decided to move on to a more ambitious initiative. She created "Fundación También." In English, *también* means *me also*, a clear appeal that those living with disabilities be fully included in the joys of sports participation. This is a non-profit organization that focuses on the youngest children so that they can enjoy their free time on equal terms. Through the foundation, participants receive adapted material, the necessary logistics, and possible subsidies to cover the costs of courses, trips, and activities for people with "different" abilities. This is carried out at national level in Spain, reaching more than 9,000 beneficiaries and 200 associations. The foundation is a qualified referral for adaptive sports in Spain.

The mission of the foundation is to create spaces for inclusion in the world of sports. This is a unique learning opportunity that challenges perceptions of what is possible. Sports provide the catalyst for personal growth. Through participating in sports like skiing, sailing, and kayaking, self-esteem grows in those living with disabilities. More importantly, for someone living with a disability, their perception of what is possible for themselves changes. That shift is seen by others. This brings about a fundamental change in the psychology of the individual, leading to self-improvement. The thought being:

> If I can ski that slope, maybe I can get that job. If I can kayak a river, maybe I can face a challenge in another area of my life.

Silva remains faithful to her sporting spirit and practices sailing and alpine skiing. She is a Spanish Champion in Adapted Alpine Skiing and a Madrid Champion in Adapted Sailing. Throughout her professional career she has received several awards.

She talks about the importance of normalizing the lived experience of children who have disabilities. The educational value of doing so benefits both the children with disabilities as well as those without them. Attitudes and perceptions change on both sides.

Unsurprisingly, speaking with Silva brings to mind the bracing, icy breeze from a mountain slope while skiing at top speed. She is a force to be reckoned with. Everything started for her as a child. She describes herself as a pioneer in sports. Her father bought windsurfing lessons for her as a child and told her, "You can learn and teach me." He cultivated her independence and determination from a young age, instilled in his eldest of seven children a deep love and passion for a variety of sports, ranging from cycling to table tennis to skiing. Silva gets emotional when discussing her father, suggesting that she learned many of her leadership skills from the example that he set. He was an attorney. She describes her father as her role model because he was "an honest, hard worker and good to others."

Silva was injured at the age of 30. The severity of her injuries causes her to observe, "I should have died." Silva has been in a wheelchair for over 30 years and has dealt with countless surgeries as a result of her initial injury. With warmth in her voice, she shares:

> Life gave me another opportunity. I cried a lot. But I put on a brave face. Cracked jokes. I saw my family, so sad, and my boyfriend, so sad. I did everything to make them feel better. I spent nine months in the hospital to recover. When I saw the [severity of the] other injured people [in the paraplegia ward], I talked to myself. I said, "You are very lucky."

A few years after her accident, coaches from the United States came to teach a workshop on adaptive skiing techniques. Silva recalls that she mastered it on the first day. It changed her mind completely about what was ahead of her. It helped redefine a sense of her own future. She called everyone and said:

> I am the same Teresa as before because I am able to ski again.

She felt free. She felt happy:

> While I was skiing, I forgot all my disabilities. I'm here, alive because now my life has a new sense.

Her decision was to share this newly found freedom with people in her situation. That was why she created the organization. Her father told her that if she were going to create a foundation, it would be a lifelong endeavor. He explained she would need financing, sponsors, members, and all of the infrastructure. It would require enormous hard work. The materials for adaptive sports were expensive, as was the cost of trained personnel. Her determination to make these opportunities available to others is the purpose of Fundación También. Silva says her work will never end as long as she can provide opportunities for others.

Central to the success of the organization is her deeply committed team of 12 people. Silva credits her team as invaluable. She further acknowledges the vital work done by the volunteers who participate with the organization. Silva is also grateful for the expression of care shown by families whose children are entrusted to them. Perhaps most importantly, her husband is also an integral part of the foundation team. He is the boyfriend who was with her before her injury and has remained with her throughout the years.

Teresa Silva's dream is to continue her work. The ability to receive people from any country in the world to participate in her program would be ideal. For that, funding is needed. She works 12-hour days with a light heart:

I don't consider myself a leader. I'm a normal person.

Just a normal person. Perhaps that epitomizes the modern leader.

The Voices of History on "Hope"

After a series of major defeats in World War II, this is Winston Churchill taking over as leader:

I have nothing to offer but blood, toil, tears and sweat. We have before us an ordeal of the most grievous kind. We have before us many, many long months of struggle and of suffering. You ask, what is our policy? I can say: It is to wage war, by sea, land and air, with all our might and with all the strength that God can give us; to wage war against a monstrous tyranny, never surpassed in the dark, lamentable catalogue of human crime. That is our policy. You ask, what is our aim? I can answer in one word: It is victory, victory at all costs, victory in spite of all terror, victory, however long and hard the road may be; for without victory, there is no survival.

He didn't sugar-coat it, but the hope was there with the repetition of the world "victory." This is an important word for the British. All over the country parks were named Victory Park. It was also the name of Nelson's flagship at the Battle of Trafalgar. Victoria was the name of the longest-serving monarch. Five years later, Britain had won through. Like Nelson, Churchill secured a great victory and, like Nelson, he was gone a short time afterward. Churchill was soundly defeated in the election of 1945.

Some leaders are like Churchill. They are naturally pugnacious and full of light and dark. Leaders need this quality. Not everyone is naturally pugnacious, but it can be developed. Think of all the things that you'd fight for, such as becoming a parent, being a parent, or loving someone. These are usually the things you hold most precious. These are usually also the positive things in your life.

Neither is "hope" the preserve of political conservatives. It was former US First Lady Michelle Obama who said:

You may not always have a comfortable life and you will not always be able to solve all of the world's problems at once but don't ever underestimate the importance you can have, because history has shown us that courage can be contagious, and hope can take on a life of its own.

It is an abiding theme for all those fighting for civil rights. For instance, Desmond Tutu, South African Anglican bishop and theologian, described hope as:

being able to see that there is light despite all of the darkness.

Tutu is famous for saying:

There comes a point where we need to stop just pulling people out of the river. We need to go upstream and find out who is pushing them in.

It was a consistent theme in all civil rights movements. Martin Luther King said:

We must accept finite disappointment, but never lose infinite hope.

This brings us to where hope springs eternal. The concept of the right brain was discussed in earlier chapters. Hope resides in the right brain. It takes this quiet time to imagine the circumstances of success or how things will improve. If you are in pain or in sorrow, understand that this too will eventually pass. There has to be a deliberate intent to foster positivity, even in the face of its absence.

A piece in *Psychology Today* entitled "The Healing Power of Hope," says that being hopeful can improve mental health treatment outcomes:

Hope is a powerful tool for addressing some of our most prevalent mental health concerns. People who have hope for recovery see improved treatment outcomes of many mental health issues.[8]

What Happens When We Lose Hope?

At one time or another, all of us will lose hope. Situations don't always turn out as expected. Yet hope can be one of the most powerful tools at the leader's disposal.

Anxiety is the most common mental health issue in the world today. This includes worry, fear, and panic attacks, symptoms that can feel difficult to manage and frightening to experience. The research, however, indicates that hope plays a role in shaping how people can cope with anxiety. Hope can foster an attitude that empowers people to confront their fears.

How does one foster hope? Developing hope while dealing with significant mental health issues is a multifaceted process, but it is possible with the right support and strategies.

One crucial aspect is fostering a sense of connection and social support, whether through therapy, support groups, or trusted relationships. Setting realistic goals and focusing on small, achievable steps can provide a sense of progress and accomplishment.

One of the problems with leadership is responsibility. Not everyone wants it. In fact, most people shun it. Most don't want everyone else's problems added to their own. Besides, people leadership is more complicated than ever due to an employee-centric approach brought on by the scarcity of staff, shifting HR policies, social media, sensitivities around language use, an increasingly litigious environment, and remote working practices. It's easy to get it wrong. Who would want to be a leader?

There is, though, a great deal of leadership that's done by people who don't seek it, nor do they want the adulation, approbation, recognition, or reward.

Financial Gain and Leadership

For some, leadership is all about financial gain. You can measure everything financially. You can definitely assess your leaders on how much money they make. There's nothing wrong with that. Adam Smith's principles still hold good. Yet we need a wider field of vision. What we've been saying throughout this book is that the pandemic changed a lot of things. It accelerated and deepened a lot of divisions. Remember the words of Matthew 16:26: "For what is a man profited, if he shall gain the whole world and lose his own soul?"

As we write this text, it's the 2024 annual meeting of the World Economic Forum in Davos. Over 1,000 private planes fly into the meeting from around the world.[9] There will be many high-profile, highly intelligent, talented, experienced, powerful, and wealthy leaders present. Arguably, the leaders of the human race. Will any of them read this book? Perhaps. World leaders are serious, busy people. They talk the language of geopolitics, high finance, and global alliances. Nothing wrong with that, but it's not the language of hope that the rest of the world uses.

The Soul Within Leadership

We know an individual's whole self comes to work every day. And these are difficult times. One might say, "We all have a cross to bear." The stronger of us bear that burden; we pay more in tax. Yet there's another tax levied on leaders. In the words of George Washington:

Labor to keep alive that little spark of celestial fire, called conscience.

This is perhaps the challenge for world leaders. Or even to display the compassion and care you might apply to yourself. A gesture of kindness can redirect a colleague's day. Seeing and being seen matter. If you have the chance to be decent to another human being, take it. We tell ourselves that we are too busy, too stressed, and maybe too important. Every day is a decision and a chance to get it right.

Those around us are more vulnerable than they appear. If we look beyond their anger, we may see the depth of fear. If we look beyond their cynicism, we might see their deep desire for hope.

If the soul is intangible then certainly, feelings and emotions are too. The exploration of the intangible requires us to examine other areas of our lives that are similar. They play such a significant part in who we are and how we engage in the world around us. Faith, hope, grace, and charity are concepts that speak to the higher sense of self.

Many people are born into constellations of chaos that surround them in the form of their families. None of us get to choose our families or our social class. Was your birth met with joy or trepidation? Were you surrounded by a setting of safety and security or fear and chaos? What were you rewarded for? How important was hope to you? What did you hope for?

The most wonderful aspect of hope is that it shows up when you expect it least. This is also another manifestation of the right brain. It's been discussed before that many report that their best ideas come when they are on their own, not working and not even trying. This is when the idea arrives. Just like hope, it arrives as divine inspiration.

Really, what are these Damascene interventions but hope, made practical? This is why hope is so often found at the heart of despair.

Is There Hope Concerning Racism?

There is no greater moment of despair for Black people than being called the "N" word for the first time. It's an unholy, diabolic baptism—a date they will remember as long as they live. This is the day they were named something "other," told they were something *less*. Parents experienced it. They dread the moment when their children hear it. There was a before. There is a lifetime after. Less enlightened people will respond:

"But we hear this word all the time."

"The word is used in song lyrics."

"Our children picked this word up."

This doesn't make it right. If we are a society desensitized by denigration, then it's time to recognize the importance of our language. Don't get it? Look closer at the word denigrate. It means to blacken, to make less. Ironic, no?

Racially hateful language persists. Why? Derrick Bell, in *Faces at the Bottom of the Well: The permanence of racism*,[10] explains that most Black people see racism as a permanent part of the American scene. Only with this recognition can solutions be sought. To deny its persistence and prevalence prevents the development of strategies.

Bell, when asked why his book was "unremittingly despairing," responded:

> I get that question again and again. Very few Black [people] would ask that… particularly professional civil rights people… if you really are a part if this thing, you sense where you are, regardless of how much money you may make, you are part of a group that's at the bottom of the societal well… The truth is not despairing when you see it as the truth. In fact, it's enlightening.[11]

W. E. Du Bois was an American sociologist, historian, and civil rights activist. His thinking about racism is summarized here:

> In any land, in any country under modern free competition, to lay any class of weak and despised people, be they white, black, or blue, at the

political mercy of their stronger, richer, and more resourceful fellows,
is a temptation which human nature seldom has withstood and seldom
will withstand.[12]

It's not a matter of being woke or politically correct. It's actually
simpler than that—it's about being human. You can't be human
without humanity. Those who would deliberately and ignorantly
use the language of division are not striking a blow for free speech.
Or rebelling against what they think is an orthodoxy. They're just
showing their lack of consideration, deficit of emotional intelligence, and bad manners.

Bad manners show a lack of humanity. Of course, you can order
a cup of coffee without the words "please" and "thank you," but
most decent people don't. Why? It's about respect and consideration. Politeness is the first sign of leadership. It doesn't stop the
ability to get things done. Quite the contrary. It doesn't stop you
being dynamic or making decisions. It helps.

Maybe you think the world is already too polite? If so, you
clearly haven't been anywhere near the world in which our
youngest generation is developing. The lack of respect can spiral
out of control to anonymous bullying online and to violence and
self-harm.

Words Matter

If you're serious about leadership then your language matters. It
matters especially toward minority groups or to the marginalized.
The argument against woke is seldom made by anyone other than
those in a majority. They say it's all gone too far. They complain
how it impinges on their world. They complain about how it makes
them feel. And that's just it. It is about them.

When it comes to the consideration of minority groups, we're
not made stronger by pointing out how different we are. Leaders
make everyone see similarities, not differences. How else can you
create common cause? How else can you unify?

It's not up to the well-fed to decide who has enough to eat. Only the hungry can tell you when they are full. There will still be the fat. There will still be the thin. The world is full of different people. This is the way of things. But you can't lead a team—at any level—that only sees how unlike each other they all are.

W. E. Du Bois again:

> The equality in political, industrial, and social life which modern men
> must have in order to live, is not to be confounded with sameness.
> On the contrary, in our case, it is rather insistence upon the right of
> diversity; upon the right of a human being to be a man even if he does
> not wear the same cut of vest, the same curl of hair or the same color
> of skin. Human equality does not even entail, as it is sometimes said,
> absolute equality of opportunity; for certainly the natural inequalities
> of inherent genius and varying gift make this a dubious phrase. But
> there is more and more clearly recognized minimum of opportunity
> and maximum of freedom to be, to move and to think, which the
> modern world denies to no being which it recognizes as a real man.

We raise this to say a leader's language *matters*. It needs to be used carefully *with consideration*. You cannot preach a vision of darkness. You cannot unify with division. Hatred creates only further unknowable landscapes of fear, horror, death, and hopelessness.

In the 1941 film *Pimpernel Smith*, Leslie Howard plays bookish professor of archaeology Horatio Smith, who leads a double life. He performs a series of daring extractions of Jewish refugees from Germany in World War II. At the same time, he's also a mild-mannered teacher of his students. The role echoed a part he played in an earlier film, *The Scarlet Pimpernel*, where again he played a man with a double life. Sir Percy Blakeney was a foppish English aristocrat on the surface whilst underneath being the savior of French aristocrats fleeing Revolutionary France.

Here he is in *Pimpernel Smith* addressing his Nazi tormentor:

> May a dead man say a few words to you, General, for your
> enlightenment? You will never rule the world... because you are
> doomed. All of you who have demoralized and corrupted a nation are

doomed. Tonight, you will take the first step along a dark road from which there is no turning back. You will have to go on and on, from one madness to another, leaving behind you a wilderness of misery and hatred. And still, you will have to go on... because you will find no horizon... and see no dawn... until at last, you are lost and destroyed. You are doomed, Captain of Murderers, and one day, sooner or later, you will remember my words.

You can find the clip here:

"You're Doomed":
Pimpernel Smith Monologue

SOURCE Toby E Carson, https://www.youtube.com/watch?v=7evSk4SSUy8

Howard was born Leslie Howard Steiner to a British mother, Lilian (née Blumberg), and a Hungarian Jewish father, Ferdinand Steiner, in London. He anglicized his name during the First World War, although his military service records were still in his original name. He had ample motivation for the role he played here.

Howard epitomized a type of long-forgotten leader – a seemingly effortless, inspirational, amiable, polite, loyal, modest, self-sacrificing, servant–leader, who retains a secret heroic dynamism. It was a role he played in many different movies, most notably *Gone with the Wind*, where he played opposite Clarke Gable.

He was killed when his civilian airliner was shot down by German aircraft on June 1 1943. He was 50 years old. His untimely demise was a storyline that could have been taken from any of his movies.

LEADERSHIP PROFILE
Heather Bradley: Pittsburgh Bereavement Doulas

Pittsburgh Bereavement Doulas

SOURCE https://pittsburghbereavementdoulas.com/

You may ask why we have chosen this organization to feature in a chapter on hope. The answer should be obvious on reading the text below. As Leonard Cohen said in his song "Anthem":

There is a crack, a crack in everything. That's how the light gets in.

This team are the ultimate bringers of light in the midst of great darkness. Heather Bradley, Founder and Executive Director, Pittsburgh Bereavement Doulas, says:

Bereavement doulas are not the heroes here. You're a navigator, you're a listener, you're a companion, to facilitate this baby being honored.

When a baby dies, no one wants to talk about it. We don't have the vocabulary. How do people lead in the face of unimaginable pain? That is the task of the Pittsburgh Bereavement Doulas. The introduction on the website is:

If you are reading this, you are experiencing something unexpected and sad. You probably didn't think this would happen to you and you aren't prepared to deal with what is happening to you emotionally, physically, and spiritually. You may not have been so intimately involved in death before. When your baby dies, you may be at a loss as to what to do next. Our experienced bereavement doulas will support you during the birth of your baby by miscarriage, stillbirth, or life-limiting diagnosis. They will also guide you through your options, suggest ways to honor and remember your baby, and help you find the support you need afterwards as you grieve.

Heather Bradley is changing the conversation around the way the death of a baby is handled. An experienced doula in her own right, Bradley witnessed the experience of a mother whose child died in the womb at 37 weeks. The mother was not treated with evidence-based research. She received no quality perinatal bereavement care. The result was that she was left feeling unsupported. Bradley was shocked that there was no one offering specialized care.

Bradley knew this mom, this family, would experience a lifetime of loneliness and heartbreak. Countless people are walking around carrying this pain. She wanted to determine how this experience could be changed to support the family and honor the dead. She shares:

We quietly model what quality bereavement care can look like. Did I want to start a non-profit at that point in my life? No, but I just, I couldn't not do it. There were people out there with no one helping them and you see people suffering.

She explains that the typical path through which someone learns of them is through their care provider when the death or imminent delivery of a stillborn child is about to happen.

An aspect of her leadership role is that she trains doulas to assist families in these painful circumstances. Her outlook shifts the perspective on how life is viewed, regardless of the stage. Learning to make decisions out of love, not fear, even in the face of the worst sorrow:

You have to remind them like this is a love story. Did you forget about that love? People say, "How can you do this?" I see these human moments that are just incredible and that's what draws everyone when they're doing the work.

Reframing the conversation to provide information to parents at this challenging time is key. The option to hold the baby, touch the baby, introduce the baby to siblings, take family photos, bathe the baby, wash the baby's hair should be shared. At the very least, the choice should be in the hands of parents.

*Let's have a conversation about that. Why are you afraid to bring your
children to meet their sibling? This is the only opportunity you have for
a family photo. And it's never as bad as you think it's going to be in
your mind.*

By explaining to families that they are going to meet their baby helps to
remove the fear. The doulas reintroduce the love that the parents have held
for this child. They are helping the family to see the beauty in their child
rather than amplifying the pain of the loss:

*People want to know everything they can do to have a safe pregnancy. I
mean you're telling them not to eat sushi and not to eat lunch meat or clean
the litter boxes. Why? Because your baby could die. So, let's talk about these
other things. We're not having these conversations prenatally. We know that
some stillbirths are preventable.*

There are practical steps that should be communicated to all families. There
is an app for counting kicks. This helps mothers stay tuned to the activity of
the baby based upon what is consistent with that particular pregnancy.
There are myths that need to be debunked about babies becoming less
active as they near delivery. There are practical steps such as measuring the
placental size, which can provide information that may prevent a stillbirth
or other life-ending outcomes. In addition to warning women away from
eating sushi, we need to prepare them for potentially serious eventualities.
Information is a prophylactic to potential trauma.

Bradley says that in the same way that lactation specialists have become
standard in most hospital settings, bereavement doulas should have a
financially supported presence in all hospitals:

They need to step up and realize this is part of patient care.

Many families report that the trauma they experienced in the ER or with a
technician has added to the trauma of the loss of their child. Training,
education, and open communication must occur. Physicians and nurses do
not necessarily receive training in how best to manage the conversations.
And doulas have the time. They have the many hours that may be required,
that the medical professionals do not have, to sit with the family, explain
and explain again what's going on. Trained bereavement doulas have the
vocabulary. They have the compassion.

Information about cremation, taking the baby home with you, inducing the baby intact are important considerations for the parents to understand. They are not commonly known or talked about. The grief that the family will experience is comprehensive and will require clergy, mental health support, and other practitioners. It takes a coordinated community response to support a family through this sort of trauma.

Bradley reflects that she didn't know this could happen to wealthy, well-educated White people with good insurance. This stems from her understanding of the landscape of the birth experience for American Black women. In the United States, Black women are two to three times more likely to experience trauma surrounding birth. Having doulas who reflect the community is an important priority for Pittsburgh Bereavement Doulas. Regardless of race or sexual orientation, trauma occurs. Being culturally responsive is key in supporting people through difficulties. Unexpected death is tragic. Depending on how it is managed, trauma can be reduced, and love can be reclaimed.

Hope and Fear

We assume that most people have predictable markers in their lives that involve education, development, movement into career, family life, aging, and ultimately death. Yet the course of life is rarely that linear. We pepper in an illness or two. A crisis or five. We are confronted with the unpredictable and our introduction to worlds we never knew can lead us to places we never thought we'd experience. Good and bad. As in the case of the Pittsburgh Bereavement Doulas, grief and loss can touch any one of us. And those experiences catapult us back to the age of vulnerability. Many of the causes we've highlighted come from a place of crisis, innovation, disruption, or vulnerability. Their leaders have innovated and changed the narrative for both the organization and what it is to be a leader.

They won't have the resources, nor the experience of those at the 2024 World Economic Forum at Davos. They inspire despite, and because of this.

Martha Nussbaum is a professor of law and philosophy at the University of Chicago and the author of more than 20 books. This is what she says about the relationship between hope and fear:

We come into a world with which we are not ready to cope. The discrepancy between the very slow physical development of the human infant and its rapid cognitive development makes fear the defining emotion of infancy. Adults are amused by the baby's futile kicking and undisturbed by its crying because they know they are going to feed, clothe, protect, and nurture it. The infant, however, knows nothing of trust, regularity, or security. Its limited experience and short time horizons mean that only the present torment is fully real, and moments of reassurance, fleeting and unstable, quickly lead back to insufficiency and terror. Even joy is tainted by anxiety, since to the infant it seems all too likely to slip away.

We usually survive this condition. We do not survive it without being formed, and deformed, by it. Neurological research on fear has shown that the scars of early fright stimuli endure and become a continuing influence on daily life.

Fear is not only the earliest emotion in human life; it is also the most broadly shared within the animal kingdom. To experience other emotions, such as compassion, you need a sophisticated set of thoughts: that someone else is suffering, that the suffering is bad, that it would be good for it to be relieved. But to have fear, all you need is an awareness of danger looming. The thoughts involved don't require language, only perception and some vague sense of one's own good or ill.

Fear is not just primitive; it is also asocial. When we feel compassion, we are turned outward: we think of what is happening to others and what is causing it. But you don't need society to have fear; you need only yourself and a threatening world. Indeed, fear is intensely narcissistic. An infant's fear is entirely focused on its own body. Even when, later on, we become capable of concern for others, fear often drives that concern away, returning us to infantile solipsism.[13]

If the leader's message is to bring hope, then an understanding of fear is vital. Martha Nussbaum again:

Hope is the inverse of fear. Both react to uncertainty, but in opposing ways. Hope expands and surges forward, fear shrinks back. Hope is vulnerable, fear is self-protective. This is the difference.

Perhaps the best example of the fear in a young life is related by Dr. Chan Hellman. He is the Founding Director of the Hope Research Center and Professor at the University of Oklahoma. After a childhood of despair and homelessness, he found his way. He ascribes this miraculous turnaround to hope. He talks through his experience here:

The Science and Power of Hope: Dr. Chan Hellman

SOURCE TEDx Talks, https://www.ted.com/talks/chan_hellman_the_science_and_power_of_hope

Chan Hellman has spent his life studying the art and science of hope. As hope rises, he sees positive outcomes for health and education. Equally with rising trauma, hope declines and the likelihood of positive outcomes decreases with it. He says well-being is more than just the reduction of the things that are wrong with us. Hellman makes the point that hope is a way of thinking. It is something that can be taught:

Hope is the belief that your future will be better than today and that you have the power to make it so.

Imagination is the instrument of hope. We have to be able to imagine ourselves in the situation. This is the basis for what we learned in Chapter 7 about the OSCAR model of coaching. The subject must be able to imagine the state into which they wish to develop. Only then can hope power them to go beyond optimism into action. However, the goals must be wanted. Once hope is established, it can then feed on itself. Hope begets hope.

Hellman says there's a big difference between hoping and wishing. Hope involves identifying pathways to get from one place to another. Wishes need to be granted by an external source, thus excluding the role of the individual. They are a dream that has no pathway back to reality. He points out that you can be highly motivated while still lacking pathways and willpower.

Hellman says something interesting about the connection between willpower and the physical state. He says that willpower is a limited resource. It needs energy, specifically glucose and high-energy nutrition. Willpower is not enough to power hope. It's too difficult to sustain. To keep going with willpower alone becomes harder. You run out of energy, physically and mentally. Like all other aspects of excellence, hope is not a single event. Hope is a habit.[14]

The Loneliness of Leadership

If we really care about leading a team, understanding fear and hope is vital. Why? When you're in a position of leadership you can do vastly more damage and devastation than any one individual. You have a responsibility. This is not to say you should not be obsessive and driven. This is not to say you have to be easy going. This is not to say you need to be everyone's friend. You can be friendly with members of your team, but it's difficult to be their friend. Why? You may have to push them beyond what they think they're capable of doing. For this reason, if leaders have friends in the team, then there must be a tacit understanding of the conflicts. Passionate, energetic people can be a pain in the derriere. It's the way of things.

It is a consistent problem with those in leadership positions. They may have position, power, money, and even fame and notoriety, but they still have problems. For instance, they never know if their friendships are based on their position or on who they are as people. Some will only ever see them as a position and not a person. This happens frequently to politicians and those "in power." They are respected more often than they are loved. They all too frequently sacrifice intimacy for integrity. These are great sacrifices and leaders should not expect them to be universally applauded.

Leaders need to understand the role of hope and fear. They also need to be on the lookout for despair. It's essential that leaders look out for the well-being of others. Quite frequently the loudest voices do not represent the largest groups. The largest are the ones that suffer in silence. We know this from Martha Nussbaum's work. We all have a battle to fight against fear.

As we learned in Chapter 2, our physical connectedness is one of the single biggest generators of hope. Hope is the social gift that comes from physical community. That's why people are better off at least spending time together in fellowship, whether it be at the office, working on a joint cause, in the pub, breaking bread at a restaurant, enjoying theatre, watching a sports event, or participating in one. Teams are made of more than just work.

Civil Rights theologian Howard Thurman defines hope:[15]

Look well to the growing edge! All around us worlds are dying, and new worlds are being born; all around us life is dying, and life is being born. The fruit ripens on the tree, the roots are silently at work in the darkness of the earth against a time when there shall be new leaves, fresh blossoms, green fruit. Such is the growing edge! It is the extra breath from the exhausted lung, the one more thing to try when all else has failed, the upward reach of life when weariness closes in upon all endeavor. This is the basis of hope in moments of despair, the incentive to carry on when times are out of joint and men have lost their reason, the source of confidence when worlds crash and dreams whiten into ash. The birth of the child—life's most dramatic answer to death—this is the growing edge incarnate. Look well to the growing edge!

Leadership is Changing

Thank God. It needs to change. It needs to condemn less, understand more, and be less certain about itself.

It's time we recognized its critical importance in everything we do. Whatever humanity's goals, be it developing and preparing our children for the world they are entering, ending wars, building a stronger economy, better healthcare, greater care for the elderly, we need better. We need better in government, in business, in medicine, in education, in our military, and our third sector of charities, social enterprises, and voluntary groups.

The great historian and biographer Stephen Ambrose wrote:

The past is a source of knowledge, and the future is a source of hope.
Love of the past implies faith in the future.

This brings us finally to love. The Paratrooper, Airborne Ranger and Green Beret, family law mediator and adoptions specialist José N. Harris once said:

There comes a time in your life when you walk away from all the drama and people who create it. You surround yourself with people who make you laugh. Forget the bad and focus on the good. Love the people who treat you right, pray for the ones who do not. Life is too short to be anything but happy. Falling down is a part of life, getting back up is living.[16]

And, of course, the esteemed poet, author, educator, playwright, and civil rights activist, Dr. Maya Angelou:

Love recognizes no barriers. It jumps hurdles, leaps fences, penetrates walls to arrive at its destination full of hope.

Wilferd Peterson was an American author who wrote a monthly column for *Science of Mind* magazine. In his book *The Art of Getting Along*,[17] he wrote:

The world needs less heat and more light. It needs less of the heat of anger, revenge, retaliation, and more of the light of ideas, faith, courage, aspiration, joy, love, and hope.

We need our leaders to know the difference between right and wrong. We need them to be genuinely committed to communities. We need them to understand that success comes as much in service as it does with a soaring stock price. They are not mutually exclusive. They walk hand in hand. Leaders can be driven by the spread of surplus, not just the accumulation of it.

The final word is for the wonderful people we've written about here.

This book tells of their love and logic. Love has its own logic. It elevates us.

Love is both the provenance and destiny of their leadership.

It's been a privilege to elevate it here.

SUMMARY: CHAPTER 8

Hope is a theme that pervades the human story. Some of the greatest thinkers in every walk of life have reflected upon the important role that hope plays. The use of words and language matters greatly. Whether on social media, in a simple text or spoken, words can impact powerfully. Words are used to cancel, to harm, to dismiss, to diminish. Yet, words can also inspire, inform, educate, and shine light onto a broken world.

Hope and fear are closely connected. Often fear is the precursor to the finding of hope. Modern leadership demands that a leader operate from a position of hope. That is not to say that despair will not happen. Yet, the battle against fear is ongoing and hope must triumph. Otherwise, society cannot dream nor imagine the concept of "better." That the world will be a better place. That people will aspire to do better. The invitation to everyone who reads this book is to "do better."

Aspirational Note

- As a result of having read this chapter, what might you do differently in terms of your own leadership style?
- What facts, stories, quotes, or points stood out for you?
- What might you explore further?

PLAYLISTS

SOURCE TEAM LEWIS https://www.youtube.com/playlist?list=PLCy37yMUxPUP1Q8
ilzxEjlmyZ4dbzHiY3

SOURCE TEAM LEWIS https://www.youtube.com/playlist?list=PLCy37yMUxPUNCl
evSV6hFvOGFhYUDPQsp

ACKNOWLEDGMENTS

Thanks to Sarah Aitchison, Sarah Aitchison and Sarah Aitchison, Rob Alexander, Dr Alicia Altorfer-Ong, Muneerah Bee, Kyle Biller, Simon Billington, George Blacklock, Matt Bowie, Heather Bradley, Professor David Brown, Lauren Bushell, Jacqui Campbell, Lord Chartres, Professor Peter Checkland, Iolanda Chirico, Dr Ian Cole (the brilliant), Professor Sir Cary Cooper, Jessica Cross, Chris Cudmore, Samuel Dean, Umang Dokey, Ken Ford, Professor Russell Foster, Derrick & Hillary Fox, Steve Frampton, Brianna Hernandez, Sharon E. Horton, Alex Humphries, Dan Jacobson, Monte Jones, Jason King, Stephanie McLemore, Sir Geoffrey Leigh (for the J-word), Georgia Lewis, Jo Lewis, Pip Lewis, Sophie London, Iain McGilchrist, The Rt Hon Penny Mordaunt MP, Fallon Murray, Clifton Odom, James Oehlcke, Peter Pereira Gray, Desiree Phlegar, Julianne Power, Charlie Quinn, Leticia Recarte, Kelly Redding, Jo Roberts, Laura Robinson, Joe Schipani, Donna Schoenherr, Sir Anthony Seldon, Teresa Silva, David Stanley, Brigadier General USAF (Ret) Ken Todorov, Pamela Tor Das, Zapporah Turner, Roy Tuscany, Yvonne van Bokhoven, Reuban Yuvaraj.

GONE TOO SOON

Richard Levick

Sir Christopher Meyer

Sir Ken Robinson

Merlyn Isabelle Owens-Robinson

Katherine Kavanaugh Ryan

ABOUT THE AUTHORS

Chris Lewis is an entrepreneur, writer, and philanthropist. He created TEAM LEWIS, one of the largest independent marketing consultancy practices in the world. It runs commercial and community campaigns all over the world. He splits his time between America and Britain. He was made a Freeman of the City of London but remains trapped in his own office. He is the author of:

Greater: Britain after the Storm, Biteback

The Infinite Leader: Balancing the demands of modern business leadership, Kogan Page Inspire

The Leadership Lab: Understanding leadership in the 21st century, Kogan Page Inspire

Too Fast to Think: How to reclaim your creativity in a hyper connected work culture, Kogan Page Inspire

Inez Robinson-Odom is a consultancy professional who has coached and mentored people on varied subjects including faith and hope in the modern world. She earned her master's degree in communication from Stanford University. She puts humanity first in all of her interactions. Her mother, a Yale-educated nurse practitioner, modeled treating everyone with dignity and compassion, and Robinson-Odom has made this the throughline of her life's work.

Robinson-Odom is Vice President of Professional Development for TEAM LEWIS. In this role, she provides executive coaching, training, and culture-building to its global team of marketing, media, and PR professionals. Showing up with full authenticity is her main tenet.

During the span of her career, Robinson-Odom has operated her own multimedia company, creating thought-provoking documentary content for Frontline and PBS. She has counseled families and inspired countless students in her long-standing executive roles at

La Jolla Country Day School and the Academy of Our Lady of Peace. Robinson-Odom has hosted a range of business podcasts. She has taken on some of the most complex topics pertaining to the evolving state of leadership in the 21st century. She approached it all in the spirit of optimism for the future.

A watershed moment occurred for Robinson-Odom early on during her work on the award-winning series *Eyes of the Prize*, a PBS documentary on the American Civil Rights Movement. Robinson-Odom saw first-hand the power of storytelling when applied to questions of social justice. It inspired her to follow in the footsteps of the project's esteemed series producer and brought her to Stanford University, where she completed a master's degree in communications. She went on to found IMO Productions, a multi-media production company. Her projects gave voice to marginalized and vulnerable populations, from children to crime victims to elders.

Robinson-Odom also employs storytelling in her individualized work with clients. As a coach who cares deeply about her fellow humans, she excels at helping people find solutions. Robinson-Odom's superpower? Holding space for vulnerability. It's only through vulnerability that true change can occur. Her inquiry and presence-based approach allows clients to be safely seen and heard so they can go beneath the surface and uncover their brilliance.

If I've been tasked with something, how can I elevate it in such a way that I am bringing great value to the work? I want to inspire people to show up as their best selves and do their best. It's just part of being a good human."

Inez Merlyn Robinson-Odom

Notes

2020 Vision

1   GW Today. Social media companies profiting from misinformation, June 19 2020, https://iddp.gwu.edu/social-media-companies-profiting-misinformation (archived at https://perma.cc/YA25-5U68)
2   Grassi. Nonprofit Leadership Survey Report, September 2021, http://www.grassiadvisors.com/wp-content/uploads/2021/10/GrassiNonprofitSurveyReport2021_Spread.pdf (archived at https://perma.cc/Z4W4-5ZKG)
3   Small Charities Data. The impact of COVID-19 on small charities, https://smallcharitiesdata.org/topic/the-impact-of-covid-19-on-small-charities/ (archived at https://perma.cc/ZZM3-98U2)

Why We Wrote This Book

1   Ipsos. Around the world, people yearn for significant change rather than a return to a "pre-COVID-19 normal", September 16 2020, https://www.ipsos.com/en/global-survey-unveils-profound-desire-change-rather-return-how-life-and-world-were-covid-19 (archived at https://perma.cc/3E2K-3SXF)
2   A Pressman. How Apple uses the Channel Island of Jersey in tax strategy, Fortune, November 6 2017, http://fortune.com/2017/11/06/apple-tax-avoidance-jersey/ (archived at https://perma.cc/8RBF-NEZ6)
3   K Ridley and K Freifeld (2015) Deutsche Bank fined record $2.5 billion over rate rigging, Reuters, April 23 2015, https://www.reuters.com/article/us-deutschebank-libor-settlement/deutsche-bank-fined-record-2-5-billion-over-rate-rigging-idUSKBN0NE12U20150423 (archived at https://perma.cc/QZN3-LDT9)
4   BBC. HSBC bank 'helped clients dodge millions in tax', February 10 2015, http://www.bbc.com/news/business-31248913 (archived at https://perma.cc/HD6J-XZLE)

5 D Rushe. HSBC 'sorry' for aiding Mexican drugs lords, rogue states and terrorists, Guardian, February 10 2015, https://www. theguardian.com/business/2012/jul/17/hsbc-executive-resigns-senate (archived at https://perma.cc/MH2D-Z3JP)

6 K Rapoza. Tax haven cash rising, now equal to at least 10 percent of world GDP, Forbes, September 15 2017, https://www.forbes.com/ sites/kenrapoza/2017/09/15/tax-haven-cash-rising-now-equal-to-at-least-10-of-world-gdp/?sh=29b4a50370d6 (archived at https://perma. cc/P4CD-ZH8N)

7 J Treanor. RBS facing £400m bill to compensate small business customers, Guardian, November 8 2016, https://www.theguardian. com/business/2016/nov/08/rbs-facing-400m-bill-to-compensate-small-business-customers (archived at https://perma.cc/DBM4-PB35)

8 J Cumbo. MPs raise concerns over 'brewing pensions scandal', Financial Times, October 27 2017, https://www.ft.com/ content/87f72e9e-bafb-11e7-9bfb-4a9c83ffa852 (archived at https:// perma.cc/V65Z-D8UA)

9 N Mathiason. Three weeks that changed the world, Guardian, December 28 2008, https://www.theguardian.com/business/2008/ dec/28/markets-credit-crunch-banking-2008 (archived at https:// perma.cc/4WMK-497Z)

10 S Yang. 5 Years ago Bernie Madoff was sentenced to 150 years in prison – here's how his scheme worked, *Business Insider*, July 1 2014, http://www.businessinsider.com/how-bernie-madoffs-ponzi-scheme-worked-2014-7 (archived at https://perma.cc/RMC5-3TCR)

11 A Ash. 20 years since the U.K.'s massive gold sales, here's the big lesson for gold investors, *Forbes*, May 3 2019, https://www.forbes. com/sites/greatspeculations/2019/05/03/20-years-since-the-uks-massive-gold-sales-heres-the-big-lesson-for-gold-investors/ #51fb3a932ac6 (archived at https://perma.cc/2S87-TKK8)

12 M Park. Timeline: A look at the Catholic Church's sex abuse scandals, CNN, June 29 2017, https://www.cnn.com/2017/06/29/ world/timeline-catholic-church-sexual-abuse-scandals/index.html (archived at https://perma.cc/ZAQ7-NF7B)

13 BBC. Oxfam Haiti scandal: Thousands cancel donations to charity, February 20 2018, http://www.bbc.co.uk/news/uk-43121833 (archived at https://perma.cc/2Y9T-9U99)

14 BBC. Baby Peter 'was failed by all agencies', October 26 2010, http:// www.bbc.com/news/education-11621391 (archived at https://perma. cc/H8CH-48Y2)

15 N Allen. MPs' expenses: Sir Peter Viggers claimed for £1,600 floating duck island, Telegraph, May 21 2009, https://www.telegraph.co.uk/news/newstopics/mps-expenses/5357568/MPs-expenses-Sir-Peter-Viggers-claimed-for-1600-floating-duck-island.html (archived at https://perma.cc/VR62-A2CF)

16 K Schallhorn. The 7 biggest political scandals of 2017, Fox News, December 25 2017, http://www.foxnews.com/politics/2017/12/25/7-biggest-political-scandals-2017.html (archived at https://perma.cc/EL2U-UXSD)

17 L Shane III. Report: Wars in Iraq, Afghanistan cost almost $5 trillion so far, Military Times, September 12 2016, https://www.militarytimes.com/news/your-military/2016/09/12/report-wars-in-iraq-afghanistan-cost-almost-5-trillion-so-far/ (archived at https://perma.cc/622U-W4QX)

18 NBC News. Study: Bush led U.S. to war on 'false pretenses', January 23 2008, http://www.nbcnews.com/id/22794451/ns/world_news-mideast_n_africa/t/study-bush-led-us-war-false-pretenses/ (archived at https://perma.cc/ZRC3-WUVX)

19 M Bentham and C McDonald-Gibson. 'Damn': EU referendum result shocks world leaders as Britain backs Brexit, The Standard, June 24 2016, https://www.standard.co.uk/news/politics/damn-eu-referendum-result-shocks-world-leaders-as-britain-backs-brexit-a3280031.html (archived at https://perma.cc/SW27-RHF9)

20 F Perraudin. Thousands of teachers caught cheating to improve exam results, Guardian, February 11 2018, https://www.theguardian.com/education/2018/feb/11/thousands-of-teachers-caught-cheating-to-boost-exam-results (archived at https://perma.cc/MSH4-46YH)

21 A Jauregui. Dishonor roll: 10 most notorious teacher sex scandals of 2013, Huffington Post, https://www.huffpost.com/entry/teacher-sex-scandals-2013_n_4392614 (archived at https://perma.cc/U2UT-WX5K)

22 J Thompson. BAE Systems pays $400m to settle bribery charges, Independent, February 6 2010, http://www.independent.co.uk/news/business/news/bae-systems-pays-400m-to-settle-bribery-charges-1891027.html (archived at https://perma.cc/YD5G-A75T)

23 PWC. CEO Success Study 2018, https://www.strategyand.pwc.com/gx/en/insights/ceo-success.html (archived at https://perma.cc/J85N-F3WW)

24 BBC News. Volkswagen: The scandal explained, December 10 2015, https://www.bbc.co.uk/news/business-34324772 (archived at https://perma.cc/79GZ-VKTD)

25 D Carrington. Four more carmakers join diesel emissions row, Guardian, October 9 2015, https://www.theguardian.com/environment/2015/oct/09/mercedes-honda-mazda-mitsubishi-diesel-emissions-row (archived at https://perma.cc/A6NF-P5VR)

26 Y Wakatsuki. Ex-Nissan chief Carlos Ghosn has fled Japan for Lebanon, CNN Business, December 31 2019, https://edition.cnn.com/2019/12/30/business/carlos-ghosn-lebanon/index.html (archived at https://perma.cc/DJ6Z-J245)

27 BBC News. Southern Water punished over 'shocking' wastewater spills, https://www.bbc.co.uk/news/business-48755329 (archived at https://perma.cc/LRP6-VMU8)

28 BBC News (2023) Harvey Weinstein timeline: How the scandal has unfolded, February 24 2023, http://www.bbc.co.uk/news/entertainment-arts-41594672 (archived at https://perma.cc/LDG7-ANWH)

29 R Greenslade. Newsnight's McAlpine scandal – 13 days that brought down the BBC's chief, Guardian, February 19 2014, https://www.theguardian.com/media/greenslade/2014/feb/19/newsnight-lord-mcalpine (archived at https://perma.cc/TNA6-NAXZ)

30 L Watson. 'Atmosphere of fear' at BBC allowed Jimmy Savile to commit sex crimes, report finds, Telegraph, February 26 2016, https://www.telegraph.co.uk/news/uknews/crime/jimmy-savile/12172773/Jimmy-Savile-sex-abuse-report-to-be-published-live.html (archived at https://perma.cc/7TNZ-7Q9U)

31 BBC Sport. Russia doping: Country still suspended by IAAF and could face permanent ban, 6 March 2018, http://www.bbc.co.uk/sport/athletics/43301116 (archived at https://perma.cc/69PJ-QX58)

32 D Campbell. Mid Staffs hospital scandal: the essential guide, Guardian, February 6 2013, https://www.theguardian.com/society/2013/feb/06/mid-staffs-hospital-scandal-guide (archived at https://perma.cc/36K8-A985)

33 O Bowcott. Phil Shiner: Iraq human rights lawyer struck off over misconduct, Guardian, February 2 2017, https://www.theguardian.com/law/2017/feb/02/iraq-human-rights-lawyer-phil-shiner-disqualified-for-professional-misconduct (archived at https://perma.cc/X7NL-2VBX)

34   Busby, M (2018) How many of Donald Trump's advisers have been convicted? Guardian, September 14 2018, https://www.theguardian.com/us-news/2018/aug/22/how-many-of-trumps-close-advisers-have-been-convicted-and-who-are-they (archived at https://perma.cc/2KY4-XPFE)

35   D Scharfenberg. Trillions of dollars have sloshed into offshore tax havens. Here's how to get it back, Boston Globe, January 20 2018, https://www.bostonglobe.com/ideas/20/01/20/trillions-dollars-have-sloshed-into-offshore-tax-havens-here-how-get-back/2wQAzH5DGRw0mFH0YPqKZJ/story.html

36   J Desjardins. The $80 trillion world economy in one chart, Visual Capitalist, October 10 2018, https://www.visualcapitalist.com/80-trillion-world-economy-one-chart/ (archived at https://perma.cc/M3S9-JDA5)

37   The Leadership LAB 2018 reproduced with the kind permission of Kogan Page Ltd

38   M O'Sullivan. How has COVID-19 changed the world? Forbes, August 26 2023, https://www.forbes.com/sites/mikeosullivan/2023/08/26/how-has-covid-changed-the-world/?sh=132f35351ebe (archived at https://perma.cc/CD82-C2U7)

39   D Trujillo. Engaging Gen-Z, our most purpose-driven generation, Forbes, https://www.forbes.com/sites/forbesnonprofitcouncil/2023/09/15/engaging-gen-z-our-most-purpose-driven-generation/?sh=7154d31872a2 (archived at https://perma.cc/FD6K-GZPY)

40   A Gaskell. COVID-19 saw an exodus of over-50s from the workforce, Forbes, August 11 2022, https://www.forbes.com/sites/adigaskell/2022/08/11/covid-saw-an-exodus-of-over-50s-from-the-workforce/?sh=5d82e10758f5 (archived at https://perma.cc/E4E7-SEHB)

Chapter 01: How Did the Pandemic Change Us?

1   A Maher et al. Relationship between income level and hospitalization rate in COVID-19 cases; an example of social factors affecting health, Archives of Academic Emergency Medicine, 2022, 10 (1), https://www.ncbi.nlm.nih.gov/pmc/articles/PMC9078072/ (archived at https://perma.cc/AJ6V-8RUN)

2   N Johnson and J Mueller, Updating the accounts: global mortality of
    the 1918-1920 "Spanish" influenza pandemic, Bulletin of the History
    of Medicine, 2002, 76 (1), https://pubmed.ncbi.nlm.nih.gov/11875246/
    (archived at https://perma.cc/XKV8-L2EW)

3   S F Fujimara. Purple death: The great flu of 1918, Perspectives in
    Health, 2003, 8 (3), https://www.paho.org/en/who-we-are/history-
    paho/purple-death-great-flu-1918 (archived at https://perma.cc/
    Q9CC-U7YE)

4   I Backman. Nurses and essential workers: the "sacrificial lambs" of US
    pandemics in 1918 and 2020, Yale School of Medicine, 8 November
    2022. https://medicine.yale.edu/news-article/nurses-and-essential-
    workers-the-sacrificial-lambs-of-us-pandemics-in-1918-and-2020/
    (archived at https://perma.cc/KJ3U-ZCGE)

5   The Conversation. People dropped whisky into their noses to treat
    Spanish flu. Here's what else they took that would raise eyebrows
    today, Indian Express, September 20 2021, https://indianexpress.com/
    article/lifestyle/health/whisky-spanish-flu-cure-covid-7521765/
    (archived at https://perma.cc/4YZX-RKG7)

6   G Daugherty. Amid 1918 pandemic, bootleg whiskey became a
    respectable medicine, History.com, May 1 2022, https://www.history.
    com/news/1918-flu-pandemic-whiskey-remedy-prohibition (archived
    at https://perma.cc/KLF9-L2VG)

7   World Health Organization. The true death toll of COVID-19, May
    20 2021, https://www.who.int/data/stories/the-true-death-toll-of-
    covid-19-estimating-global-excess-mortality (archived at
    https://perma.cc/JAE8-7KK4)

8   Centers for Disease Control. End of the Federal COVID-19 Public
    Health Emergency (PHE) Declaration, September 12 2023, https://
    www.cdc.gov/coronavirus/2019-ncov/your-health/end-of-phe.html
    (archived at https://perma.cc/8ESN-WSQK)

9   R Lea. Sales of the new Rolls Royce Spectre have reached record
    levels, The Times, January 8 2024, https://www.thetimes.co.uk/
    article/spectre-hits-forecourts-as-rolls-royce-sales-set-new-records-
    ppq899zfz (archived at https://perma.cc/N3GC-TPY3)

10 M John. Pandemic boosts super-rich share of global wealth, Reuters,
    December 7 2021, https://www.reuters.com/business/pandemic-
    boosts-super-rich-share-global-wealth-2021-12-07/ (archived at
    https://perma.cc/8DWS-DP43)

11   Statista. Value of COVID-19 fiscal stimulus packages in G20 countries as of May 2021, as a share of GDP, 2024, https://www.statista.com/statistics/1107572/covid-19-value-g20-stimulus-packages-share-gdp/ (archived at https://perma.cc/22WH-CTXS)

12   HM Treasury. Twelfth Report of Session 2021-22. COVID-19: Cost tracker update, https://committees.parliament.uk/publications/7872/documents/81760/default/ (archived at https://perma.cc/TFM7-J2KS)

13   K Gooch. 85 strikes in 2021: why healthcare workers are 'more emboldened to act', Beckers Hospital Review, June 6 2023, https://www.beckershospitalreview.com/hr/85-strikes-since-2021-why-healthcare-workers-are-more-emboldened-to-act.html (archived at https://perma.cc/2Y8R-KKL2)

14   K Gooch. US healthcare workers walk off the job: 27 strikes in 2023, November 28 2023, Becker's Hospital Review, https://www.beckershospitalreview.com/hr/us-healthcare-workers-walk-off-the-job-7-strikes-in-2023.html (archived at https://perma.cc/VKX2-887P)

15   F Richter. The most aggressive tightening cycle in decades, Statista, December 14 2014, https://www.statista.com/chart/28437/interest-rate-hikes-in-past-tightening-cycles/ (archived at https://perma.cc/N9PG-PVXV)

16   M Goldberg. The 7 largest bank failures in US history, Bankrate, May 1 2023, https://www.bankrate.com/banking/largest-bank-failures/ (archived at https://perma.cc/2BY4-QRPV)

17   Office for National Statistics. Long-term international migration, provisional: year ending June 2023, November 23 2023, https://www.ons.gov.uk/peoplepopulationandcommunity/populationandmigration/internationalmigration/bulletins/longterminternationalmigrationprovisional/yearendingjune2023 (archived at https://perma.cc/SAW9-6MZD)

18   A Caldwell. Migrant surge overwhelms border agents as smugglers target remote stretches, Wall Street Journal, December 18 2018, https://www.wsj.com/us-news/migrant-surge-overwhelms-border-agents-as-smugglers-target-remote-stretches-d2b0ce07 (archived at https://perma.cc/YQ65-SHTE)

19   I Schwartz, D Boulware and T Lee. Hydroxychloroquine for COVID-19: The curtains close on a comedy of errors, The Lancet, May 5 2022, https://www.thelancet.com/journals/lanam/article/PIIS2667-193X(22)00085-0/fulltext (archived at https://perma.cc/89BT-8X3K)

20 I Backman. Nurses and essential workers: the "sacrificial lambs" of US pandemics in 1918 and 2020, Yale School of Medicine, November 8 2022, https://medicine.yale.edu/news-article/nurses-and-essential-workers-the-sacrificial-lambs-of-us-pandemics-in-1918-and-2020/ (archived at https://perma.cc/P9JW-RBLS)

21 J Maben et al. 'You can't walk through water without getting wet' UK nurses' distress and psychological health needs during the COVID-19 pandemic: A longitudinal interview study, Internationl Journal of Nursing Studies, 2022, 131, https://www.sciencedirect.com/science/article/pii/S0020748922000712 (archived at https://perma.cc/4SW8-UAEM)

22 Pan American Health Organization. COVID-19 Pandemic Disproportionately Affected Women in the Americas, 8 March 2022, https://www.paho.org/en/news/8-3-2022-covid-19-pandemic-disproportionately-affected-women-americas (archived at https://perma.cc/WD4V-M72H)

23 Oxfam International. COVID-19 cost women globally over $800 billion in lost income in one year, April 29 2021, https://www.oxfam.org/en/press-releases/covid-19-cost-women-globally-over-800-billion-lost-income-one-year (archived at https://perma.cc/HF8V-7H5H)

24 E Smith et al. The economic and societal effects of COVID-19 on our brains, Brookings, June 23 2022, https://www.brookings.edu/articles/the-economic-and-societal-effects-of-covid-19-on-our-brains/ (archived at https://perma.cc/86FT-5ZNQ)

25 The COVID-19 Tracking Project. The COVID-19 racial data tracker, 2021, https://covidtracking.com/race (archived at https://perma.cc/4KXM-J2X6)

26 E Smith et al. The economic and societal effects of COVID-19 on our brains, Brookings, June 23 2022, https://www.brookings.edu/articles/the-economic-and-societal-effects-of-covid-19-on-our-brains/ (archived at https://perma.cc/MP6D-HE7C)

27 The COVID-19 Tracking Project. The COVID-19 racial data tracker, 2021, https://covidtracking.com/race (archived at https://perma.cc/Q8L5-DX6W)

28 K Toure et al. How George Floyd and COVID-19 are highlighting structural inequities for vulnerable women, children and adolescents, International Journal for Equity in Health, 2021, 20 (193), https://equityhealthj.biomedcentral.com/articles/10.1186/s12939-021-01540-0 (archived at https://perma.cc/YU5J-JMGN)

29   S Pappas and B Radford. 20 of the best conspiracy theories, Live Science, July 11 2023, https://www.livescience.com/11375-top-ten-conspiracy-theories.html (archived at https://perma.cc/ME7M-72DJ)

30   The British Academy. The COVID-19 Decade: understanding the long-term societal impacts of COVID-19, 2021, https://www.thebritishacademy.ac.uk/publications/covid-decade-understanding-the-long-term-societal-impacts-of-covid-19/ (archived at https://perma.cc/T7MU-63HT)

31   K Harmon. How important is physical contact with your infant? Scientific American, May 6 2010, https://www.scientificamerican.com/article/infant-touch/ (archived at https://perma.cc/HUH9-Z5UC)

32   H Cho et al. The bright and dark sides of social media use during COVID-19 lockdown: Contrasting social media effects through social liability vs. social support, Computers in Human Behaviour, April 24 2023, https://www.ncbi.nlm.nih.gov/pmc/articles/PMC10123536/ (archived at https://perma.cc/K8F3-CCHM)

33   J Taylor. Bots on X worse than ever according to analysis of 1m tweets during first Republican primary debate, Guardian, September 9 2023, https://www.theguardian.com/technology/2023/sep/09/x-twitter-bots-republican-primary-debate-tweets-increase (archived at https://perma.cc/6APC-TSA5)

34   S H R Ahamed et al. Doctors vs. nurses: understanding the great divide in vaccine hesitancy among healthcare workers, Proceedings of the International Conference on Big Data, https://www.ncbi.nlm.nih.gov/pmc/articles/PMC10208360/ (archived at https://perma.cc/D5BU-2N67)

35   Unicef. 5G technology does not cause or spread coronavirus, July 12 2021, https://www.unicef.org/montenegro/en/stories/5g-technology-does-not-cause-or-spread-coronavirus (archived at https://perma.cc/UEJ4-ZRAX)

36   G Driver. Coronavirus conspiracy theories are rampant, here are the most hilarious, Elle, April 21 2020, https://www.elle.com/uk/life-and-culture/a31892113/coronavirus-conspiracy-theories/ (archived at https://perma.cc/2H4N-88ZP)

37   C Itkowitz. Trump again uses racially insensitive term to describe coronavirus, Washington Post, June 23 2020, https://www.washingtonpost.com/politics/trump-again-uses-kung-flu-to-describe-coronavirus/2020/06/23/0ab5a8d8-b5a9-11ea-aca5-ebb63d27e1ff_story.html (archived at https://perma.cc/AW8Y-NE5S)

38 N Ruiz et al. Many Black and Asian Americans say they have experienced discrimination amid the COVID-19 outbreak, Pew Research Center, July 1 2020, https://www.pewresearch.org/social-trends/2020/07/01/many-black-and-asian-americans-say-they-have-experienced-discrimination-amid-the-covid-19-outbreak/ (archived at https://perma.cc/2WQC-RTAU)

39 S Pappas and B Radford. 20 of the best conspiracy theories, Live Science, https://www.livescience.com/11375-top-ten-conspiracy-theories.html (archived at https://perma.cc/8PFL-ESMY)

40 S Shen and V Dubey. Addressing vaccine hesitancy, Canadian Family Physician, March 2019, https://www.ncbi.nlm.nih.gov/pmc/articles/PMC6515949/ (archived at https://perma.cc/AV2D-VCEQ)

41 B Spencer and E Wilkinson. Measles vaccine: NHS to write to millions of parents as a third of children go unprotected, The Times, January 20 2024, https://www.thetimes.co.uk/article/measles-children-mmr-vaccine-jab-parents-adults-djbgdgfn9 (archived at https://perma.cc/5M56-HE83)

42 R Murray and G Lewis. Millions of women lost jobs in 2020 — here's how they're coming back, LinkedIn, 8 March 2021, https://www.linkedin.com/business/talent/blog/talent-strategy/many-women-rejoining-workforce-after-covid-cost-millions-job (archived at https://perma.cc/5ZBM-4Z3Q)

43 Z Williams. Why are we living in an age of anger – is it because of the 50-year rage cycle? Guardian, May 16 2018, https://www.theguardian.com/science/2018/may/16/living-in-an-age-of-anger-50-year-rage-cycle (archived at https://perma.cc/73VF-7ZET)

44 B Golden. Fear and anger: similarities, differences, and interaction, Psychology Today, March 20 2021, https://www.psychologytoday.com/us/blog/overcoming-destructive-anger/202103/fear-and-anger-similarities-differences-and-interaction (archived at https://perma.cc/TA7Z-VNEK)

45 W Brangham and M Fecteau. How homeschooling's rise during the pandemic has impacted traditional school enrolment, PBS News Hour, May 18 2023, https://www.pbs.org/newshour/show/how-homeschoolings-rise-during-the-pandemic-has-impacted-traditional-school-enrollment (archived at https://perma.cc/NEV8-8BH8)

46 M Savage. Why the pandemic is causing spikes in break-ups and divorces, BBC, December 6 2020, https://www.bbc.com/worklife/article/20201203-why-the-pandemic-is-causing-spikes-in-break-ups-and-divorces (archived at https://perma.cc/X9U2-XAZC)

47   https://www.shrm.org/topics-tools/news/benefits-compensation/
potential-downside-to-remote-work-higher-rates-depression
(archived at https://perma.cc/847A-247R)

48   https://www.forbes.com/sites/forbesbusinesscouncil/2021/07/22/5-
common-problems-plaguing-remote-workers-and-what-to-do-about-
them/?sh=75ee148b4c57 (archived at https://perma.cc/Z8SU-C496)

49   E Smith et al. The economic and societal effects of COVID-19 on our
brains, June 23 2022, Brookings, https://www.brookings.edu/articles/
the-economic-and-societal-effects-of-covid-19-on-our-brains/
(archived at https://perma.cc/LG5M-37VZ)

50   K Mayer. A potential downside of remote work? Higher rates of
depression, Harvard Business Review, March 10 2023, https://hbr.
org/2021/08/you-dont-need-a-college-degree-to-land-a-great-job
(archived at https://perma.cc/S449-6KY6)

51   E Smith et al. The economic and societal effects of COVID-19 on our
brains, Brookings, June 23 2022, https://www.brookings.edu/articles/
the-economic-and-societal-effects-of-covid-19-on-our-brains/
(archived at https://perma.cc/9ZT2-LQTW)

52   T Goodrich. Workplace communication study during pandemic finds
managers should talk less, listen more, Baylor University, April 12
2021, https://news.web.baylor.edu/news/story/2021/workplace-
communication-study-during-pandemic-finds-managers-should-talk-
less (archived at https://perma.cc/Y4XZ-W3QG)

53   K Marshall and D Hale. COVID-19 related substance use disorder
in the older population, Home Healthcare Now, July/August 2021,
https://journals.lww.com/homehealthcarenurseonline/citation/
2021/07000/covid_19_related_substance_use_disorder_in_the.8.aspx
(archived at https://perma.cc/BC8M-GZEF)

54   S Indap et al. WeWork files for bankruptcy amid office market
downturn, Financial Times, November 7 2023, https://www.ft.com/
content/775ec01c-1f57-4105-bbc2-b048865056f7 (archived at
https://perma.cc/S7UT-M6MH)

55   A R Sorkin. Adam Neumann gets a new backer, New York Times,
September 29 2022, https://www.nytimes.com/2022/08/15/business/
dealbook/adam-neumann-flow-new-company-wework-real-estate.
html (archived at https://perma.cc/45T3-C8SM)

56   Gallup. Confidence in Institutions, https://news.gallup.com/
poll/1597/confidence-institutions.aspx (archived at https://perma.
cc/4N3V-F5H5)

57 Office for National Statistics. Trust in government, UK, 2023, https:// www.ons.gov.uk/peoplepopulationandcommunity/wellbeing/ bulletins/trustingovernmentuk/2023 (archived at https://perma.cc/ EJ2J-GVQW)

58 OECD. Trust in government, https://data.oecd.org/gga/trust-in-government.htm (archived at https://perma.cc/N8XU-C8GW)

59 N Baker and A Weedon. What is the '15-minute city' conspiracy theory? ABC News, February 26 2023, https://www.abc.net.au/ news/2023-02-27/the-15-minute-city-conspiracy/102015446 (archived at https://perma.cc/4F7U-8KKL)

60 National Oceanic and Atmospheric Administration. Global carbon dioxide growth in 2018 reached 4th highest on record, March 22 2019, https://www.noaa.gov/news/global-carbon-dioxide-growth-in-2018-reached-4th-highest-on-record (archived at https://perma. cc/2F9N-CNE8)

Chapter 02: How Did We End Up So Divided?

1 Macrotrends. China GDP 1960-2024. https://www.macrotrends.net/ countries/CHN/china/gdp-gross-domestic-product (archived at https://perma.cc/KSB8-7UWY)

2 Statista. Manufacturing labor costs per hour for China, Vietnam, Mexico from 2016 to 2020, https://www.statista.com/statistics/744071/ manufacturing-labor-costs-per-hour-china-vietnam-mexico/ (archived at https://perma.cc/6PLT-DGUZ)

3 D Goodhart (2017) *The Road to Somewhere: The populist revolt and the future of politics*, Hurst

4 K Robinson. Changing education paradigms, TED, October 2010, https://www.ted.com/talks/sir_ken_robinson_changing_education_ paradigms (archived at https://perma.cc/EMY6-2SLM)

5 D Stanley. David Stanley BEM: From teacher to entrepreneur, King's College London, December 22 2022, https://www.kcl.ac.uk/david-stanley-teacher-to-entrepreneur (archived at https://perma. cc/586W-JF7V)

6 Darpa. https://www.darpa.mil/ (archived at https://perma.cc/36P9-W29R)

7   The Times. What are the rules when commenting on The Times website? https://www.thetimes.co.uk/help/articles/what-are-the-rules-when-commenting-on-the-times-website?utm_source=email&utm_medium=CRM&utm_campaign=FY23_TML_Real-Name-Commenting_TML-TS-E-SER1-1-0005 (archived at https://perma.cc/J4EV-WFPZ)

8   A Pellish and K Maher. Haley calls for name verification on social media, drawing pushback from GOP rivals, CNN, November 15 2023, https://www.cnn.com/2023/11/14/politics/haley-name-verification-social-media/index.html (archived at https://perma.cc/9BYX-VG6W)

9   N Confessore. Cambridge Analytica and Facebook: The scandal and the fallout so far, New York Times, April 4 2018, https://www.nytimes.com/2018/04/04/us/politics/cambridge-analytica-scandal-fallout.html (archived at https://perma.cc/5XNK-MX8B)

10 Federal Communications Commission. Telecommunications Acts of 1996, https://www.fcc.gov/general/telecommunications-act-1996 (archived at https://perma.cc/98KX-DN8L)

11 A Satarino. British ruling pins blame on social media for teenager's suicide, New York Times, October 1 2022, https://www.nytimes.com/2022/10/01/business/instagram-suicide-ruling-britain.html (archived at https://perma.cc/QW5E-GXP7)

12 N Camut. Putin's (still) not dead, Kremlin insists, Politico, October 27 2023, https://www.politico.eu/article/vladimir-putins-still-not-dead-kremlin-say/ (archived at https://perma.cc/XEQ2-YAFB)

13 Marca. A look at 19 celebrities who were falsely reported dead, October 11 2023, https://www.marca.com/en/lifestyle/celebrities/2023/08/10/64d54b0322601d750e8b45a7.html (archived at https://perma.cc/3ABY-AL5K)

14 V Stepanenko. Poland, NATO say missile strike wasn't a Russian attack, AP News, November 16 2022, https://apnews.com/article/russia-ukraine-g-20-summit-nato-biden-government-and-politics-c76bead57a11bc8397a30ee7bb06264e (archived at https://perma.cc/5JYR-K8VX)

15 E Maxwell. No, these videos do not show Israeli soldiers at Al Shifa hospital, France 24, November 17 2023, https://www.france24.com/en/tv-shows/truth-or-fake/20231117-no-these-videos-do-not-show-israeli-soldiers-at-al-shifa-hospital (archived at https://perma.cc/K4RC-Z7VG)

16 WHO. COVID-19 pandemic triggers 25% increase in prevalence of anxiety and depression worldwide, March 2 2022, https://www.who.int/news/item/02-03-2022-covid-19-pandemic-triggers-25-increase-in-prevalence-of-anxiety-and-depression-worldwide (archived at https://perma.cc/8RR3-LM2F)

17 Cats that look like Hitler, http://www.catsthatlooklikehitler.com/cgi-bin/seigmiaow.pl (archived at https://perma.cc/DZ7W-4J65)

18 JTA News. Things that look like Hitler, YouTube, May 29 2013, https://www.youtube.com/watch?v=arUE6KuZo_U (archived at https://perma.cc/PP6N-9N2C)

19 E Ortiz-Ospina. The rise of social media, Our World in Data, September 18 2019, https://ourworldindata.org/rise-of-social-media (archived at https://perma.cc/BB5H-8N8G)

20 Ione Wells. Twitter, November 24 2023, https://twitter.com/ionewells/status/1728072528906604766 (archived at https://perma.cc/PST7-X859)

21 R Mason. Sideways tool use earns Rishi Sunak hammering on social media, Guardian, November 24 2023, https://www.theguardian.com/politics/2023/nov/24/sideways-use-of-a-hammer-earns-rishi-sunak-social-media-mockery (archived at https://perma.cc/FC43-FXRJ)

22 O Darcy. Putin's brutal war on Ukraine vanishes from news coverage amid raging conflict in Gaza, CNN, November 17 2023, https://www.cnn.com/2023/11/17/media/gaza-ukraine-war-news-coverage/index.html (archived at https://perma.cc/WL9N-QTMY)

23 A Connaughton. Social trust in advanced economies is lower among young people and those with less education, Pew Research Center, December 3 2020, https://www.pewresearch.org/short-reads/2020/12/03/social-trust-in-advanced-economies-is-lower-among-young-people-and-those-with-less-education/ (archived at https://perma.cc/V2QT-CYY4)

24 Ibid.

25 Ibid.

26 Wikipedia. Godwin's Law, nd, https://en.wikipedia.org/wiki/Godwin%27s_law (archived at https://perma.cc/84QX-ZG8S)

27 J Waterson. News of the World: 10 years since phone-hacking scandal brought down tabloid, Guardian, July 10 2021, https://www.theguardian.com/media/2021/jul/10/news-of-the-world-10-years-since-phone-hacking-scandal-brought-down-tabloid (archived at https://perma.cc/BVR7-HUVD)

28 C Mayer. Piers Morgan tomorrow? The hacking scandal laps at the British star, Time, August 4 2011, https://world.time.com/2011/08/04/piers-morgan-tomorrow-the-hacking-scandal-laps-at-the-british-star/ (archived at https://perma.cc/CU6S-QBWG)

29 Daily Mail. About MailOnline, https://www.dailymail.co.uk/home/article-10538781/About-MailOnline.html (archived at https://perma.cc/BNX8-DQM2)

30 Stanford University. Watts Rebellion (Los Angeles), nd, https://kinginstitute.stanford.edu/watts-rebellion-los-angeles (archived at https://perma.cc/2DFA-H27S)

31 I Parogni. The history of Cinco de Mayo and how it's celebrated, New York Times, May 5 2022, https://www.nytimes.com/article/cinco-de-mayo-celebration.html (archived at https://perma.cc/Y5VC-VGD9)

32 National Museum of African American History & Culture. The seven principles of Kwanzaa, nd, https://nmaahc.si.edu/explore/stories/seven-principles-kwanzaa (archived at https://perma.cc/3UBZ-6ZBZ)

33 Ghetto - from the Italian borghetto, or borough

34 Wikipedia. On Liberty, nd, https://en.wikipedia.org/wiki/On_Liberty (archived at https://perma.cc/2L6Z-27YY)

35 https://hbr.org/2022/09/emotions-arent-the-enemy-of-good-decision-making?utm_campaign=hbr&utm_medium=social&utm_source=linkedinnewsletter&tpcc=linkedinnewsletter (archived at https://perma.cc/8QFQ-PRC5)

Chapter 03: What Actually Is Leadership?

1 C Strauss Einhorn. Emotions aren't the enemy of good decision-making, Harvard Business Review, September 9 2022, https://www.theguardian.com/theguardian/2006/sep/29/features11.g2 (archived at https://perma.cc/3AKA-SJM4)

2 McKinsey. What is Leadership? August 17 2022, https://www.mckinsey.com/featured-insights/mckinsey-explainers/what-is-leadership (archived at https://perma.cc/7SE8-PT62)

3 A Boynton. Nine things that separate the leaders from the managers, Forbes, March 31 2016, https://www.forbes.com/sites/andyboynton/2016/03/31/want-to-be-a-leader-not-just-a-manager-do-these-nine-things/?sh=4dbec0de51e0 (archived at https://perma.cc/CNK6-8P43)

4   Aspire 2Be. What is 'Appreciative Inquiry'? YouTube, January 30
    2018, https://www.youtube.com/watch?v=l3RjC5vllZ4 (archived at
    https://perma.cc/3RBX-R8LB)

5   National Institute on Aging. Optimism linked to longevity and
    well-being in two recent studies, December 8 2022, https://www.nia.
    nih.gov/news/optimism-linked-longevity-and-well-being-two-recent-
    studies (archived at https://perma.cc/9QCH-WHWM)

6   Ibid.

7   Ibid.

8   The Sunday Times Rich List 2023, https://www.thetimes.co.uk/
    sunday-times-rich-list (archived at https://perma.cc/W2HS-8EPN)

9   A Chow. The 100 most influential people of 2022: Sam Bankman
    Fried, Time, May 23 2022, https://time.com/collection/100-most-
    influential-people-2022/6177770/sam-bankman-fried/ (archived at
    https://perma.cc/ZPQ8-58LU)

10 R Greenleaf. The servant as leader, 1970, https://www.gonzaga.edu/-/
    media/Website/Documents/Academics/School-of-Leadership-Studies/
    DPLS/IJSL/Vol-1/IJSL-Vol-1-04-Greenleaf.ashx?la=en&hash=373F48
    91C38322A1E5543DFE2976DA9C2746E6BA (archived at https://
    perma.cc/GTD8-NF4P)

11 M Block. After going for gold, athletes can feel the post-Olympic
    blues, The Torch, September 8 2016, https://www.npr.org/sections/
    thetorch/2016/09/08/493111873/after-going-for-gold-athletes-can-
    feel-the-post-olympic-blues (archived at https://perma.cc/S43Q-8KZS)

12 Fortune Editors. Founder Adam Neumann explains why Marc
    Andreessen invested $350 million in Flow, his new company that
    sounds a lot like WeWork, Fortune, June 13 2023, https://fortune.
    com/2023/07/13/adam-neumann-why-marc-andreessen-invested-
    flow-wework/ (archived at https://perma.cc/64BG-95JD)

13 R Dalio (2021) *Principles for Dealing with the Changing World
    Order: Why nations succeed and fail*, Avid Reader Press w

14 From the German verb Führen, to lead.

Chapter 04: How Does Leadership Need to Change?

1   C Zhang et al. Why capable people are reluctant to lead,
    December 17 2020, Harvard Business Review, https://hbr.org/2020/12/
    why-capable-people-are-reluctant-to-lead (archived at https://perma.
    cc/9J3C-SDYB)

2 N Stoddard and C Wykoff. The costs of CEO failure, Chief Executive, nd, https://chiefexecutive.net/the-costs-of-ceo-failure/ (archived at https://perma.cc/R3FM-RRSD)

3 D Marcec. CEO tenure rates, Harvard Law School Forum on Corporate Goevernance, May 9 2024, https://corpgov.law.harvard.edu/2018/02/12/ceo-tenure-rates/ (archived at https://perma.cc/J6QE-JK73)

4 M Ettore. Why most new executives fail—and four things companies can do about it, Forbes, 13 March 2020, https://www.forbes.com/sites/forbescoachescouncil/2020/03/13/why-most-new-executives-fail-and-four-things-companies-can-do-about-it/?sh=13fc666f7673 (archived at https://perma.cc/9CBD-NSRB)

5 Korn Ferry. Age and tenure in the C-suite, nd, https://www.kornferry.com/about-us/press/age-and-tenure-in-the-c-suite (archived at https://perma.cc/TD62-FG4T)

6 P-O Karlsson et al. Are CEOs less ethical than in the past? Strategy + Business, Summer 2017, https://www.pwc.com/ee/et/publications/pub/sb87_17208_Are_CEOs_Less_Ethical_Than_in_the_Past.pdf (archived at https://perma.cc/75PG-BLQA)

7 R Teachout. More CEOs being fired for ethical lapses, study finds, SHRM, 5 June 2017, https://www.shrm.org/topics-tools/news/ceos-fired-ethical-lapses-study-finds (archived at https://perma.cc/LA3C-GRG8)

8 Hourly History (2023) *George Washing Carver: A life from beginning to end*, Hourly History

9 S Achor et al. 9 out of 10 people are willing to earn less money to do more-meaningful work, Harvard Business Review, November 6 2018, https://hbr.org/2018/11/9-out-of-10-people-are-willing-to-earn-less-money-to-do-more-meaningful-work (archived at https://perma.cc/5MR5-DS5J)

Chapter 05: Understanding the Leader's Thinking

1 AARP. The positive impact of intergenerational friendships, May 2019, https://www.aarp.org/content/dam/aarp/research/surveys_statistics/life-leisure/2019/friendship-across-the-ages.doi.10.26419-2Fres.00314.002.pdf (archived at https://perma.cc/C7S3-6UGW)

2 PM Flynn and MA Quinn. Economics: Good choice of major for future CEOs, SSRN, November 28 2006, https://www.aeaweb.org/content/file?id=744 (archived at https://perma.cc/54UZ-A3AT)

3 Study.eu. The academic backgrounds of the world's most powerful CEOs, December 13 2021, https://www.study.eu/article/the-academic-backgrounds-of-the-worlds-most-powerful-ceos (archived at https://perma.cc/AWZ6-JZF2)

4 T Chamorro-Premuzic (2019) *Why Do So Many Incompetent Men Become Leaders?* Harvard Business Review Press

5 A Sayer. Reductionism in social science, Lancaster University, September 2005, https://www.lancaster.ac.uk/fass/resources/sociology-online-papers/papers/sayer-paris1.pdf (archived at https://perma.cc/S6YK-UK5K)

6 P Checkland (1999) *Systems Thinking, Systems Practice*, JW 1

7 K Katahira K et al. EEG correlates of the flow state: A combination of increased frontal theta and moderate frontocentral alpha rhythm in the mental arithmetic task, Frontiers in Psychology, March 2018, 9: 300, doi: 10.3389/fpsyg.2018.00300 (archived at https://perma.cc/G3QW-8FVX)

8 J Gold and J Ciorciari. A review on the role of the neuroscience of flow states in the modern world. Behavioral Sciences (Basel), September 9 2020, 10 (9):137, doi: 10.3390/bs10090137 (archived at https://perma.cc/Y3M2-C9TZ)

9 M Csikszentmihalyi (2008) *Finding Flow: The psychology of engagement with everyday life*, Basic Books

10 C Lewis and P Malmgren (2020) *The Infinite Leader: Balancing the demands of modern business leadership*, Kogan Page

11 BBC Left-Handers Day: Amazing facts about lefties, August 13 2022, https://www.bbc.co.uk/newsround/53739189 (archived at https://perma.cc/634K-TKMF)

Chapter 06: What Does Leadership Look and Sound Like?

1 M Gladwell (2007) *Blink: The power of thinking without thinking*, Back Bay Books

2 Zippia. Entrepreneur demographics and statistics in the US, nd, https://www.zippia.com/entrepreneur-jobs/demographics/ (archived at https://perma.cc/R4TM-SUTZ)

3 W Hoover. Corporate America spawned the fastest-growing group of entrepreneurs: Black women (but not for a good reason), Fast Company, March 14 2022, https://www.fastcompany.com/90730716/ corporate-america-spawned-the-fastest-growing-group-of-entrepreneurs-Black-women (archived at https://perma.cc/48R8-8P8Z)

4 American Express Newsroom. Women-owned business are growing 2x faster on average than all business nationwide, https://www.nasdaq. com/press-release/woman-owned-businesses-are-growing-2x-faster-on-average-than-all-businesses (archived at https://perma.cc/368H-7Q2P)

5 M Schwantes. Warren Buffett says this 1 simple habit separates successful people from everyone else, Inc, January 18 2018, https:// www.inc.com/marcel-schwantes/warren-buffett-says-this-is-1-simple-habit-that-separates-successful-people-from-everyone-else.html (archived at https://perma.cc/R5ZS-UVGY)

6 J Campbell (2014) *The Hero's Journey: Joseph Campbell on his life and work*, New World Library 1

7 T Coombes. About, World Justice Project, nd, https:// worldjusticeproject.org/world-justice-forum-vi/thomas-coombes (archived at https://perma.cc/HS8Y-XD6J)

8 I Player (1997) *Zululand Wilderness: Shadow and soul*, David Philip

Chapter 07: The Unexpected Roles of the Leader

1 HSE. Working days lost in Great Britain, 2023, https://www.hse.gov. uk/statistics/dayslost.htm (archived at https://perma.cc/Y2WC-5BAJ)

2 WHO. COVID-19 pandemic triggers 25% increase in prevalence of anxiety and depression worldwide, March 20 2022, https://www.who. int/news/item/02-03-2022-covid-19-pandemic-triggers-25-increase-in-prevalence-of-anxiety-and-depression-worldwide (archived at https:// perma.cc/VE82-F5LF)

3 M Seligman (2006) *Learned Optimism: How to change your mind and your life*, Vintage 1

4 S Lurye. How the pandemic affected women's health, US News and World Report, April 6 2022, https://www.usnews.com/news/health-news/articles/2022-04-06/how-the-covid-pandemic-affected-womens-health (archived at https://perma.cc/YW5V-5X94)

5 F Garcia et al. The four faces of rumination to stressful events: A psychometric analysis, Psychological Trauma, November 2017, https://pubmed.ncbi.nlm.nih.gov/28594202/ (archived at https:// perma.cc/C2B5-K9A4)

6   Mind. Mental health problems – and introduction, nd, https://www. mind.org.uk/information-support/types-of-mental-health-problems/ mental-health-problems-introduction/causes/ (archived at https:// perma.cc/DH2S-KAK9)

7   UK Parliament. House of Commons trends: The age of MPs, nd, https://commonslibrary.parliament.uk/house-of-commons-trends-the-age-of-mps/ (archived at https://perma.cc/F2ST-BS3J)

8   Blind recruitment involves the removal of all identification details from resumes and applications. It helps your hiring team evaluate on their skills and experience instead of factors that can lead to bias.

9   M Dimock. Defining generations: Where Millennials end and Generation Z begins, Pew Research Center, https://www.pewresearch. org/short-reads/2019/01/17/where-millennials-end-and-generation-z-begins/ (archived at https://perma.cc/L9TT-MTZG)

10 TJ Smith. The greatest wealth transfer in history is here, with familiar (rich) winners, New York Times, May 23 2023, https://www.nytimes. com/2023/05/14/business/economy/wealth-generations.html (archived at https://perma.cc/JCE4-UCJ4)

11 Rainmaker Thinking. Post-pandemic work: What each generation needs for success, nd, https://rainmakerthinking.com/post-pandemic-work-what-each-generation-needs-for-success/ (archived at https:// perma.cc/HU6C-KQ7K)

12 M Faverio and M Anderson. For shopping, phones are common and influencers have become a factor – especially for young adults, Pew Research Center, November 21 2022, https://www.pewresearch.org/ short-reads/2022/11/21/for-shopping-phones-are-common-and-influencers-have-become-a-factor-especially-for-young-adults/ (archived at https://perma.cc/UN2J-YHW3)

13 McKinsey. What is Gen Z? March 20 2023, https://www.mckinsey. com/featured-insights/mckinsey-explainers/what-is-gen-z (archived at https://perma.cc/4CSB-7GJZ)

14 T Francis and F Hoefel. True Gen': Generation Z and its implications for companies, McKinsey, November 12 2018, https://www. mckinsey.com/industries/consumer-packaged-goods/our-insights/ true-gen-generation-z-and-its-implications-for-companies (archived at https://perma.cc/G98L-PQCN)

15 S Krause. BlackRock: Companies should have at least two female directors, Wall Street Journal, February 2 2018, https://www.wsj. com/articles/Blackrock-companies-should-have-at-least-two-female-directors-1517598407 (archived at https://perma.cc/KQ6A-VWDP)

16 T Francis and F Hoefel. True Gen': Generation Z and its implications for companies, McKinsey, November 12 2018, https://www.mckinsey.com/industries/consumer-packaged-goods/our-insights/true-gen-generation-z-and-its-implications-for-companies (archived at https://perma.cc/E7ZQ-7E7M)

17 H Shortland. Italy's Eni fined Eur5 mil for Green Diesel advertising breach, SP Global, January 15 2020, https://www.spglobal.com/commodityinsights/en/market-insights/latest-news/coal/011520-italys-eni-fined-eur5-mil-for-green-diesel-advertising-breach (archived at https://perma.cc/3PGK-HH25)

18 W Crisp. Science Museum sponsorship deal with oil firm included gag clause, Guardian, February 16 2023, https://www.theguardian.com/culture/2023/feb/16/science-museum-sponsorship-deal-with-oil-firm-included-gag-clause (archived at https://perma.cc/CG9C-EWPN)

19 J Cleeton. The end of pink washing: why waving the rainbow flag as a marketing strategy can no longer fly, The Drum, July 3 2018, https://www.thedrum.com/news/2018/07/03/the-end-of-pink-washing-why-waving-the-rainbow-flag-marketing-strategy-can-no-longer (archived at https://perma.cc/M3DH-VBXG)

20 B Drenon. Vinyl records outsell CDs for first time in decades, BBC, March 13 2023, https://www.bbc.com/news/64919126 (archived at https://perma.cc/KTY6-ENCE)

21 McKinsey. What is Gen Z? 20 March 2023, https://www.mckinsey.com/featured-insights/mckinsey-explainers/what-is-gen-z (archived at https://perma.cc/JST8-KQ4H)

22 PwC. How prepared are employers for Generation Z? https://www.pwc.com/ug/en/press-room/how-prepared-are-employers-for-generation-z-.html (archived at https://perma.cc/8PY5-ZW2K)

23 Selective mutism is an anxiety disorder where a person is otherwise capable of speech becomes unable to speak when exposed to specific situations.

24 G Thunberg. Ted Talk transcript: school strike for climate, Rev, nd, https://www.rev.com/blog/transcripts/greta-thunberg-ted-talk-transcript-school-strike-for-climate (archived at https://perma.cc/W9MW-ZU7W)

25 PwC. How prepared are employers for Generation Z? https://www.pwc.com/ug/en/press-room/how-prepared-are-employers-for-generation-z-.html (archived at https://perma.cc/ZU4L-SFDX)

26 J Haidt and Z Rausch. What we learned in 2023 about Gen Z's mental health crisis, After Babel, December 31 2023, https://www.afterbabel. com/p/best-of-2023 (archived at https://perma.cc/AX7P-UHH9)

27 CDC. Youth risk behaviour survey, 2021, https://www.cdc.gov/ healthyyouth/data/yrbs/pdf/YRBS_Data-Summary-Trends_ Report2023_508.pdf (archived at https://perma.cc/7VR4-9L8Y)

28 Y Kelly et al. Social media use and adolescent mental health: Findings from the UK Millennium Cohort Study, eClinical Medicine, January 4 2019, https://www.thelancet.com/journals/eclinm/article/ PIIS2589-5370(18)30060-9/fulltext (archived at https://perma.cc/ LA4U-RDNJ)

29 J Haidt. Social media is a major cause of the mental illness epidemic in teen girls. Here's the evidence, After Babel, February 22 2023, https://www.afterbabel.com/p/social-media-mental-illness-epidemic (archived at https://perma.cc/5HDH-7HCQ)

30 PwC. How prepared are employers for Generation Z? https://www. pwc.com/ug/en/press-room/how-prepared-are-employers-for- generation-z-.html (archived at https://perma.cc/ZA28-K9VJ)

31 H Farah and D Milmo. TikTok allowing under-13s to keep accounts, evidence suggests, Guardian, December 19 2023, https://www. theguardian.com/technology/2023/dec/19/tiktok-allowing-under-13s- to-keep-accounts-evidence-suggests (archived at https://perma.cc/ CB95-KDNY)

32 Courts and Tribunals Judiciary. Three Is: Independence, Impartiality and Integrity, nd, https://www.judiciary.uk/about-the-judiciary/ our-justice-system/three-is/ (archived at https://perma.cc/4W26- 359H)

33 T Fredberg. Why good leaders pass the credit and take the blame, Harvard Business Review, October 6 2011, https://hbr.org/2011/10/ why-good-leaders-pass-the-cred (archived at https://perma.cc/95T6- Z98X)

34 M Timms. Blame culture is toxic. Here's how to stop it, Harvard Business Review, February 9 2022, https://hbr.org/2022/02/blame- culture-is-toxic-heres-how-to-stop-it (archived at https://perma. cc/8ZXZ-4F7D)

35 K Benson. The magic relationship ratio, according to science, The Gottman Institute, nd, https://www.gottman.com/blog/the-magic- relationship-ratio-according-science/ (archived at https://perma.cc/ J6C6-6LRZ)

36 J Rogers. *Manager as Coach: The new way to get results*, 2012, https://jennyrogerscoaching.com/product/manager-as-coach-the-new-way-to-get-results/ (archived at https://perma.cc/9QHB-HZYT)

37 D Silsbee (2008) *Presence-Based Coaching: Cultivating self-generative leaders through mind, body, and heart*, Jossey-Bass

Chapter 08: The Future and Hope

1 L Hughes. Hope, https://sevengoodthings.com/hope-langston-hughes/ (archived at https://perma.cc/C95G-6ABR)

2 J Weber. Hope is not 'a' strategy: it's the only strategy, War Room, February 27 2018, https://warroom.armywarcollege.edu/articles/hope-not-strategy-strategy/ (archived at https://perma.cc/CB23-P9JM)

3 H Fiazal (2020) *We Hunt the Flames*, Square Fish

4 J Weber. Hope is not 'a' strategy: it's the only strategy, War Room, 27 February 2018, https://warroom.armywarcollege.edu/articles/hope-not-strategy-strategy/ (archived at https://perma.cc/K973-UYTW)

5 J Vespa et al. Demographic turning points for the United States: Population projections for 2020 to 2060, https://www.census.gov/content/dam/Census/library/publications/2020/demo/p25-1144.pdf (archived at https://perma.cc/93RB-NGWA)

6 The Athletic. Premier League hope-o-meter 2023-24: How every club's fans are feeling, August 11 2023, https://theathletic.com/4757831/2023/08/11/premier-league-hope-o-meter-2023-24/ (archived at https://perma.cc/R5ZR-939B)

7 A Stern. Hope: Why it matters, Harvard Health Publishing, July 16 2021, https://www.health.harvard.edu/blog/hope-why-it-matters-202107162547 (archived at https://perma.cc/D458-N4MF)

8 C Scharff. The healing power of hope, Psychology Today, May 16 2023, https://www.psychologytoday.com/us/blog/ending-addiction-for-good/202305/the-healing-power-of-hope (archived at https://perma.cc/DJ7E-MEP6)

9 Greenpeace. Hundreds of ultra-short private jet flights to Davos revealed, as global leaders head into World Economic Forum, January 13 2023, https://www.greenpeace.org/international/press-release/57867/hundreds-of-ultra-short-private-jet-flights-to-davos-world-economic-forum/ (archived at https://perma.cc/HR9T-F2VF)

10 D Bell (2018) *Faces at the Bottom of the Well: The permanence of racism*, Basic Books

11 C-Span. Booknotes: Faces at the Bottom of the Well, September 24 1992, https://www.c-span.org/video/?34630-1/faces-bottom-well (archived at https://perma.cc/UV72-8NPY)

12 WEB Dubois (2014) *The Souls of Black Folk*, CreateSpace Independent Publishing Platform 1

13 M Nussbaum. Naked and afraid, Harper's, August 2018, https://harpers.org/archive/2018/08/naked-and-afraid-the-monarchy-of-fear-martha-nussbaum/ (archived at https://perma.cc/3U74-XM4P)

14 C Hellman. The science and power of hope, TED, May 2021, https://www.ted.com/talks/chan_hellman_the_science_and_power_of_hope (archived at https://perma.cc/URN9-HU25)

15 Wisdom for the Way. The growing edge, Stanford, May 11 2020, https://orsl.stanford.edu/news/growing-edge (archived at https://perma.cc/DNG2-C3CP)

16 JN Harris (2010) *Mi Vida: A story of faith, hope and love*, Xlibris 9

17 WA Peterson (2012) *The Art of Getting Along: Inspiration for triumphant daily living*, Literary Licensing

INDEX

Page numbers in *italic* denote information within a figure.

LATEST NEWS FROM THE AUTHORS

 More content related to *The Silent Rebellion: Becoming a Modern Leader*